To Dr Mary Francis Berry

To a person who has spent a
long distinguished career fighting
for the rights of people from all
walks of life. Your life has been
truly guided by the ancient commune
of Isaiah, "to endure their heavy
burdens + let the oppressed go free

Joe White
2/22/2000 .

Black Man
Emerging

Black Man Emerging

Facing the Past and

Seizing a Future

in America

Joseph L. White / James H. Cones III

W. H. FREEMAN AND COMPANY/NEW YORK

Text and Cover Designer: Blake Logan
Cover Image: James Gerwat/FPG International

Page 93: "WE REAL COOL," by Gwendolyn Brooks © 1991 from the book "BLACKS,"
published by Third World Press, Chicago, 1991.

Library of Congress Cataloging-in-Publication Data

White, Joseph L., 1932–
    Black man emerging : facing the past and seizing a future in America /
Joseph L. White, James H. Cones III.
        p.   cm.
    Includes bibliographical references (p.   )
    ISBN 0-7167-2895-8
    1. Afro-American men—Psychology. 2. United States—Race relations.
3. Racism—United States—Psychological aspects. I. Cones, James H. II. Title.
E185.625.W46   1999   98-39165
305.38'896073—dc21   CIP

Printed in the United States of America

First printing 1998

W. H. Freeman and Company
41 Madison Avenue, New York, NY 10010
Houndmills, Basingstoke RG21 6XS, England

To THE BLACK MEN IN OUR LIVES who have lived in the purpose of creating viable, dignified masculine roles as friend, father, grandfather, husband, brother, uncle, cousin, nephew, son, coach, clergyman, and mentor, despite pervasive de facto and de jure racism in American society. They toiled in the shadows of invisibility so we could finally emerge into the light and secure a clear presence in the future. They taught us pride in Blackness, how to keep the faith, and how to overcome the inevitable obstacles that young Black men face growing up in America. From our esteemed elders, we learned to improvise, create oportunities for ourselves and others, recover from setbacks, and renew the never-ending struggle for fair play, justice, and equality.

Especially to James H. Cones, Jr. (1933–); James H. Cones, Sr. (1903–1982); Donnie Payton (1950–1995); Joseph L. White, Sr. (1907–1963); Robert W. Lee (1915–1985); and David J. Lee (1924–).

Contents

Part I

THE PRESENT AND THE PAST:
CURRENT VOICES/HISTORICAL TRACES

Part II

CONTEMPORARY IMAGES
AND EXPRESSIVE STYLES

Acknowledgment

We would like to express our thanks to a number of people who helped us along the way in the production of this book. First, we thank our spouses, Lois White and Brenda Stevenson Cones, for the patience, understanding, and support they provided during the many months it took to complete this project. Next, we take this opportunity to express appreciation to our secretaries, Edna Mejia and Cheryl Larsson, for their assistance in preparing the early and final drafts of the manuscript. We are especially grateful to those who read and critiqued the manuscript, Professors Robert Guthrie, Daryl Rowe, and Hal Fairchild, and to our editor, Melissa Wallerstein, who helped fine-tune what we wanted to say. We would like to thank Lissa Forehan-Kelly for her research assistance.

Joseph L. White
James H. Cones III

My partner in passion, Brenda Stevenson Cones, made sacrifices alongside me through the accomplishment this book represents. The sharing of our work and our love is refreshing play for my spirit. Our daughter, Emma Carrie Cones, the product of our passions—her gaze, filled with the wisdom of the Ancestors, continually reminded me of the importance of this work for our futures. The students in my classes as well as those who completed independent readings on race and gender participated with me in an exchange of mind and soul,

bringing their lived experiences into our discussions and investiga-
tions. And my coauthor, Joseph L. White, the ultimate mentor, engaged
me in hours and hours of gracious dialogue over the past five years. He
validated my quizzical stirrings with the rich wisdom of his life.

James H. Cones III

Part
I

THE PRESENT AND THE PAST:

CURRENT VOICES/

HISTORICAL TRACES

Chapter 1

Introduction

The prevailing image of Black men in America is an overwhelmingly negative one. As two Black men who have been subjected over the course of our lifetimes to the negative image recorded in history and statistics, and reported by the various news media, it is our hope to cast a new, more positive light on African-American masculinity.

Our Voices

In the chorus of negative reports and opinions, the voice of Black men themselves is rarely heard. While we acknowledge and sympathize with the oppression felt by other minority groups, and by our Black Sisters in particular, they are not the focus of this book. In the past ten years, the intensely negative view of Black men has far surpassed the disfavor in which other oppressed peoples are held. Black men have been typecast as America's villains. It is our desire to show their true measure. We were taught by the Black men in our lives to carve out a positive template of Black male identity; we hope that this book will serve, in turn, as a message of hope to other Black men—and as a lesson to society as a whole, so that people may not only better understand the individual Black man but also comprehend the challenges he faces in his life. It was this same spirit of hope, optimism, and rebirth that inspired the Million Man March.

For seven hours on a sunny fall day in October 1995, upwards of 800,000 Black men (some say at least a million) stepped out of the shadows of invisibility and negative stereotypes to gather on the Mall in our nation's capital to remind America of their presence. They were peaceful and respectful. No incidents of violence marred the day and there was only one arrest for drunk and disorderly conduct. In what was billed as the Million Man March, there were Brothers (African-American men) as far as the eye could see. Wide-angle lenses couldn't capture the whole crowd. Although White folks joked that most of the Black men were able to attend the march because they were welfare freeloaders, in actuality, the Brothers came from all walks of life. There were northerners and southerners; urbanites and Brothers from rural areas; doctors and blue-collar workers; policemen, attorneys, and ex-convicts; young and old; students and school dropouts; poor and wealthy; employed, underemployed, and unemployed; and gang members and ex–gang members. They sang, prayed, hung out with each other, listened to the speeches, and shared brotherly love and fellowship. Using the Black call-response form of dialogue, the speakers and the audience signified, played the dozens, and put the bad mouth on White folks. But, more importantly, they affirmed each other and vowed to take responsibility for their actions. They were there to remind America that the business of race and equality will not be sidetracked, even at a time when there is a conservative backlash against programs designed to help Blacks win congressional seats, gain admission to universities and graduate schools, secure high-paying jobs, and attain lucrative business contracts with government agencies. Black men are a force to be reckoned with; they will not disappear or fade away quietly into obscurity.

Although the press concentrated on the controversy and drama surrounding the convener of the march, Nation of Islam leader Louis Farrakhan, and speculated on why retired General Colin Powell, the most popular Black man in America, wasn't there, the real message of the Million Man March was bigger than either Minister Farrakhan or General Powell. The real message sent from the sea of Black men gathered on the Mall was a grassroots affirmation of spiritual strength, dignity, atonement, hope, responsibility, love, and forgiveness. Warring enemy gang members sought forgiveness for past killings and reached out to each other. Absent fathers pledged to reunite with their children and guide them away from the destruction of drugs and crime. Husbands and boyfriends promised to respect their wives and girlfriends. The marchers showed America that Black men were not an endangered species. They were willing to commit themselves to the virtues of self-reliance and take responsibility for improving their lives and the communities they live in. Isn't personal responsibility and family values what politicians like President Bill Clinton and conservatives like former Vice President Dan Quayle are talking about? Some called it the largest family-values rally America has ever witnessed. Others said it was the greatest event in the history of African-American men.[1]

The legions of men assembled at the Mall in Washington, D.C., were also there to protest the dismal sociological and economic conditions of life in America that many Black males encounter as they make the passage from cradle to grave. Some sections of inner cities where African-American men reside resemble bombed-out European cities after World War II. Black men are more likely than their White male counterparts to be homicide victims, high school dropouts, unemployed, incarcerated or on parole; and they are more likely to have a shorter life expectancy, debilitating medical problems, and poor occupational training. Statistically speaking, being born a male with White skin confers certain advantages with respect to education, employment, career advancement, political and economic power, health care, and neighborhood residence. Conversely, dark skin places an undue burden on Black men in their struggle for self-definition and identity, education, access to networks providing employment and career information, political and economic power, and decent neighborhoods in which to rear their children.

The Million Man March was a profound psychological vindication for Black men who have been cast in public debates and political discussions as representing the low end of the bell curve measuring mental ability, as Willie Hortons, and as unqualified affirmative action hires and welfare freeloaders. The Brothers showed America an indomitable spirit that will not be denied, and they reminded their fellow citizens that it is an error to stereotype all Black men as dangerous, drug-hustling criminals, gangsta rappers, and TV sitcom clowns. Just like everyone else, most Black men have jobs, pay taxes, raise kids, struggle to pay their bills, and work hard to achieve a better life for their families and their children.

After reciting a pledge to improve themselves and their communities mentally, spiritually, morally, economically, and politically, the marchers departed from Washington with fresh resolve. They promised to get their lives together and heal the broken homes, deteriorating schools, and violence-ravaged streets of their communities, while working to empower Black men with the tools and skills to transform their lives. In July 1996, organizers of the original march (October 16, 1995) held a two-day follow-up conference in Chicago, which drew participants from around the country. The conference was sponsored by Million Man March, Inc., and the National Leadership Summit. Speakers included Louis Farrakhan, who called for more Black political participation. The chair of the conference, the Reverend Benjamin Chavis, former director of the NAACP, told the news media that the purpose of the meeting was to draft an urban policy agenda and start the process of building a God-centered mass movement. Among the urban policy agenda items were combating drugs; obtaining quality education, more job training, and better medical care; preserving public housing; revitalizing affirmative action; reversing the expansion of the nation's prison system; carving out a bigger role for Blacks in the nation's economy; and challenging the news media to confront White racism on TV, in newspapers, and other instruments of mass communication. As part of an organizing effort geared toward expanding political participation, millions of people across the country were informed of the urban agenda drafted by the conference. A national political convention was planned for September 20, 1996, to be followed by a world day of atonement on October 16, 1996—the first anniversary of the Million Man March—at the United Nations in New York.[2]

Spike Lee's October 1996 film *Get on the Bus*, released on the anniversary, is a docudrama that attempts to capture the spirit of a group of Black men who journey to Washington to participate in the march. *Get on the Bus* follows the group on a three-day trip via Spotted Owl Coach from the First African Methodist Episcopal Church in Los Angeles to the capital. The characters, portrayed by actors, represent a composite of male personality types in the Black community bound together by their desire to participate in the event. There is an old-timer, left over from the 1960s, who still addresses the Brothers with Black power salutes, a UCLA film student and student of African drums, a gay couple struggling to keep their relationship alive, a self-centered actor who wants to outshine movie star Denzel Washington, a conservative entrepreneur, and a follower of the Nation of Islam. There are also an estranged father and son; the son is a gangbanger ordered chained to his father by the courts. (The men on the bus call the chained father and son "The Defiant Ones.")[3]

The film focuses on the psychological and social challenges African-American men face as they struggle to define who they are, build and maintain relationships, cope with racism, and search for strengths in the African-American way of being. On their three-day journey, the men engage in what can be described as a combination of a nonstop talkathon and intensive group psychotherapy. They discuss, debate, and argue about such topics as gang violence, male-female relationships, sexual preference, politics, Black Nationalism, skin color, and Black-White conflicts. One of the major dilemmas confronting Black men in America is brought to the forefront when the Spotted Owl bus is arbitrarily stopped by Tennessee state troopers who think the men may be transporting drugs.

For the men on the bus trip, the ultimate essence of the march is not a cure-all for the ills facing Black men in America, nor is it a coronation of the march leader, Louis Farrakhan. What the men experience in the process is a journey into self-discovery, personal empowerment, and reconciliation. Looking inward, they discover the power to create a better vision of themselves.[4]

Two major conclusions can be drawn from the Million Man March. First, race is an inescapable complication in American life that must be resolved. Whether it be overt or covert, individual or institutional, social or economic, blatant or subtle, racism needs to end before Black males can start life on a level playing field of equal opportunity. The second conclusion to be drawn is that Black men are willing to take responsibility for initiating interventions that will transform themselves and the Black community. They are willing to provide constructive, responsible definitions of masculinity and to work to enhance the development of skills and abilities necessary to achieve an optimal level of masculine functioning. However, no amount of individual or group transformation will change the economic or social obstacles with which Black men are confronted in a racist society. Solving problems surrounding racism will require the joint efforts of Blacks and Whites.

The Black/White Perceptual Gap

A discernible difference between Blacks and Whites with respect to how race and race-related events are perceived and assessed interferes with the search for biracial solutions to the social and economic road-blocks Black American males encounter. The reactions to the not-guilty verdict handed down in the O. J. Simpson murder trial in the fall of 1995 not only confirmed that race is a major factor in American society but brought out into the open the vast perceptual gap between Blacks and Whites.

Several polls taken after the trial showed that two-thirds of Whites believed that O. J. was guilty of murdering his ex-wife and her friend Ron Goldman. Conversely, two-thirds of Blacks believed that he was innocent. While Blacks and Whites seemingly viewed the same trial on TV, they apparently focused on different events. Whites looked at the overwhelming evidence indicating that O. J. was at the scene of the crime and had a history of domestic violence, and concluded that the police would not have charged him if he were not guilty. Blacks, based on their long history of oppression and brutality by the police and the criminal justice system, had no problem believing that the evidence could have been tampered with and that the police picked on O. J. because he was a successful Black man married to a White woman.

Detective Mark Fuhrman's use of the word "Nigger," captured on audiotape during interviews with the screenwriter Laura Hart McKinney (after having denied he'd used it in the past ten years), convinced Blacks that racist police officers involved in the case could have been motivated to set O. J. up, or, at the very least, had tampered with the evidence. Aware of the fact that Blacks live in an experiential/psychological space that contains a long history of individual and collective racism and negative experience with the police, the lead attorney for Simpson, Johnnie Cochran, had no problem playing the race card. In addition to bringing up Fuhrman's use of the N-word, Cochran appealed to the predominantly Black jury's racial suspicions by tossing out a list of racial buzzwords and quotations from famous Black figures like Martin Luther King, Jr., and Frederick Douglass, who, Cochran implied, would have voted for acquittal. Not surprisingly, his strategy worked. In a press conference after the trial, Cochran admitted he had interjected the race card into the trial. He indicated that he would have been held liable for malpractice if he had passed by a perfect opportunity to appeal to a predominantly Black jury's suspicions about fairness in the criminal justice system.

Bypassing lengthy deliberations on the mountain of evidence presented in the ten-month trial, pointing toward Simpson's guilt, the jury handed down the not-guilty verdict in less than five hours. The quickness of the verdict surprised the attorneys, the presiding judge, the news media, and the American public. In TV pictures released as the verdict was being read, Whites appeared to be stunned, shocked, and angry. Blacks in colleges, beauty shops, barbershops, and restaurants were shown cheering and clapping. Ironically, Black women in a shelter for battered women cheered the not-guilty verdict despite strong evidence suggesting Simpson had a history of beating his wife.[5]

How can two groups of people watching the same widely publicized trial on TV and hearing it discussed on talk shows come to such different conclusions? Why the vast perceptual gap? The most straightforward explanation is that Blacks and Whites live in different experiential/psychological worlds, which ultimately leads to different perceptions and interpretations of race-related events. Based on a long history of abuse by law enforcement, Blacks did not find it hard to believe that the police could have manipulated the evidence against O. J. Whites, on the other hand, could not believe that the police would charge a prominent Black man with double murder if he were not guilty.

Public opinion polls consistently show that Blacks and Whites interpret racial events differently, view the meaning of racial progress differently, and assess racial spokesmen from a different perspective. In a poll conducted by the *Los Angeles Times* in 1991, 66 percent of Whites said they felt the civil rights movement had gone far enough or too far. This may explain why Whites are showing much greater opposition to special programs like affirmative action, designed to give Blacks and other minorities a boost. In the same poll, 86 percent of Blacks said the civil rights movement had not gone far enough. Blacks generally feel that while the nation has made major strides toward equality and opportunity, much remains to be done. More recent evidence that Blacks and Whites continue to view racial issues through different lenses comes from a 1997 survey by the Gallup Organization. In the poll, 58 percent of Whites thought that the quality of life for

Black Americans had become better over the past decade, whereas only 33 percent of Blacks surveyed thought that the quality of life for Black Americans had improved. Looking at the current racial scene, which seems to be a mix of stalled progress and retrogression, many Blacks feel a sense of despair. Seventy-six percent of Black college graduates in the poll said that race relations would always be a troublesome problem in America.[6]

Compounding the Black/White perceptual split in viewing racial concerns is the fact that many Whites cling to racial stereotypes. A poll conducted in 1991 by the University of Chicago's National Opinion Research Center found that 56 percent of Whites believed Blacks were likely to be less intelligent than Whites. In another poll conducted by the University of Chicago, Whites said that Blacks were more likely than Whites to prefer living on welfare. It is generally acknowledged by researchers and racial experts that many Whites tend to associate Blacks with crime, homelessness, drugs, and AIDS.[7]

Louis Farrakhan, the controversial Nation of Islam leader who orchestrated the Million Man March, is perceived differently by Blacks and Whites. A poll by *Time* magazine taken shortly after the march found that 59 percent of Blacks felt Minister Farrakhan spoke the truth; only 12 percent of Whites felt the same way. Fifty-six percent of Blacks thought that Farrakhan was a good role model for Black youths, as compared to 12 percent of Whites. Finally, 50 percent of Blacks viewed him as a positive force in the Black community. Only 33 percent of Whites saw him in the same light.[8]

Stalled Progress

From the perspective of the Black community, the accelerated pace of racial progress set into motion by the civil rights movement of the 1960s has stalled since the beginning of the Reagan administration in the 1980s. Programs to increase Black enrollment in universities and professional schools, ensure representation of Black elected officials in predominantly Black communities, increase access of women and minorities to government contracts, and implement affirmative action hiring are being threatened or eliminated. Conservative politicians have become very skillful in the use of innuendo, employing loaded words like welfare, drugs, crime, quotas, and merit-based hiring, to heap abuse on Black males. At the same time, they call for the building of more prisons, presumably to house additional Black males, who are already overrepresented in the prison population. Neoconservative magazines like *The New Republic* and the *American Spectator* routinely put the bad mouth on Black welfare mothers and at the same time call for cuts in educational, housing, and health care and nutrition programs—cuts that negatively affect Black families and children in need of assistance.

At the same time that conservative politicians decry welfare and crime, they cleverly avoid discussing corporate and middle-class welfare and White-collar crime. One of the best-kept secrets in America is that the biggest welfare recipients are corporate and middle-class Whites. In 1994, Labor Secretary Robert Reich noted that the United States spends billions of dollars annually in corporate welfare, mostly in the form of tax breaks and subsidies. Executives who have been laid off receive unemployment insurance, well-to-do senior citizens draw sizable social security checks, homeowners deduct mortgage interest, middle-class college students get educational loans, and businesses and farmers rely on federal subsidies.[9]

In 1997, a group of liberal members of the U.S. House of Representatives estimated that the government could save $261 billion over five years, more than enough to balance the federal budget, if tax breaks for government programs the congressional representatives referred to as corporate welfare were reduced. Among the corporate welfare programs and tax write-offs the representatives would end or reduce are those that benefit insurance firms, companies doing business overseas, business executives who incur entertainment expenses, and large and profitable multinational corporations.[10]

In the Savings and Loan Association scandal of the 1980s, White businessmen ripped off the government for over $100 billion, yet only a few were prosecuted and served jail time. The White men who run Wall Street investment companies annually line their pockets with millions of dollars gained in illegal insider trading deals to which Black men don't have access.

The concept of affirmative action has been demonized by conservatives and neoconservatives. Through endless repetition of loaded words and phrases like color blind, content of character, merit-based employment, lowering standards, reverse discrimination, quotas, unqualified hirings and university admissions, they have saturated discussions of affirmative action with negative implications and sinister stories (mostly false) of qualified Whites being denied opportunities in order to meet mandated quotas for hiring or admitting unqualified or inferior Blacks and other minorities. Political ads show a glum-looking White man telling someone he wasn't hired because the company was required to give the job to an unqualified minority. Opponents of affirmative action seem to be trying to convince the American public that abolishing it will solve all of our racial problems. In the strange twists of racial logic that typify America's racial scene, White conservatives accuse Blacks of being unfair and dividing America. The oppressor, in essence, is accusing the victim of doing the oppressing.

In the venom that has been heaped on affirmative action to create a divisive issue between the races, the original purpose of affirmative action programs has been obscured. These programs started in the 1960s as a way of beginning to level an uneven playing field of opportunity, the result of centuries of racial discrimination. Speaking in 1965 at Howard University, a predominantly Black institution, President Lyndon Johnson made it crystal clear when he said that 350 years of slavery and Jim Crow de facto and de jure segregation prevented Black men and women from being where they would be in society if, historically, they had been given the opportunity to compete fairly. Given that White folks had an over 300-year head start, it was obvious that something had to be done to give Blacks a chance to start the process of catching up. Affirmative action was an attempt to do this by creating special outreach programs to increase minority representation in education, job training, employment and promotions, business development, and the holding of government contracts. In President Johnson's view, society had a responsibility to take active (affirmative) steps to right the wrongs and ensure greater opportunity for people who had been denied the advantages granted to White Americans.[11]

Despite the furor surrounding affirmative action, labeled as reverse discrimination, and the repeated accusations that White men are being deprived of jobs, Blacks are still a long way from equality in high-paying jobs, education, government contracts, and executive positions in Fortune 500 companies. Measurable benefits for Blacks in terms of increases in wages and employment have been quite small. Bureau of Labor statistics show that Whites still hold 88.8 percent of managerial positions.[12] Prospective Black home buyers are still being denied mortgage loans in certain neighborhoods, and Black-owned businesses are still grossly underrepresented in securing government contracts. The fact that Blacks have not achieved parity after thirty years of affirmative action means there is still a long way to go before equal opportunity becomes a reality, despite what the critics claim. Willie Brown, mayor of San Francisco and former speaker of the California State Assembly, one of America's most influential Black politicians, compares the critics of affirmative action to a group of cheaters at a card game who have illicitly collected a stack of chips. When discovered, they want to keep playing without paying back the chips they obtained unfairly. Like the players in the poker game, Whites have benefited from chips gained unfairly. Now they don't want to give back a few of their advantages to help those who have been denied a chance to catch up.[13]

Conservative Whites, who still have the advantages that come with skin color, now frequently quote the Reverend Martin Luther King's statements about how he hoped his children would be judged on the content of their character rather than on the color of their skin. People who dismissed King as Communist-inspired while he was alive now deify his call for a color-blind society. They carefully omit his call for a beloved community where all men and women could sit down together at the table of brotherhood and sisterhood. At the core of King's theology was a belief in diversity, inclusion, and shared decision making between Blacks and Whites. He believed America could undergo a spiritual transformation so that the races could come together in harmony and mutual respect.

Dr. King left behind a clear record of support for programs like affirmative action to move America toward racial equity and an expanding base of opportunity for Blacks. In his major speeches and writings, recently published in one large volume, *Testament of Hope* (1996), edited by James Washington, King argued convincingly that society must engage in some form of affirmative social engineering to help African-Americans overcome the disadvantages of centuries of economic, political, and social discrimination.[14] In his book *Why We Can't Wait,* published in 1963, he wrote that given America's long history of racism, African-Americans deserved special compensation in jobs, education, and other areas. In 1967, writing in *Where Do We Go from Here: Chaos or Community?,* King encouraged America to do something positive for African-Americans after hundreds of years of discrimination. In still other writings and speeches, he continued to point out that since society had already set precedents for special opportunities in education, bank loans, and civil service to be granted military veterans and other groups, society could surely do something affirmative to right wrongs where Blacks were concerned. It is a supreme irony that the concept of color blindness, which Dr. King used in standing up for the rights of Blacks, is now being used by White conservatives to maintain an unequal status quo.[15]

Facing the Problem of Race

Before Black men can take their rightful place in society, America will have to resolve the inescapable complications associated with race. Finding effective solutions to racial problems will require the combined efforts of Blacks and Whites working together. What's missing in America, however, is an ongoing, candid Black/White dialogue about the role of race in society, a dialogue about how it influences attitudes, perceptions, opinions, and behaviors and how it confers advantages and disadvantages and opens up or closes down opportunities. Race is a topic that Americans are uncomfortable discussing, however. After major events like the Rodney King beating, the 1992 Los Angeles rebellion, the O. J. Simpson trial verdicts, or the Million Man March, race becomes a major discussion topic for a few days, then disappears from public attention.

The Black/White perceptual gap, compounded by generations of suspicion and hostility, interferes with the mutual understanding and communication that is essential for effective biracial problem solving. Black and White Americans are like two people who have a bad marriage but for complex reasons have decided not to divorce or even establish separate households. A divorce would cost too much in alimony and involve splitting up the assets, so they are faced with the dilemma of trying to get along on a day-to-day basis. In order to solve common household problems and domestic issues, they must learn to communicate. Some years ago, Elijah Muhammad, then leader of the Nation of Islam, called for a "divorce" between Black and White Americans. Reasoning that White folks were inherently evil, he felt that the best course of action for Blacks would be to have their own nation of several states inside United States borders. The U.S. government would provide the land and start-up money as reparations for the riches White America had amassed during 350 years of exploiting Blacks as slaves and cheap labor. The government balked; the plan was too costly politically, legally, and economically, so Blacks and Whites remain bound together in the same geographic space. Like the husband and wife in the bad marriage, the cost of divorce or physical separation is so high that we must sit down and work out a way of living together in the same household.

Blacks and Whites do not have to love each other to get along, but they must be able to communicate openly and frankly in order to solve pressing social problems of mutual interest. To reach across the perceptual divide and achieve the level of mutual understanding and empathic awareness that is an essential condition for productive dialogue, each side will have to express, confront, and come face-to-face with intense, and sometimes painful, emotions. Blacks will most surely express anger and resentment about America's racial history and their personal experiences of what it is like to live in a society where Whites control the political, economic, and legal power, as well as the mass media. Blacks are likely to be a bit more reluctant to express hurt and fear, as it is not easy for them to reveal their vulnerability in front of Whites. In a frank dialogue, Whites would probably express anger and resentment toward Blacks for wanting what Whites perceive as special preferences in university admissions, employment opportunities, career advancement, business loans, and awarding of government contracts. Whites will also, no doubt, accuse Blacks of not taking responsibility for the violence, crime, drugs, teen pregnancies, welfare, and gangs that plague inner-city neighborhoods. For their part, however, the African-American men who attended the Million Man March clearly signaled a willingness to engage in self-examination and take their share of responsibility for improving the conditions that hamper the progress of Black males. Efforts are already under way in the Black community to address issues involving fatherhood, mentorship and manhood training, education, nonviolent resolution of conflict, helping high-risk youths, prison and drug rehabilitation, and outreach to gangs. Several of these interventions are discussed in Chapters 14 and 15.

Along the way in a mutual effort to solve racial issues, both Blacks and Whites will have to look within and examine troublesome thoughts, feelings, attitudes, and concerns. The three most difficult problems for Whites, no doubt, will be developing empathy for the Black experience, acknowledging that White skin carries certain advantages in American life, and working through the psychological defense mechanisms that have prevented them from understanding the devastating effects that centuries of overt and covert oppression have had on the lives of African-American men. Black men will have to face up to their responsibility for the Black-on-Black crime and violence in the inner cities, teen pregnancies, paternal absence, and family deterioration. A more detailed discussion of the call for biracial dialogue is presented in the final chapter of this book.

Chapter 2

Beginnings

The story of Black men in American life has three
beginnings. The first beginning can be traced
back to Africa. The second beginning started
with the coming of the slave ships to James-
town, Virginia, in 1619. The third beginning
represents a period after the Civil War, from
1865 to 1896, when hopes for full participation
in American life were raised only to be disappointed by de facto and de jure segregation
practices supported by science and religion.

As we move through this discussion of
precolonial African life, slavery in America, and
postslavery existence, the emergence of two
very different constructions of social reality will
be apparent. One construction of reality advances the view that Africa was a large, dark
hole inhabited by beings who made very little in
the way of positive contributions to civilization,
and that American slaves of African origin were
a cultural creation of the slave masters. Because

they brought no culture with them from Africa and were entirely molded by the American experience, they were deemed inferior beings, subhumans who deserved to be treated as property. The second view holds that African people who came to America as slaves brought with them an epic psychological memory, a way of being, and a strong will toward self-determination and self-definition that was suppressed by the injustices of slavery and racism. The former view was constructed by Whites out of a need to justify slavery and oppression; the latter view has been adopted by Blacks out of a need to survive that justification.

Beginnings I: Ancient Africa

Fifteen centuries before the birth of Christ and more than three centuries before Greek and Roman civilizations came into prominence, African peoples had developed advanced civilizations in what is now Egypt. The Sahara at that time was green savannas supporting the intermigration and thriving of cultures from the west, south, north, and east of Africa. This historical fact, corroborated by archaeological and anthropological evidence, demonstrates that Egyptian culture and civilization was indeed influenced by the descendants of those who eventually became slaves in the Americas.[1]

Today it seems absurd to still debate whether African-Americans can claim lineage to the Egyptian contributions to contemporary civilization and scientific knowledge. However, in the past decade, this discussion has been a point of considerable controversy. The Euro-American academy, supported by notions of White supremacy, strongly minimized and denied the influence of Africa on Western civilization. Courageous scholars like Yosef A. A. Ben-Jochannan, Martin Bernal, John Henrik Clarke, Cheikh Anta Diop, Asa Hilliard III, Ivan Van Sertima, and Carter G. Woodson challenged the academy and revealed these connections. The result gave birth to a revision of the basic tenets on which White supremacy is based. Their work established central the place of Africa's contributions to the development and progress of Western civilization.

Currently, many scientists even challenge the value and legitimacy of the notion of race altogether.[2] In its most reduced form, race is a biological term that designates a unique set of inherited characteristics that could be identified as independent from other groups. However, the variations among groups as well as the languages spoken can be explained by tracing the gradual waves of migration from East Africa, the origin of humanity.[3] Instead of there being races, the research indicates one race of people who have only minute genetic differences across groups.

To understand the role of race in history, one must appreciate the meanings that have more or less been attributed to these relatively mild variations in people. It is the social and psychological meanings of these differences over historical time that have given the notion of race its power. It may be accurate from a biological standpoint to assert that race does not exist; some, however, may make such a claim as though to take a moral higher ground. Nevertheless, take into consideration the social, psychological, and historical contexts in which Blacks find themselves in American life. In context, race exudes a compelling existential force regardless of the salutary intentions of those who would wish to erase the legacy of inhumanity (disenfranchisement, genocide, slavery) which was justified through notions of biological determinism and Darwinian views of human value. This book addresses a notion of race that is embedded in psychosocial and historical meaning. Whether the meaning is derived from others, from history, or from Blacks themselves, there have accumulated mounds of material that have been used wrongly to support an idea that Blacks are an inferior and undeserving racial variant. It is against this trend that this book stands while exposing the unique meanings and pressures that must be negotiated by African-American men.

The African males who came to the New World as slaves in the seventeenth, eighteenth, and nineteenth centuries left a world in which they were part of a well-organized culture with clearly defined masculine roles.

Socialization

The socialization of African boys in the tribal cultures of West Africa involved a carefully delineated series of steps designed to facilitate psychosocial maturation and prepare them for their adult male roles and responsibilities. Beginning in childhood and continuing through late adolescence, male children were guided through the rites of passage by village elders. In precolonial African societies, a high value was placed on children. Children, as extensions of the ancestors and spirits, represented the future of the tribe. Children were guided not only by the tribal elders, but the biological family, extended family, and the entire village were integral components of the child-rearing process. Hence, the old African saying: "It takes an entire village to rear a child." As central figures in the psychological and social development of young males, tribal elders acted as their mentors. Mentors taught youths the tribal culture, the village's history, and the role of God and spiritual ancestors in everyday life. As future tribal leaders, males were expected to preserve the village culture and pass it on to the next generation. Boys were taught their responsibilities as husbands and fathers, proper care of the body, and appropriate sexual behavior. The elders passed on the survival skills that would enable these young men to take care of themselves and others. Adolescents learned crafts, hunting and farming, and self-defense. By successfully testing themselves against the expectations, boys were gradually able to develop a sense of mastery, personal power, and shared values—significant psychological qualities essential for an adequate definition of self, identity, and masculinity. The rites of passage culminated in an initiation ceremony in which the youth was formally recognized as an adult.[4]

Role of the Adult Male

In precolonial Africa, gender role identity followed a patriarchal pattern in community and family life.[5] Adult males were providers for and protectors of women and children, had the primary decision-making responsibility in family matters, and were expected to provide leadership in community affairs. The family was a central feature of African tribal life. Marriages were not just a union of two persons but joined family lineages. Extended families reached beyond the nuclear family to grandparents, uncles, aunts, cousins, nieces, nephews, and quasi-kin, who were all part of the family's day-to-day activities. Although males held the final decision-making authority, women occupied powerful roles. In addition to childbearing, child rearing, household management, and providing companionship to their husbands, women were involved in village commerce and trading. They participated in communal decision making and were encouraged to speak up and present their views at tribal and community meetings. The African family operated under the principles of mutual aid, reciprocity, role interchange, and respect for the elderly. Although there were separate male and female duties, no stigma was attached to males doing female work, and vice versa. The goal in family and community life was to function harmoniously with others and to create a balance between fulfilling the needs of self and those of others.[6]

Worldview

Underlying precolonial African marriage and family life, child rearing, community affairs, and daily living was a well-defined psychological frame of reference, or worldview—a set of assumptions, beliefs, values, ideas, and behaviors shared by a particular group of people that are handed down from one generation to the next. It is a cultural ethos that filters reality and gives meaning to life experiences. It functions like a psychological lens, enabling a people to focus reality and interpret events.[7] The African psychological frame of reference can be described by seven primary characteristics: spirituality, interdependence, holism, humanism, emotional vitality, rhythm, and the oral tradition.

African existence is deeply spiritual. There is a deep-seated belief that a creative, life-affirming force controlled by God permeates the universe.[8] A spiritual force or élan vital in all living organisms gives power, meaning, and inspiration to life. Spirituality connects the person, the family, the community, the society, and the universe in an interdependent manner. All elements of the universe—people, plants, animals, and inanimate objects—are thus interrelated; there is no separation between spiritual and material, sacred and secular. The human condition and its relationship to the universe are depicted as holistic.

The African psychological perspective does not recognize the mind/body, cognitive/affective, material/spiritual dualisms that are prevalent in European thought. Emphasis is placed on oneness, unity, and reconciliation of opposites and dichotomies through creative synthesis. The human organism is perceived as a totality made up of interlocking psychological systems that perform the functions of sensing, perceiving, feeling, and experiencing. For Africans, the construction and verification of knowledge—epistemology—is not solely the province of mental functions. In addition to rational knowing, understanding reality can occur through the feelings, intuition, sensations, and life experiences. Both knowledge and feeling are necessary for an accurate perception of reality. A person should be able to know the truth in a rational sense and feel the truth as a personal reality. Knowledge and feeling are inextricable.[9]

African philosophy fosters a humanistic conception of life. The rules of living are geared toward mutual aid, collective survival, and interdependent relationships. The basic human unit is the tribe or village, not the individual. Since survival of the group is of primary importance, enhancement of cooperative, harmonious interpersonal relationships is a major cultural value. People exist to benefit one another in an altruistic fashion. Maintenance of positive relationships is more important than power, control, competition, or acquiring material possessions. Individual psychological identity is part of a collective identity. The self cannot exist apart from the group.[10]

African living is saturated with rhythm, motion, and emotional vitality. There is a quality of aliveness, intensity, and animation in music, dance, song, religion, gestures, talk, and body motions in African lifestyles. Rhythmic expressions of joy, possession by spirits, love, sensuousness, awe, and reverence characterize ceremonies and festivals. Cyclical rhythms govern the flow of events in the universe, such as the rising and setting of the sun and the coming and going of the seasons. The stages, or seasons, of life, beginning with birth and continuing through childhood, adolescence, and old age, follow a certain cyclical rhythm. The essence of life is to be able to move harmoniously with the flow of life's internal clock rather than becoming obsessed with controlling life and the universe.[11]

The spoken word is supreme in the African way of life. *Nommo,* the power of the spoken word, carries meaning to generations of people across historical time and geographic space. Words come alive when the speaker breathes life into them through the power of *Nommo.* Nothing exists, including a newborn baby, until it is named with the power of *Nommo.* Through the call-response pattern in spoken dialogue, speaker and listener are joined together in a message unit, with each affirming the presence of the other. The speaker sends out a call (talks) and the listener responds.[12]

Historically, the African male did not have to justify his existence as a human being, nor was he forced to contend with race as a barrier to self-worth. He was not dehumanized and considered a subspecies of humankind based on skin color and hair texture. Precolonial African society provided a psychological frame of reference in terms of which a person could achieve his potential and personal effectiveness in an interpersonal environment of productive relationships with others,

supported by the spiritual presence of a protective God and the ancestors. He could derive his identity and definition of self from his own
experiential base of beliefs, values, and traditions, without being negatively compared to other ethnic groups.

Beginnings II: Africa to America—
The Psychological Transition

When young men like Alex Haley's Kunta Kinte were shipped from
Africa in chains and forced into slavery in America, they no doubt
experienced profound psychological, spiritual, and philosophical
shock.[13] An orderly, predictable pattern of living was interrupted and
replaced with a new kind of life in an environment that was antitheti-
cal to their well-being. The slavery of Africans in America, starting in
the English colonies early in the seventeenth century and continuing
until Abraham Lincoln announced the implementation of the
Emancipation Proclamation on January 1, 1863, was a journey into
existential absurdity. When Africans first arrived on American shores,
they carried with them no history of family instability, juvenile delinquency, disrespect for the elderly, or rampant crime. In preslavery
Africa, young men could realistically aspire to roles as fathers,
providers, heads of families, protectors of women and children, and
decision makers in community governance, following an orderly,
clearly defined set of rules and customs. In America, African males
would be redefined as subhuman property.

In the psychological dislocation of slavery, two major aspects of
the African male experience would undergo significant change. First,
African male slaves in America would no longer have legal rights or
political power. During slavery and long after, Euro-American males
would attempt to maintain a monopoly on legal and civil rights and
political power. Second, African males in America would be forced to
live according to a Euro-American worldview, which differed dramatically from the one that had shaped their lives in Africa. The social construction of reality by descendants of Europeans living in America
would come to value competition and conflict over cooperation, individualism over interdependence, power and control over harmonious
relationships, property rights over human rights, and the rights of
Whites over the rights of Blacks. For example, on the eve of the Civil

War, the U.S. Supreme Court would rule in the case of the runaway slave Dred Scott that Black slaves had no rights that the White man was bound to respect because the Black man was his property.[14]

There are opposing psychological theories about Black male slavery. The traditional view describes the Black male slave as a passive pawn who was almost totally controlled, psychologically and socially, by the slave owner. The revisionist view, which has become more popular since the 1960s, describes the Black male slave as a person who actively and passively resisted the devastating psychological effects of slavery, expressed a clear pattern of self-determination, and created a cultural style that is still visible as we enter the twenty-first century.[15]

The Traditional View of Slavery

The traditional psychological view of Black male slavery, advanced by Uirich Phillips, Stanley Elkins, and Orlando Patterson, revolved around two interrelated psychosocial themes: the overwhelming power of the slave master and the influence of social conditioning. In his book *Slavery* (1968), Stanley Elkins describes the slave master as having almost total control over Black slaves from birth to the grave. Slaves had no legal or human rights, the master could not be punished for how he treated them, and their children were automatically slaves. The male slave was stripped of his role as family head and community leader; he could not protect his women or children. The White slave master determined who was allowed to have conjugal relationships and long-term male/female relationships. The slave master could arbitrarily break up slave families at any time by selling off its members, and could have sexual relationships with slave women at any time. Through social conditioning, according to Elkins's view, the master created a childlike dependency. Like instrumental conditioning of a laboratory animal in a psychological experiment, the slave master punished unacceptable behavior by beatings, extra work assignments, threats of sexual abuse, and near starvation. Acceptable behavior was rewarded. Sometimes the absence of punishment was perceived as a reward.[16]

Orlando Patterson supports Elkins's account.[17] After years of conditioning, the Black male slave came to believe in his own inferiority. His major goal in life was to please the master. Through a syndrome termed "identification with the aggressor," the slave came to believe in the master and sought to be like him. Lacking the "innate ability" of the White man, he could only become an inferior model of the powerful White male. To make all the pieces fit in this model of the passive, childlike, Sambo, male slave personality, it was necessary to assume that Blacks brought very little in the way of psychological beliefs or cultural patterns with them from Africa. Social institutions and psychological coping styles that existed in Africa soon disappeared. The slave relinquished his old personality, values, life-guiding principles, and self-assertion. According to Uirich Phillips, the dean of classical slavery historians, the Black male was totally a creation of the White slave master.[18] He embraced the master's values but lacked the ability, resourcefulness, and self-direction to achieve the level of competence expected of an adult male in American society. As late as 1963, two leading social scientists would maintain that although other American ethnic groups had cultural and historical backgrounds to assist in defining themselves, American Blacks were only American and nothing else. The Black man had no history or culture to protect himself and use as a basis for defining his identity.[19]

This view of the childlike male slave who lacks the discipline, self-assertiveness, and ability to think logically necessary to take on the expected male role would become the basis for the twentieth-century deficit/deficiency psychological theories designed to explain Black male social pathology. These theories advanced the belief that Black males, in essence, lacked the right stuff. A combination of genetic and cultural deficiencies is responsible for the failure of the Black male to assume positions of power and authority in American society. The deficit/deficiency model has spawned many popular Black male stereotypes, such as the clown, the brute, the sexual savage, the pimp, the dunce, and the absent father. To place these stereotypes in proper perspective, major observational errors, which are mistakenly assumed to represent Black reality, need to be addressed. The social pathology stereotype, or deficit/deficiency model of Black male behavior, is an observation created by White males from their perspective that is passed off as objective. It is more self-serving than accurate. It does not represent how Black males themselves say they view the world from their vantage point, or what they think about White folks; nor does the social pathology image reflect the superhuman struggle that Black males have engaged in to survive and to thrive in the face of obstacles placed in front of them by White males.

The Revisionist View of Slavery

In rethinking the past, revisionist historians and sociologists have seriously challenged the notion that male slaves were merely passive, childlike creations of the master or empty psychocultural vessels who were shaped by the dictates of their owners. Using slave narratives, testimonials, journals, letters, diaries, and memories handed down through the oral tradition, revisionist scholars have ample evidence to demonstrate that despite powerful controls exercised by the slave owners, Blacks in captivity actively created a social/psychological environment that combined elements of African culture with their experiences in America. Contrary to traditional beliefs, African captives did not arrive in America with a blank psychological slate. They brought with them cultural and ancestral memories that helped sustain them in the harsh realities of slave life. Melville Herskovits was one of the first students of African-American slavery to demonstrate that traces of African social and cultural patterns existed in the folklore and storytelling, music, dance, religion, speech and language patterns, family and community organizations, and other social culture of African-American slaves. Family and community life, active and passive resistance, and religion and spirituality, three areas studied extensively by revisionist historians, show clear evidence of attempts by African-American slaves to construct their own social institutions, seize control of their destiny, and create a sense of self-determination and self-worth.[20]

Family and Community Life

Contrary to the traditionalist belief that the African-American family was destroyed during slavery, John Blassingame and George Rawick, two African-American historians who have conducted extensive studies of African-American family life on slave plantations, argue convincingly that Black family life reemerged in the form of an extended family.[21] The Black family was broken and degraded during slavery, but was revived and sustained throughout plantation society by large numbers of Blacks. In their own words, graphic portrayals of family life were given by ex-slaves in interviews conducted by the Federal Writers' Project in the 1930s.[22]

Tribal identity was reorganized and reconstructed to bring together slaves who were united by their common ancestral heritage and by their enslavement. The extended family on the plantation consisted of biologically related and quasi-related adults, children, marital partners, grandparents, uncles, aunts, cousins, and friends, linked together in a kinship or kinlike network. The value system of the slave extended family emphasized collective survival, mutual aid and solidarity, cooperation, and responsibility for others, just as it had in precolonial Africa. In the extended family, conjugal unions coexisted within the overall kinship network. While slave marriages were not legally recognized, long-term conjugal unions or unofficial slave marriages were acknowledged by fellow slaves and frequently sanctioned by slave owners. Marriage was a highly valued institution among slaves. After the Civil War, thousands of newly freed Blacks rushed to courthouses to have their marriages legally registered. Until 1925, according to the historian Herbert Gutman, who compiled Black family statistics based on plantation records, U.S. Census Bureau data, and regional and local population records, 75 percent of Black children were born into families that had two married parents.[23]

Under slavery, Black males no longer had the patriarchal decision-making authority they held in Africa. The ultimate decision maker and patriarchal authority on the plantation was the slave owner and his overseers. Nonetheless, male slaves in America played a significant role in the life of the extended family and plantation community. Both males and females worked in the fields or in the "big house" and shared child-rearing responsibilities. On some plantations, male slaves were able to develop a cooperative working relationship with the slave masters. Harsh punishment on the part of the slave master was relaxed in return for acceptable work performance. Improvisation brought its own rewards; at times, male slaves were able to supplement family rations by hunting and fishing and by developing ways to increase crop yields and store food.[24]

Socialization of children was one of the most important functions of the slave family. According to George Rawick, the slave community was a genuine extended kinship community, similar to African tribal culture, in which all the adults looked after all the children.[25] Children were accepted whether they were legitimate or not. Within the core family and extended family kinship network, slave children could receive the love and support they needed to cushion the shock of bondage. Adults could teach children survival skills and transmit aspirations and hopes for freedom someday, in this world or in the next. Memories of life before slavery could be communicated.

Children could be shielded from the master's psychological devaluation by being taught that they were worthwhile.[26] Kinship networks were also a vital source of emotional support, empathy, and belonging for adults. Psychological bonding and companionship within kinship units meant that one was not alone; there were others who understood and were there to share in the pain of human captivity. Within the slave community, away from the prying eyes of the master, the slaves could begin to fashion an identity in which they viewed themselves as adequate and competent human beings who deserved to have legal and human rights.

Resistance

Before and after arriving in America, African captives expressed self-determination by engaging in active and passive resistance. Revisionist historians have documented evidence to show that African-American slaves engaged in a variety of overt and covert behaviors to undermine the power and control of the master. In his book *A Journey in the Seaboard Slave States,* Frederick Law Olmsted describes a repeated pattern of work slowdowns, destruction of property, pretenses of ignorance, and self-liberation by escape.[27] In *The Negro in Our History,* Carter G. Woodson devotes a chapter to slave resistance and assertive behavior.[28] The resistance started on the slave ships and continued on slave plantations. Joseph Carroll attacks the myth of the passive, contented slave by providing detailed accounts of slave revolutions and insurrections.[29]

The three most widely known slave revolts were led by religious Black men. In 1800, Gabriel Prosser, a slave preacher, devised a plan to attack Richmond, Virginia, with a thousand men. At the last minute, he was betrayed, and he and his followers were hanged. In 1822, Denmark Vesey, a free Black minister in Charleston, South Carolina, led an insurrection. He was also betrayed, by a slave who informed his master, and he and forty-six of his followers were executed. In 1831, Nat Turner, another Black preacher, led a slave uprising in which fifty-seven Whites in Southampton County, Virginia, were killed. The authorities finally put down the uprising. Nat Turner was captured and executed.

On the eve of the Civil War, Robert Smalls, a Black slave who worked as a merchant along the docks in South Carolina under a special arrangement with his owner, stole a Confederate warship,

The Planter, and delivered it to the Union forces. For the rest of the war, the Union forces allowed Smalls to serve as captain of the ship. At the end of the war, he sailed victoriously into Charleston harbor with his family and a delegation of leading abolitionists on board.[30]

Long before the Civil War, Black males as ex-slaves and freedmen became part of a tradition of political and social activism in the Black community that continues to the present day. In addition to the efforts of Harriet Tubman, known as "the Moses of her people," and of the abolitionist Sojourner Truth, Black males, too, assisted in the successful escape of over 100,000 slaves through a system of safe houses stretching from the South to the North and on to Canada via the Underground Railroad. The Reverend Henry Highland Garnet (1815–1882), a confidant of John Brown, was a strong advocate of emancipation. Frederick Douglass (1817–1895), who was born into slavery, is recognized as a leader in the abolitionist movement by both Blacks and Whites. He was a powerful speaker, lecturer, and newspaper editor, and an organizational catalyst. In 1847, Douglass began publishing *The North Star,* which became one of the most successful Black newspapers published in the United States prior to the Civil War.[31]

The proponents of slavery apparently had trouble understanding the meaning of resistance, revolt, and rebellion on the part of Black slaves, ex-slaves, and freedmen. Their belief in the image of the childlike, contented slave, no doubt, prevented them from understanding why Blacks would risk beatings, imprisonment, and death to escape or change the system. Nat Turner pointed out to an interviewer before he was executed that southern Whites had clearly understood resistance and revolutionary behavior when the American colonies were trying to gain freedom from England. Yet, when it came to Blacks, resistance and revolutionary behavior were condemned as savage and, in some cases, diagnosed as mental illness. Samuel Cartright, a faculty member of the University of Louisiana in the antebellum South, labeled runaway Blacks as suffering from a psychological illness called "drapetomania," an irresistible, unrestrainable propensity to run away. It was part of a larger syndrome of mental diseases called "dysaesthesia," meaning stupidity of mind. Dysaesthesia was a mental disease that would cause slaves to engage in mischief, break and destroy equipment, steal from the master, slow down their work, generally engage in passive/aggressive behavior, and even have the audacity to argue with the master periodically.[32]

Spirituality and Religion

Spirituality and religion were powerful forces in the lives of Black slaves. The power of religion as a sociopsychological force in the African-American community can be traced back to the spiritual worldview fostered in Africa. Africans lived in a society that revolved around the presence of spiritual forces as the guiding elements of life and the universe. Religion permeated all areas of existence; there was no distinction between the sacred and the secular. In the New World, Africans combined the slave owners' Christianity with African cultural patterns involving the oral tradition, music, rhythmic motion, and dance. One hundred years after slavery, the Reverend Martin Luther King, Jr., would draw upon the power of African-American soul force to lead the civil rights movement of the 1960s.[33]

Slave owners taught their slaves that God was aware of their bondage and approved of it. According to the slave owners' interpretations of biblical texts, slaves were required to obey their masters humbly. It was God's will. Slave preachers, however, interpreted the Bible differently. From their perspective, slavery was unjust, undeserved, and not the will of God. Slave preachers provided leadership in secular matters, also. As has been pointed out, the three major slave revolts were led by men with deep religious convictions, who taught that life was abundant at the spiritual level and that there was room for everyone in God's kingdom on Earth and in Heaven. Belief in God strengthened the slaves' sense of self-worth and helped them develop an internal fortitude that outward conditions were unable to destroy. Slave preachers interpreted biblical stories, particularly in the Old Testament, in ways that had relevance to the life of slaves. Thus, African captives in America came to identify with the oppressed Israelites. They believed that just as surely as God had delivered the Hebrew children from the fiery furnace, Daniel from the lion's den, and Jonah from the body of the whale, he would deliver them from bondage.[34] In America, slave preachers replaced the African wisemen and griots. Using the oral tradition, they handed down ancestral memories from African and American life. They taught day-to-day survival lessons, often using ironic, gallows humor to describe the conditions of slave life. Here's an example of ironic slave humor:

We raise the wheat, dey gib us de corn;
We bake de bread, dey gib us de crust;
We sif de meal, dey gib us de huss;
We peal de meat, dey gib us de skin;
  And dat's de way dey takes us in.
We skims de pot, dey gib us de liquor,
An' say, dat's good enough fer a nigger.

Anonymous

In order to understand fully the psychological dynamics underlying the Black male experience during slavery, it is necessary to avoid the pitfalls of one-dimensional thinking. Viewed only from the perspective of the slave owner, the Black male appears to lack the essential male qualities of leadership, active mastery, and self-directedness. From this vantage point, it appears that the slaves (except for a few bad apples) passively conformed to the master's dictates because they were inherently inferior human beings or because they feared the master's lethal weapons and legal power. Viewed from the perspective of the slaves, Black males fused African memories and common experiences to create a way of being that reflected continuity in family patterns and sex roles, religion and spirituality, and self-determination through active and passive resistance. Out of the slave experience emerged a psychological style that became the basis of Black male pride, Black identity, Black power, and the Black revolution of the twentieth century.[35]

Beginnings III: Post–Civil War

The Social Construction of White Male Superiority and Black Male Inferiority

When the Civil War ended in 1865, newly freed Blacks looked forward to full participation in American life and the possibility of 40 acres and a mule to help them get started after 250 years of legal bondage. Neither the promise of full participation nor the 40 acres and a mule were to materialize. Despite the passage of the Thirteenth, Fourteenth, and Fifteenth Amendments guaranteeing Black citizenship, equal protection under the law, and voting rights, the reconstructed Union reneged on its commitment to support the human and legal rights of ex-slaves in the South and free Blacks in the North. In 1875, Federal troops sent to protect Blacks were withdrawn from the South. In 1883, the Equal Access to Public Accommodations section of the Civil Rights Act of 1875 was declared unconstitutional. In 1896, the U.S. Supreme Court upheld the separate but equal racial separation doctrine in the famous *Plessy v. Ferguson* decision.[36]

Building on the residual images of Black degeneracy developed during slavery, Euro-Americans constructed a social reality grounded in a belief in White male superiority and, conversely, Black male inferiority that was to last for the next 100 years and beyond. The hell of slavery was replaced by the purgatory of second-class citizenship. The patriarchal basis for White male superiority/Black male inferiority was based on three psychobiological and psychological concepts: masculinity, race, and victim-blame.

Masculinity

Masculinity was defined in terms of highly desirable sociopsychological traits or personality propensities. In the gender trait theory of masculinity, White males, as compared to White females, Black males, and Black females, were believed to possess greater psychobiological potential in logical thinking, leadership, ability to plan ahead, resourcefulness, and emotional control. Additional characteristics associated with White male masculinity included assertiveness, toughness (physically and psychologically), dominance, decisiveness, independence, ambitiousness, self-reliance, forcefulness, reliability, analytical ability, and competitiveness. While most psychologists now believe that these traits are learned during the socialization process, the theory that the traits are associated with gender and are inherited was a generally held belief in science and popular culture until well into the 1960s.

Race

On the surface, race was generally categorized by identifiable physical characteristics such as skin color and hair texture. In the social construction of race, it was assumed by Euro-Americans that race represented underlying biological or genetic differences that were responsible for the sociopsychological and personal superiority of White males over

Black males. This assumption was supported by scientific and religious forces who deemed Blacks a subhuman species created by God in a separate act of creation. As a result, Blacks had received different genetic material that was responsible for their character defects.

The theory of racial personality traits was based on assumptions of sameness, inheritability, social desirability, and immutability of attributes. In its most simplified version, the theory holds that members of the same racial group breed with one another, thus passing down the same inferior or superior characteristics from generation to generation. Each race (Black and White) shares certain traits that are inheritable because the races are from different human stocks, a concept handed down from animal husbandry. Value judgments are made about which qualities are the most socially desirable. The most desirable qualities, such as leadership, intelligence, logical thinking, and the like, are assigned in greater quantities to White males.

This theory is a prime example of Euro-American dualistic or dichotomous thinking, a pattern of reasoning that places psychological traits and human biological characteristics in dualistic categories, which easily become labeled as superior/inferior, dominant/subordinate, primitive/civilized, and mature/immature. Once an attribute or personality trait is present, it is believed to be innate. Therefore, attitudes and characteristics such as intelligence, logical thinking, ability to plan ahead, and the like will not change significantly over a lifetime or from generation to generation. The belief in the sameness, inheritability, social desirability, and immutability of attributes was the basis of the White male superiority/Black male inferiority stereotype that White Americans used to lock Black males into a subservient role.[37]

Researchers studying molecular biology and DNA have now traced all human beings to a common ancestry in Africa. There are no known separate racial evolutionary trees or separate developments of subhuman species. Nevertheless, the Euro-American theory of White male superiority/Black male inferiority fabricated by earlier science and religion and used to reinforce social constructions still holds. These two "legitimate" and venerable institutions, science and religion, conspired to frame a picture of the Black man as sexually depraved. In 1900, in a best-selling book, *The Negro as a Beast: or, In the Image of God,* Charles Carroll argued that the Black male would destroy White women and humanity through the greatest of all sins, wanton miscegenation.[38] William Lee Howard echoed this sentiment in 1903 with an article in *Medicine.* According to Howard, White women were not safe around Black males, who were sexually uncontrollable, partly because of an oversized penis that lacked sensitive terminate fibers.[39] Even U.S. government officials theorized about defects in Black sexuality and behavior. Walter F. Willcox, chief statistician for the Census Bureau, in a presentation to the American Social Science Association, explained that Black males were genetically prone to sexual degeneracy, vice, and crime.[40]

Victim-Blame and the Self-Fulfilling Prophecy

The outcome of theories of White male superiority and Black male inferiority, supported by America's major social institutions, was predictable. Black males ended up ranked lower than White males on all indices of social achievement and ranked higher on measures of social pathology. Black males attained less education, worked in low-status jobs, were more likely to live in low-income communities, and occupied fewer positions of political and civic leadership. Black males experienced more family instability, health problems, and unemployment. They were overrepresented in jails and prisons. In essence, the outcome was a self-fulfilling prophecy. Powerful social institutions in America conspired to keep the Black male in an inferior social status. When the predictable result ensued, White America externalized the blame. Rather than hold themselves responsible for the inhuman conditions that Black males were forced to endure, White America blamed the Black male. It was a classic case of victim-blame: The perpetrator of injustice blamed the victim. To add insult to injury, Euro-Americans constructed the "just deserts theory," which states that Black males got what they deserved. The rationale underlying this theory is that God is just, the universe is fair, and science is objective. If Black males evolved at the bottom of society, it was just the will of God, just more evidence supporting the thesis that Black males are truly subhuman, have bad character, and need to be controlled by White folks.[41]

Popular Stereotypical Images

Language and visual images are powerful tools for shaping public opinion; they influence how we think and feel. Negative images of Black males were conveyed in stage shows, novels, movies, advertisements, newspapers, and magazines. North and South, America was saturated with images of clowning, cunning, lazy, ignorant, pleasure-seeking, childlike Black men who needed to be supervised and controlled by powerful, competent, responsible White males.

White minstrels in blackface became very popular in traveling stage shows before the end of slavery. Among the most popular minstrel performers was Thomas Dartmouth Rice, who used the stage name "Daddy Rice." In the 1870s he directed a blackface singing and dancing team known as Jim Crow. Jim Crow was famous for its caricatures of Black males as dimwitted, ridiculous-sounding, shuffling, dancing, happy-go-lucky, irresponsible creatures.[42] In his novels and essays at the beginning of the twentieth century, Thomas Nelson Page warned America that the old-line Blacks were dying off and being replaced by younger Black males who were insolent, intemperate, and dishonest and who possessed only rudimentary elements of morality.[43] In 1906, Upton Sinclair published *The Jungle,* a novel about the horrible conditions in the Chicago stockyards. He was appalled that innocent young White girls working in the stockyards came into contact with dangerous, highly sexed Black men.[44] *The Clansman,* by Thomas Dixon, Jr., published in 1905, described Black males as half animal and half child, with uncontrollable sexual urges and wild hedonistic impulses. The Black male was a being who, unsupervised, would drink and carouse all night and sleep all day. He was incapable of true love and contained the easily aroused fury of a tiger. According to Dixon, it was essential that White men, like members of the Ku Klux Klan, be prepared to defend White womanhood.[45] *The Clansman* became a popular play in theater houses across the country, and would later be transformed into the record-breaking film *Birth of a Nation.*

Produced in 1915 and directed by D. W. Griffith, *Birth of a Nation* was America's first full-length movie, lasting over three hours. It earned more than one million dollars at the box office and was a sellout nationwide. President Woodrow Wilson was given a private showing at the White House. Using close-up shots, rapid-fire editing, split-screen shots, and realistic lighting, *Birth of a Nation* became a classic that altered the concept of moviemaking in America. In 1998, the American Film Institute ranked it number 44 on its list of the "100 greatest American movies." *Birth of a Nation* was a blatant misrepresentation of Black males in positions of military and political power during Reconstruction after the Civil War. It cemented the image of the

Black male brute in the public mind. Black Union Army troops were shown looting, burning, and pillaging in the South. Black legislators were portrayed as arrogant, egotistical, idiotic, heavy drinkers who lusted after White women and were determined to abuse White folks. The film led to the rebirth of the Ku Klux Klan and justified restrictions on Black voting rights. The central message of the film was that Black men could not be trusted with political power. The image of Black males presented in *Birth of a Nation* set the tone for future representations of Black males on the screen.[46]

The images and stories that appeared in newspapers and magazines were generally congruent with the negative stereotypes projected in stage plays, novels, movies, and advertisements. In an essay in *White Racism,* edited by Barry Schwartz and Robert Disch, Rayford Logan reviews the portrayal of Black males as lazy darkies, criminals, childlike clowns, and brutes in major newspapers and magazines prior to World War I. Publications such as the *New York Times, Chicago Tribune, Boston Evening Transcript, San Francisco Chronicle, Harper's, Atlantic Monthly, Popular Science Monthly,* and *Century* lampooned, trashed, butchered, and assaulted Black males in articles and cartoons. Black males were routinely described as lazy dunces, slow-witted imbeciles, moral degenerates, and criminally prone beasts.[47] The *Encyclopaedia Britannica* supported the thesis of White racial superiority; the following description of Blacks appeared in the article "Negro," by Walter F. Willcox, in the 11th edition (1910, Vol. 19, p. 344):

> *Mentally the negro is inferior to the White. . . . The negro children were sharp, intelligent and full of vivacity, but on approaching the adult period a gradual change set in. The intellect seemed to become clouded, animation giving place to a sort of lethargy, briskness yielding to indolence. We must necessarily suppose that the development of the negro and White proceeds on different lines.*

In the period before World War II, prominent public figures, including presidents of the United States, contributed to the negative stereotypes of Blacks. Theodore Roosevelt thought it was important to maintain racial purity. In a letter to a friend, he wrote that Blacks were inferior to Whites. William Howard Taft told a group of Black students at North Carolina College that their race should adapt to the role of farmers. Woodrow Wilson supported segregation in the city of

Washington, D.C., and in civil service positions, feeling it would be in the best interest of Blacks. Before becoming president, Wilson, in an article published in 1901 in the *Atlantic Monthly*, warned the public not to expect too much from Black men, who were little more than pleasure-seeking, work-avoiding children. Warren Harding spoke of inherent racial differences, and Calvin Coolidge believed that the superior Nordic race would deteriorate if mixed with other races.[48, 49]

Supported by religion and science and by popular culture, images of Black male inferiority proved to have a deep and lasting impact on America. What started out as a social construction created by White males, predominantly, came to be reified as a virtual reality believed in, in some fashion, by most Euro-Americans in all sections of the country. As the Sambo image of Black males was handed down from generation to generation, it became frozen in the public mind as an accurate representation of a material reality. That the portrayal of Black males as subhuman has had a continuing effect on American life and thought can be illustrated by numerous examples over the last 70 years.

In 1955, Tom P. Brady, a Mississippi Supreme Court justice, wrote a book called *Black Monday* that was published by the White Citizens' Council, an organization devoted to maintaining racial segregation. In his book, Judge Brady protested the U.S. Supreme Court decision to desegregate America's public schools. His words clearly articulate the view of Blacks as subhuman, savage creatures:

> *The American Negro was divorced from Africa and saved from savagery. In spite of his basic inferiority, he was forced to do that which he could not do for himself. He was compelled to lay aside cannibalism, his barbaric savage customs. He was transported from Aboriginal ignorance and superstition. He was given a language. A moral standard of values was presented to him, a standard he would never have created for himself and which he does not now appreciate. His soul was quickened. He was introduced to God! And the men of the South, whether we like it or not, were largely responsible for this miracle. . . . The veneer has been rubbed on, but the inside is fundamentally the same. His culture is yet superficial and acquired, not substantial and innate.[50]*

As recently as the 1970s, a handbill circulated in southern states alleging that Blacks, according to scientists, were still in the apelike stage. As seen in the image reproduced on the next page and in Box 2.1, the handbill replicates the scope of the stereotype of Black inferiority.

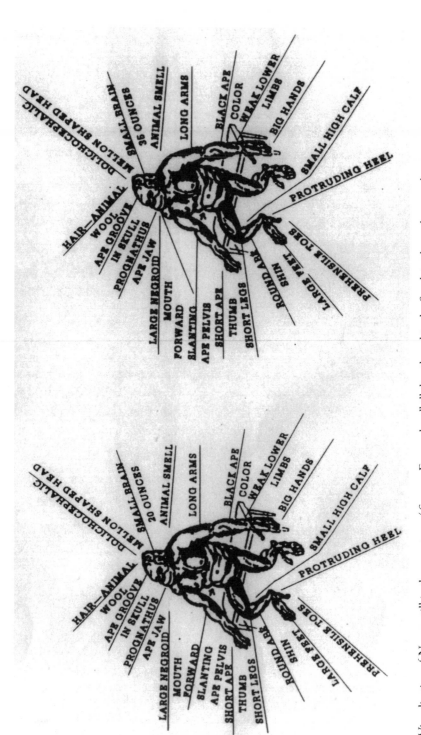

Visualization of Negro still in the ape stage. (*Source:* From a handbill distributed in the South in the early 1970s.)

Box 2.1   Scientists Say Negro Still in Ape Stage

Races Positively Not Equal

(1) The Negro's head shows the archaic form. The front of the Negro's skull is much smaller than the White man's, thus giving the Negro less room for the higher faculties, such as affection, self control, will power, reason, judgment, apperception, orientation and a feeling for the relationship of personality to environment.

(2) Formation determines the amount of intelligence that will be reflected just as the size and shape of a glass pitcher determines the size and shape of the water in it. If this were not so there would be no law governing intelligence and one organism would reflect as much mind as another regardless of its construction.

(3) The Negro's whole skull capacity is much undersize so that the Black brain weights 35 ounces as against 45 ounces for the Caucasian brain.

(4) In the Negro the cranial bones are very thick and the cranial sutures united early in life. This checks the development of the brain and explains the sudden stunting of the Negro intellect shortly before puberty.

(5) The Negro's hair is flat and without a center core of duct. It is not a true human hair but resembles the wool of the lower animals and it can be felted.

(6) The Negro's eyeball is tinged with yellow as is the ape's. The jaws protrude so that the facial angle of the Negro is 70 degrees as in the ape. The White man's facial angle is 82.

(7) The Negro's nose is concave at the bridge as is the ape's. The nostrils turn up and show the red inner lining. The lips are everted and show the red mucous membrane.

(8) In the White man the alveolar arch and palatine area of the mouth became shortened and widened and the tongue became shortened and more horizontally flattened which allows for greater refinement in pronunciation while the Negro palate and tongue remained apelike (macrodont) and he is unable to pronounce sibilant sounds. Sibilant sounds are unknown in Negro dialect.

(continued)

(9)   The Negro carries stench glands as does the dog and in his natural state these may serve as a means of identification in place of a name. This stench (from extra sweat glands) is partly under control and is put out when the Negro is excited.

(10) The Black skin of the Negro has noting to do with climate. It is caused by animal coloring matter between the true and the scarf skins. It is proven the world over that Black and yellow skins are signs of mental and spiritual inferiority and that no tinged race can create a civilization.

(11) A few mulattoes may appear to be brilliant but this brilliance never allows them to invent or create which shows they have not bridged the gap between the Black and White, for no archaic form can become a modern.

(12) The Negro is much closer to the ape than any other race physically, and consequently mentally, for form must determine mental and moral qualities and like must produce like. Every race is different physically and thereby mentally. With the Negro, the body—hence mind—is the lowest of all.

(13) No amount of imitation and apeing will instill a creative or inventive instinct into the Negro nor will education of sympathetic aid.

(14) The Negro has had just as long as the White man to develop. Tens of thousands of years have passed by and the Negro has not produced a civilization. Where is his art, his science, his religion? What single aspect of civilization has he contributed to present-day culture?

(15) The Negro has no morals. He is not immoral but non-moral. Without the White man to control him the Negro reverts to savagery and practices torture, cruelty and witchcraft. The Negro is a natural cannibal and on his native doorpost may be found choice cuts of human flesh. In Africa the Negro even sells his dead relatives and will eat human flesh after it has become decomposed.

(16) As the Black genes of the Negro are more powerful than White genes—the Negro has thereby destroyed every White civilization that he has come in contact with or has left that civilization

stagnant and rotting and dependent upon the last drop of White blood from outside to keep it going.

(17) Negro blood which differs from all other human blood and has a sickle shaped cell has destroyed Egypt, India, Carthage, Greece, Rome, and caused the deep animal sleep to fall upon China, Portugal, Spain, and Turkey.

Unless the Negro race with its deadly sickle celled blood is separated from the White race it will completely destroy America.

Mongrelization of the Races Would Destroy White Christian Civilization

Source: From a handbill distributed in the South in the early 1970s.

De Facto and De Jure Segregation

To maintain the dominant position of White males, Euro-Americans erected a system of de jure and de facto segregation. In the southern and border states between 1890 and 1910, legislators passed a flood of segregation laws. Blacks and Whites were separated in schools, theaters, buses, trains, restaurants, libraries, restrooms, parks, swimming pools, graveyards, and other public facilities. Poll taxes, impossible literacy tests, all-White primaries, and grandfather clauses were instituted to keep Blacks from voting. Interracial dating and marriage were strictly forbidden. Black men faced daily humiliation as members of a legally segregated caste. In reality, the separate but equal clause in the *Plessy* v. *Ferguson* Supreme Court decision never really translated into equal. Public facilities reserved for Blacks were always substandard compared to those for Whites.

Throughout America, Blacks faced restrictions in jobs, housing, and economic opportunities. Black and White males operated in separate work forces. By social custom, certain jobs were defined as Negro jobs. Black males, who were frequently unemployed in any case, generally could only find work as dining car waiters and train porters, yard boys, butlers, hotel doormen, shoe shine boys, garbage men, janitors, and chauffeurs. At the beginning of World War II, the president of North American Aviation said that it was against company policy to hire Blacks as aircraft workers except for jobs as janitors; he claimed the company was in sympathy with the legitimate goals of Blacks.

Black teachers, doctors, morticians, and social workers only worked in Black communities. Blacks were not employed in the skilled trades as plumbers, carpenters, sheet metal workers, engineers, railroad train operators, elevator installers, or electricians. Before the antidiscrimination laws of the 1960s, racial codes segregating Blacks in the labor force were put in writing. Box 2.2 shows the racial requirements for membership in several trade unions. As late as 1960, there were only seventy-nine Black electrical apprentices in the entire United States. By 1970, Blacks in construction unions made up only 1.7 percent of ironworkers, 0.4 percent of elevator construction workers, and 0.2 percent of plumbers.

Skin color was an implicit requirement for advancement in industry and the corporate structure. Since Black males were not hired in entry positions in banks, commercial enterprises, financial institutions, and retail sales, they could not move up to management positions. Elaborate codes of secrecy and deception were used by large White companies to keep Black males from advancing above low-status positions. In an employment discrimination case against the Detroit Edison Company in 1973, investigators armed with subpoena power searched Edison's personnel records for several months before uncovering a racial coding system, a Black dot on certain names in personnel files, that served to channel Black employees into low-paying positions.[51] In a patriarchal society where a major aspect of the masculine role consisted of being head of the household and chief economic provider, Black males were placed at a distinct disadvantage.

A combination of gentlemen's agreements, written and unwritten rules, social customs, and aggressive law enforcement was employed to keep Black males in subjugated roles. Violence, terrorism, and intimidation were directed not only at those who challenged the rules, but to instill fear in Blacks as a whole. As late as the 1960s, civil rights workers were repeatedly jailed, beaten, harassed, and even murdered with the complicity of southern law enforcement and elected officials. Attempting to register to vote could bring swift, violent retaliation. In 1961, in Amite County, Mississippi, Herbert Lee, a Black farmer, was attending voter education classes sponsored by civil rights groups. A White Mississippi state assemblyman, E. H. Hurst, attempted at gunpoint to dissuade Lee from continuing his voter education efforts. Lee told Hurst he would not talk with him until he put his gun away. Hurst aimed the gun at Lee's head and shot and killed him. The murder was ruled justifiable homicide.[52]

Box 2.2 Before Antidiscrimination Laws Forced Bigotry to Go Underground, the Racial Codes Were Put in Writing

---

The Racial Prerequisites for Membership in Trade Unions
Early Twentieth Century

Brotherhood of Locomotive Firemen "He shall be White born, of good moral character, sober and industrious, sound in body and limb, his eyesight shall be normal, not less than eighteen years of age and able to read and write the English language."

Brotherhood of Railway Carmen "Any White person between the age of 16 and 65 years, who believes in the existence of a Supreme Being, who is free from hereditary or contracted diseases, of good moral character and habits."

Clerks and Freight Handlers Union "All White persons, male or female, of good moral character."

Masters, Mates and Pilots Union "White person of good moral character, in sound health, and a firm believer in God, the Creator of the Universe."

Wire Weavers Union "Christian, White, male of the full age of 21. . . . Foreigners applying for admission must declare citizenship intentions and pay an initiation fee of $1,000."

Source: Herbert Hill, *Black Labor and the American Legal System: I, Race, Work, and the Law* (Washington, DC: The Bureau of National Affairs, Inc., 1977, pp. 19–20).

Racial Progress

Whites sought to perpetuate the image of White male superiority and Black male inferiority by controlling the definition, pace, and style of Black progress. Euro-Americans interested in maintaining the status quo in race relations defined progress in terms of gradualism and tokenism. Cosmetic or token changes were passed off as substantive.

Whites defined progress as one Black being hired as a bank clerk or a Black man being appointed to a mid-level civil service position. Blacks were encouraged to work hard, be patient, and trust the judgment of the White power structure. They were told that social agitation for civil rights, human dignity, and greater job opportunities would only alienate Whites, set back progress, and possibly invite retaliation. The general theme, consistent with the Black inferiority thesis, was that Blacks would have to prove themselves first before they could enter the mainstream of employment, voting, public accommodation, and housing. Since science, religion, and popular beliefs considered Blacks to be far behind Whites in human development, it was obvious that it would take Blacks several generations to catch up. In the meantime, Black men should be patient, faithful, and work hard and humbly at menial jobs.

Since Black leadership would inevitably push for change, Euro-Americans tried to select Black leadership that was consistent with their philosophy of gradualism and tokenism. At the beginning of this century, the Euro-American establishment was very willing to anoint Booker T. Washington as America's Black leader. Washington, a former slave and founder of Tuskegee Institute in Alabama, preached thrift, patience, and gradualism. He felt Blacks should concentrate on manual trades and building small businesses. They should avoid agitation for social equality and civil rights. By staying away from social agitation, working hard at manual labor, and developing prudent personal habits, Blacks could build a pattern of goodwill among Whites that would pay off in the long run. Conversely, W. E. B. Du Bois, a Harvard-educated Ph.D. who agitated for political and social change, was rejected by the White power structure.[53] In the 1950s and 1960s, FBI Director J. Edgar Hoover sought to prevent the emergence of a Black messiah. His attempts to discredit Martin Luther King, Jr., were part of a broader effort to replace Dr. King with a more moderate leader, presumably a person that Hoover could control.[54]

An Overview

From our discussion of the social construction of White male superiority versus Black male inferiority, four findings regarding race relations in America seem evident. First, Euro-Americans rearranged reality to create the appearance of change without changing the underlying reality of White male dominance. After 250 years, the slaves were freed and America promised to live up to the ideals of equal justice, fair play, and opportunity for all men. Despite the promises of a new and equitable social order, Euro-Americans used science, religion, and de facto and de jure segregation to re-create an image of the Black male as subhuman, reinforced by social barriers designed to keep Black men in a subordinate role. Between 1865 and the early 1960s, the fundamental power relationship between Black and White males did not change; America remained a country where White racism prevailed. Second, social forces have been used to create an illusion of objectivity and rationality. Euro-Americans started out with a belief in their superiority. Subsequently, scientific and religious pronouncements and popular cultural images were shaped to fit this ideology, which was then marketed as objective, rational, and justified by God. Sociologists refer to this phenomenon as the sociology of knowledge. According to the sociology of knowledge, powerful cultural beliefs influence scientific and theoretical conclusions. The way Whites constructed social reality resulted in a restricted range of choices for Blacks.

Third, competition for advancement and achievement was rigged in favor of White males. The game was played with a stacked deck. No matter how hard they worked, impenetrable social and legal barriers, backed up by intimidation and force when necessary, made it impossible for Black males as a group to climb above the bottom rung of the social ladder in jobs, education, income, and political power. In the rigged game, predictable outcomes favorable to White males were used to support the theory of social Darwinism, which espouses the belief that White males succeeded because they were the best and the brightest, not because the deck was stacked in their favor.

Fourth, once a set of negative images was deeply ingrained in the thinking of American society, the sociology of knowledge made it next to impossible for new images to occur without carrying the old baggage forward. Black inferiority was established as a fact, not just an opinion. Every thought regarding Blacks was then tainted by that "fact." In the 1950s and 1960s, even those social scientists attempting to move away from perceptions of the genetic inferiority of Black males created new deficit/deficiency models in the form of concepts of cultural deprivation, self-hatred, and social pathology.

In order to construct a set of positive images that present the rich human potential and strengths of Black males, it is necessary to start from a perspective that has not been contaminated by centuries of White racist thinking. It is essential to listen to the voices of the oppressed, to hear and see how they have dealt with the strain of racism and how they define themselves in light of the false definitions thrust upon them.

Chapter 3

An Opposing View: The Black Construction of Social Reality

From the end of the Civil War in 1865 to the 1960s, Euro-Americans appeared to control Black life in the United States. Operating through social custom, law, economic and political power, and stereotypical images, White power defined and maintained a subordinate status for Black males. On the surface, Euro-Americans presumed to know what Blacks were thinking, feeling, and planning, but at a level not generally available to Whites, Black Americans were constructing an alternative way of being that would have a profound impact on both African-American and Euro-American life.

The African-American Way of Being

The authentic African-American male and his way of being were, for the most part, invisible.

In the often quoted lines of Ralph Ellison's 1947 novel, *Invisible Man*, the young Black protagonist says to America:

> *I am an invisible man. No, I am not a spook like those who haunted Edgar Allan Poe; nor am I one of your Hollywood-movie ectoplasms. I am a man of substance, of flesh and bone, fiber and liquids—and I might even be said to possess a mind. I am invisible, understand, simply because people refuse to see me. Like the bodiless heads you see sometimes in circus sideshows, it is as though I have been surrounded by mirrors of hard, distorting glass. When they approach me they see only my surroundings, themselves, or figments of their imagination—indeed, everything and anything except me.*[1]

The African-American way of being can be described in terms of three primary dimensions: African-American psychology; African-American social, family, and religious institutions; and the African-American aesthetic. It evolved from a combination of three central forces: the residuals of African culture, the effects of slavery and continuing oppression in America, and partial assimilation into Euro-American society.[2]

African-American Psychology

Five major characteristics define African-American psychology: improvisation, resilience, connectedness to others, the value of direct experience, and spirituality.[3]

Improvisation

Historically, racially oppressive forces operating in Euro-American society have limited the range of important life options available to Black males. To increase their life choices, Black males have been taught to be resourceful and innovative, competencies that Black psychologists refer to under the general label of "improvisation." Effective improvisation requires three major skills. First, the person must be able to imagine possibilities that are not entirely apparent. A Black youngster growing up in the 1930s who had never seen a Black male employed as a stockbroker, accountant, or machinist would have to use his imagination to visualize himself in these roles. Second, after dreaming the dream, he would have to devise a plan to make the dream a reality. Third, he would have to be willing to risk failure, learn from inevitable setbacks, and sustain his motivation while trying to make the best of an unfair predicament.

Resilience

Resilience can be described as the capacity to rebound from a major setback or tragedy. In the Black experience, this means more than stoicism or a return to the status quo; it involves going beyond healing and recovery. The goal in moving successfully through tragedy is to become stronger in the broken places, to keep moving toward revitalization and psychological renewal. Profound sorrow and heartbreak are inevitable in a society where Whites have enslaved Blacks, subjected Blacks to de facto and de jure Jim Crow laws, and defined Black males as subhuman. A first step in learning to survive, and ultimately to transcend tragedy, is to see life as it really is, without romantic pieties. The message in the blues and in Black gospel music is that profound sorrow and heartbreak are unavoidable. In the process of living, there are dues to be paid—this is simply the way it is. In the Black ethos, personal maturity cannot be achieved until one has transcended tragedy and crossed over to a more actualized level of personal growth. In the folk poetry of gospel and the blues, and in the works of such writers as Langston Hughes and James Baldwin, overcoming tragedy is facilitated by remaining open to the life-affirming experiences of joy and sensuousness and to the tragicomic themes in African-American humor.[4, 5]

Connectedness to Others

From the cradle to the grave, Black folks are connected to each other in interdependent, reciprocal relationships. Beginning with overlapping extended families and the Black church, African-Americans are linked in a series of social networks: neighborhoods, fraternal orders and lodges, street corner groups, barbershop gatherings, social clubs, civic groups. Trying to make it in the world alone is perceived as an invitation to personal disaster and alienation. Revitalization of the human spirit is aided by the knowledge that you are not alone, that there are others who will bear witness to your joys and sorrows. In the context of relationships, Blacks are expected to be "for real." They are expected to be authentic and down-to-earth and to risk taking off the social mask to share genuine feelings and ideas. When African-Americans get together, whether at parties, funerals, religious services, weddings, poetry readings, political meetings, or other gatherings, the emotional tone is one of aliveness, of animation and spontaneity. Feelings are emotions to be shared rather than suppressed.

Spoken language in the African-American community is highly participatory. Whether at parties, on street corners, at barbershops, on playgrounds, or in the course of political speeches or church sermons, speakers and listeners engage in a verbal interaction called the call-response. The speaker sends out a call (talks) and the listener responds, acting as an echo chamber—reiterating, clarifying, validating, and affirming the message of the speaker with amens, right-ons, yes-sirs, and teach-ons. The listener's response is amplified by body gestures, head nodding, handclapping, and touching. Speaker and listener operate in a shared linguistic space, continuously acknowledging each other's presence. Black speech is rich in symbolism, tonal rhythms, metaphors, and personification. The large number of linguistic categories used to designate various forms of sociolinguistic interaction attests to the importance of the spoken word: Black linguists have identified more than forty-two categories of African-American interactive speech, including "signifyin'," "playin' the dozens," "cappin'," "whoofin'," "tommin'," "bad-mouthin'," "runnin' it down," and "jivin'."[6, 7]

The Value of Direct Experience

In the traditional African-American way of being, there is no substitute for actual experiences gained in the course of living. Life cannot be lied to. In personal relationships and matters of race, the truth will ultimately come out. African-American slaves and their descendants kept the faith that attaining freedom was just a matter of time because slavery and oppression were against the laws of humanity, the laws of God, the Declaration of Independence, and the U.S. Constitution. Respect for the elderly and distrust of Euro-American institutions, spoken proclamations, and written documents are two consequences of the value that Blacks place on direct experience.

The elderly in the Black community are valued because they have been through experiences that can only come with age. They are the reservoirs of wisdom accumulated through a lifetime and the keepers of the African-American heritage, the storehouse of the oral tradition. They have lived through the repetitive cycles of oppression, struggle, survival, backlash, and renewed struggle that have historically confronted African-Americans. The elderly have learned to improvise, rebound from setbacks, transcend tragedy, and stay connected to others. They have stood the test of time and adversity and discovered how to survive the existential contradictions of being Black in America. The store of wisdom that elderly Blacks have accumulated in the course of living is handed down from generation to generation through the oral tradition. Children and grandchildren are taught the lessons of life through a vast oral literature consisting of parables, proverbs, folktales, biblical verses, and song.

Direct experience with the legacy of slavery—Jim Crow (de facto and de jure segregation), broken promises, lies, and negative racial stereotypes projected by Euro-Americans—has taught Black males a deep distrust of America, its institutions, written words, and spokespersons. There have been too many dreams deferred and promissory notes left unpaid by the banks of American justice for Blacks to be able to trust Whites. The Kerner Commission, created in 1967 by President Lyndon Johnson to study the causes of violent rebellion in America's Black urban ghettos, concluded—after documenting the history of racism in America—that African-Americans had valid reasons for their distrust.[8] This distrust makes it difficult for Blacks and Whites to engage in honest, productive communication about racial matters. The basic assumption of Blacks is that Whites will engage in denial, deception, and other forms of psychological trickery either to stonewall or try to convince Blacks that cosmetic changes are substantive ones.

Spirituality

Spirituality is the unifying theme in African-American psychology. The spiritual élan, or soul force, provides the fundamental life-affirming power for maintaining psychological vitality, inspiration, strength, and faith in the face of adversity. Soul force generates the courage to resist oppression and find meaning despite the existential dilemmas created by racism. It is the primary psychic energy essential for renewal and revitalization as one moves through the life cycle. Soul force is the bond in loving relationships.

The traditional African-American way of being is part of a soul culture that conveys the spiritual essence in expressive forms, such as music, drama, dance, and the oral tradition. The beat, rhythm, and style of the Black church can be found in all major forms of Black music—jazz, blues, gospel, rhythm and blues, pop, and rock.[9]

Major Social Institutions

In the traditional African-American community, the way of being revolves around the extended family, educational institutions, fraternal
orders and civic groups, and the Black church. Black males have
played an instrumental role in developing and maintaining these interlocking community institutions.

The Extended Family

The strengths of the extended family can be described in terms of the
values, competencies, and relationship patterns that contribute to the
well-being of its members and its positive contribution to the African-
American community. The extended family is responsible for building
self-esteem in children and socializing them to become part of
American society without negating the African-American heritage.
One of the most notable strengths of the extended family is its willingness to help others and to absorb others into the household and kin
networks. In times of crisis, the extended family is able to expand in
response to external pressures by informally adopting dependent children whose parents have died or separated or by taking in single
teenage mothers and their children. The Black extended family is like
a social service network that helps out others with day care, financial
assistance, nursing care, and other forms of mutual aid, especially during times of personal misfortune. Spiritual and religious beliefs have
been part of the psychological foundation of the extended family. Most
Black American families hold on to a spiritual belief and an unshakable faith that conditions may improve because of a commitment to a
power greater than oneself.[10]

Education

The quest for learning has had a strong influence in the Black community, with education viewed as a vehicle through which members of
each generation could expand their range of opportunity. After the
Civil War, with the help of northern philanthropic and religious organizations, Black families and churches led the drive to build educational
institutions in the Black community. By 1890, just one generation after
slavery, one-third of Black children under age twenty-one were attending school. The gains in school attendance continued. By 1910, 45 percent

of Black children were enrolled in school, often in states where school attendance laws were nonexistent or were not enforced for Black youth. (Black children were often withdrawn by White landowners to pick cotton whenever extra help in the fields was needed.) Between 1865 and 1965, each generation received more education than the preceding generation. The gains were achieved in all major areas of education, including basic literacy, school attendance, number of grades completed, college attendance, and college graduation.[11]

Fraternal Orders and Civic Groups

A variety of organizations supplemented the Black extended family networks and educational institutions and provided leadership in business, political, and civic affairs. The Knights of Pythias, Oddfellows, Elks, and Masonic lodges helped to build strong communities. Alumni chapters of Black college fraternities contributed scholarships and guidance for Black youth.

The Black Church

The Black church is the flagship institution in the African-American community. Next to the extended family, it is the oldest continuous Black institution, addressing both spiritual and social needs. As a carry-over from their African origins, and also from slavery, Black Americans do not make rigid distinctions between secular and sacred. While not all African-Americans are active members, the Black church, with its overlapping extended families, touches every area of the community. From slavery forward, the Black church has promoted values of improvisation, resilience and redemptive suffering, connectedness to others, direct experience, and spirituality as the basic forces that connect events in this life and the world beyond. It is the Black church that has provided the spiritual beacon to help Blacks survive the strains of living in a racist society that attempts to keep them in legal, economic, political, and psychological bondage. The church has sustained African-Americans individually and collectively and has given them the strength to keep on pushing, to find meaning, and to creatively transform negative energy into positive accomplishments.

Major Black businesses, educational institutions, and political movements had their beginnings in the basements and meeting rooms of Black churches. Prominent Black entertainers, among them Duke

Ellington, Little Richard, Sam Cooke, Lou Rawls, and Aretha Franklin, began their careers in the church. Young people and adults learned public speaking, how to conduct a meeting, and how to initiate fund-raising drives in the church. Despite dead-end jobs and low-status po-sitions in mainstream America, many Black men and women have found a sense of somebodyness in the church. Black males, who were not allowed to vote, who had to step off the sidewalk to let White peo-ple pass, could be somebody in the church. They could aspire to be-come deacons or trustees, they could be elected to represent their church as delegates to state and national religious conventions. Three of the most powerful African-American spokesmen of the twentieth century, Malcolm X, James Baldwin, and Martin Luther King, Jr., came from strong spiritual backgrounds.

Worshipers in the traditional Black church were free to express themselves; during services they could holler, shout, dance, cry, and bear witness to the sorrow and joys of life's journey. African-American ministers encouraged their congregations to identify with biblical characters who kept their faith in ultimate freedom despite the over-whelming power of their oppressors. The central message of the church was that if you kept faith in divine intervention despite seem-ingly impossible odds, God would ultimately deliver you from the burdens of racial discrimination. Themes of spiritual deliverance, re-demptive suffering, and collective freedom were at the heart of the civil rights movement; the oratory, hymns, and prayers of the move-ment had their origins in the Black church.[12]

The Black Aesthetic

The Black aesthetic is the expressive component of the African-American way of being. In music, dance, literature, and sports, the special spiritual and psychological character of historical and contem-porary African-American existence is artistically communicated by those whose empathy comes from having lived the Black experience.

Black Music

In Africa and from the beginnings of their existence in America, African-Americans created music and dance. The original African-American entertainers were talented slaves who performed for other slaves and their owners on the antebellum plantations. In field hollers, work songs, prison songs, sorrow songs, and gospel music, African-Americans sang about stubborn mules, sledgehammers, chain gangs, no money, two-timing women, mean Whites, and deliverance in this world and the next. Singing was a way to ease the drudgery and freely express feelings.

Blues and gospel music evolved from African music and flow from the same bedrock of the African-American experience; they integrate joy and sorrow, love and hate, and the hopes and dreams of Black people.[13] The blues articulate a psychology of suffering and resilience. According to William Handy, "father of the blues," the blues were conceived in heartache, sorrow, pain, and suffering. The bluesman articulates the pain and suffering in a patter of African-American speech and images that the listener who has lived the Black experience can understand. By giving voice to temporary defeat brought on by hard luck, mean White folks, hardhearted women, and sometimes his own bad judgment, the bluesman experiences a catharsis. Working through rage, pain, and despair, he is able to break free of self-pity and hopes the sun will shine in his back door someday. Collectively and personally, he then deprecates and mocks the trouble that caused the blues. According to Ralph Ellison, the blues are the only consistent art form in the United States that reminds us of our limitations by encouraging us to see how far we can go in conquering those same limitations through sheer resilience and toughness of spirit.[14]

African-American gospel represents the flip side of the blues. Spirituals are a powerful emotional testimonial to the depths of despair, atonement, and redemption, juxtaposed with an unshakable faith that God will ultimately prevail. The melancholy moans, plaintive wails, and anguished cries that accompany the vocals are easily transformed into vibrant rhythms, shouts, and joyful frenzy, with arm swaying, handclapping, dancing, and the step-sway motions of the choir and congregation. To those who come to church feeling empty, alone, and abandoned, the spirituals can provide uplift. Their music and lyrics reach out and touch one, figuratively and literally, until the presence of God can be felt. It is difficult to understand the psychological force of African-American gospel music unless one has lived the Black experience.

As radio became popular in the Black community in the 1930s, 1940s, and 1950s, Black disk jockeys created large followings. Successful DJs enjoyed a strong feeling of direct communication with the radio audience; they were like de facto mayors and family psychologists in many communities. Along with playing gospel, blues, R&B, and popular hits by Black artists, the DJ would honor special requests, dispense advice and information, and encourage his listeners to keep an upbeat attitude toward life. Sunday spiritual and gospel music hours on Black-oriented radio stations were among the most popular programs.[15]

These two basic African-American musical art forms, blues and gospel, gave birth to jazz, ragtime, rhythm and blues, rock, bebop, pop, and rap.[16]

Black Dance

African-American dance has been called the poetry of motion. Rhythmic motion is an integral aspect of the pulse of the Black community. African-American dance is an act of communication. Dancers express joy, exuberance, freedom, and sensuality and spontaneity, qualities that are the essence of African-American dance. Once the basic dance steps are mastered, dancers are expected to improvise and create new steps, to let the spontaneity of the spirit move them to put their individual rhythmic marks on the performance—to do their thing, so to speak. The call-response is an integral part of African-American dance. Partners and observers on and off the dance floor provide feedback with body gestures and vocal responses. Whereas formal Euro-American dances such as the foxtrot and the waltz follow a slow, controlled, sedate linear pattern, African-American dance is characterized by pulsating rhythms, expressive freedom, and vigorous intensity. Twisting, jerking, quick rhythmic foot movements, body gestures, and movement in the pelvic region are the heart and soul of African-American dances like the Charleston, jitterbug, huckle-buck, hully-gully, Watusi, and, more recently, the freak, electric slide, and the bounce. Before and after the advent of TV, popular dances in one geographic region of the Black community would quickly spread across the country, no doubt carried by the "national Black grapevine."[17]

Black Literature

The dominant theme in twentieth-century African-American literature has been the continuing quest for self-definition in a society where

Black males have been stereotyped as lazy darkies, criminal savages, and slow-witted half-men/half-children. In rejecting such externally imposed stereotypes, Black writers have sought to define African-American male identity from within the framework of the African-American way of being, drawing on the psychological concepts of improvisation, resilience, connectedness to others, the value of direct experience, transcendence of tragedy, and spirituality. The themes of identity and self-definition and protest are prominent in the world of authors of the Harlem Renaissance of the 1920s—Claude McKay, Langston Hughes, James Weldon Johnson, and Countee Cullen. The major characters in the works of post–Harlem Renaissance writers—John O. Killens, Richard Wright, James Baldwin, and Ralph Ellison—struggle with existential conflicts involving self-determination in a racially oppressive society.[18]

In Ellison's *Invisible Man,* the protagonist, a young Black adult without a name (symbolizing his invisibility in Euro-American society), goes through a series of struggles as a college student, social activist, and angry rebel before he painfully realizes that a search for self-definition as an African-American male must come from within. He cannot discover who he is by accepting externally imposed definitions. In order to achieve his identity, he must confront his existence and take the responsibility for sorting it out by listening to the internal voice of his own experience. Written African-American literature is supplemented by an extensive oral folk literature in which powerful male characters, such as Stagolee, Shine, and John Henry, accomplish their goals in the face of oppression by a combination of resourcefulness, resilience, resistance, persistence, and sheer physical strength. In a folk poem entitled "The Signifying Monkey," a resourceful monkey uses a combination of deceit, instigation, and agitation to reduce the power of the lion, his archenemy and king of the jungle. The lesson is that a powerful enemy can be defeated with a well-devised psychological strategy.[19]

Black Athletics

The African-American expressive style has been vividly displayed in sports. The Black aesthetic changed the flow and tempo of major spectator sports in America, with basketball being a prime example. Long before it became a multi-billion-dollar enterprise and before UCLA's famous coach, John Wooden, put together a stretch of ten NCAA

National titles, Black teenagers playing on city streets were developing a brand of action that would revolutionize the game of basketball.

In Chicago in 1954, a team from Du Sable High School became the first all-Black team to reach the finals of a racially integrated, statewide basketball tournament. The Du Sable Panthers were flamboyant, to say the least. Nicknamed the young Globetrotters, they wore black capes over their red and white warm-up jerseys and sported long professional socks and slick red and white kneepads. When the Panthers came out to warm up, they thrilled the crowd with one- and two-handed dunks. At a time when most White high school teams considered the jump shot radical, the Du Sable Panthers used the jump shot to score at will. While most White high school teams scored between 30 and 40 points per game, the Panthers averaged 80 points. The key to their offense was a shifting, full-court press, an aggressive fast break, gravity-defying leaps toward the basket, quickness, jump shots, and smooth ball handling.[20]

The team was led by a flashy ball handler, Paxton Lumpkin, also known as Sugar Lump Lumpkin or just plain Lump. Lump dribbled the ball like a yo-yo. He had a joyful, magnetic quality that electrified the game. Like all great Black athletes, he was able to fuse his personality into the flow of movement of the game and trigger a call-response interaction with the audience. In addition to wanting to win, the Du Sable Panthers also wanted to put on a show for the audience, one that expressed their individual personalities and collective talents.

White coaches criticized the Black game as a circus, run and gun and undisciplined. They didn't understand that Black expressive styles involve an integration of cognitive, motor, and affective functions.[21] But the fact that the 1954 Du Sable Panthers put their stamp on basketball is now publicly recognized. Their exploits are commemorated at the Basketball Hall of Fame in Springfield, Massachusetts; and in 1974, the Illinois High School Coaches Hall of Fame inducted the Panthers, citing them for their pioneering play.

Athletics, like other forms of Black aesthetic expression, offered an alternative frame of reference that could be used to filter out negative stereotypical images. The positive images and the institutional support these forms of expression elicited were sources of affirmation and inspiration. Black males, as individuals and as a group, could perceive themselves as part of a collective experience. And within his own psychological, social, and aesthetic space, the African-American male could realize himself as powerful, strong, competent, and worthwhile.

The "Blackanizing" of America

Prior to the 1960s, social scientists, including some Black social scientists, studying race relationships and racial attitudes in the United States tended to concentrate their efforts on how well Blacks were assimilating into the dominant Euro-American society and how well they were emulating the behavioral attitudes, social norms, and lifestyles of Whites. Black emulation of White behavior is the major thesis of E. Franklin Frazier's *The Black Bourgeoisie*.[22] What social scientists seemed to miss was that a two-way assimilation was taking place. The African-American way of being, particularly the Black aesthetic, was having a profound effect on Euro-American behavior, lifestyles, and cognitions. A process of "Blackanizing" America had begun.

Even before the first commercial recordings of the blues in the 1920s, Euro-Americans were listening to Black music presented by traveling Black gospel choirs and stage shows and in nightclubs. Subsequently, radio and records increased the spread of Black sounds into the Euro-American community. By the 1940s and 1950s, hip White disk jockeys like Dewey Phillips of radio station WHBQ in Memphis, who first introduced Elvis Presley to a radio audience, mixed Black music with the standard array of country-western, popular music, and White gospel. Sam Phillips (no relation to Dewey Phillips), who initially recorded Elvis Presley in 1953, grew up listening to the sounds and rhythms of Black gospel music outside the open windows of Black churches. Convinced that the sounds, pulse, and rhythms of Black music would touch the heart of America, Sam looked for a White performer to simulate the Black sound. In his small recording studio, Sam Phillips recorded such future Black stars as B. B. King and Ike Turner.[23] As luck would have it, he found Elvis Presley—and the rest is history. Elvis opened the door for White performers who emulated the Black sound, like Bill Haley and Jerry Lee Lewis. In March 1955, six of the top ten nationwide best-sellers were Black rhythm and blues tunes performed by White artists.[24]

A similar phenomenon occurred with the crossover of Black dance patterns into the White community. Beginning with the Charleston in the 1920s and the jitterbug in the 1930s and 1940s, White teenagers and young adults have consistently imitated the steps of Black dancers. Typically, a dance would start in the Black community at house parties or high school gymnasiums, spread to dance halls in larger cities, then cross over into the White community.

Recent research suggests that there may be a Black voice at the core of American literature. In a recent book, *Was Huck Black? Mark Twain and African-American Voices,* Shelley Fishkin, a faculty member at the University of Texas, Austin, argues that the source of Mark Twain's classic *The Adventures of Huckleberry Finn* was a ten-year-old Black servant boy Twain calls "Sociable Jimmy." Fishkin's demonstrations that the cadence, dialect, and grammatical patterns of Huck's and Sociable Jimmy's speech are comparable and in some ways identical suggest strong Black roots in Huck's expressive style. Both boys use sassiness, satire, and ironic humor to express complex views about race, hypocrisy, and the social contradictions embedded in American values. Mark Twain recognized the power of African-American folk culture and its wealth of artistic potential.[25] According to Ernest Hemingway and other literary figures, all modern American literature flows from *Huckleberry Finn.* The significance of Fishkin's work is that a Black linguistic voice may be the structuring principle of this American classic novel. At the heart of White consciousness may exist a Black presence. Black writers like Toni Morrison and Ralph Ellison have long believed that there is a Black presence in American literature that has been denied, ignored, and suppressed.[26]

The influence of the Black aesthetic is readily apparent in athletics. In basketball, for example, Black athletes have revolutionized the sport; over time, the slow, deliberate pattern of the original game has been infused with the spirit and soul of the inner city. Television networks, professional basketball franchises, and participating NCAA colleges gross millions of dollars annually broadcasting games that feature three to four and sometimes even five Black players on a team's starting lineup.

Some scholars believe that the Black aesthetic is the only distinctive American artistic creation, that the African-American way of being is central to America's cultural base. The Black aesthetic has not only influenced America, but the sounds and rhythms of African-American music have been influential in Asia, Africa, Europe, and South America.[27]

Two conclusions can be drawn from the Euro-American assimilation of the Black aesthetic. First, given the opportunity, African-Americans can achieve a standard of excellence, demonstrating the skill, drive, and inventiveness deemed essential for achieving success in America. Second, like the metaphor in the title of Ellison's novel, Whites can look at a Black man without really seeing him. In other words, they can dance to Black music, use Black satire to convey ideas, and pay millions of dollars to watch gifted Black athletes perform—all without acknowledging the contributions of the Black way of being to American life and thought. To acknowledge such power, Euro-Americans would have to give up long-standing negative stereotypes. Negative stereotypes and corresponding superiority/inferiority beliefs prevent Euro-Americans from seeing things as they really are and fortify psychological defenses of denial, suppression, and minimization.

Existential Dilemmas, Rage, and Protest

Between the end of the Civil War and the beginnings of the civil rights movement, White racism in America presented the Black male with three psychological dilemmas: inclusion/exclusion, conflicts with the work ethic, and what to do with rage.

In the inclusion/exclusion dilemma, the Black male felt a double consciousness. He was simultaneously a part of America, yet apart from it. He lived in the United States and was granted the rights of citizenship by the Fourteenth Amendment, yet he was defined by the majority of Euro-American society as subhuman and excluded from large segments of American society. The African-American male was part of a long historical cultural heritage that made significant contributions to humankind, yet his heritage, both in Africa and America, was distorted, denied, and ignored. Viewed through the lens of the African-American way of being, he could visualize his authentic self. Viewed through the lens of Euro-American society, his authentic self was invisible, replaced by superficial caricatures. W. E. B. Du Bois, the great African-American scholar and social activist, spoke of this dilemma as a "twoness," a double consciousness, feeling a part of and apart, included and excluded, not being able to integrate fully the double components of one's selfhood.[28] Should the African-American male fully actualize the authentic African-American way of being and run the risk of further alienating himself from the larger Euro-American society, or should he conform to what America expects of him and lock himself into a subservient caste?

Black males faced a contradiction in a society which taught that a payoff would accrue from hard work. According to the social contract for males in America, a combination of hard work, persistent effort over time, prudent spending, and planning ahead was supposed to result in the accumulation of material goods and a wider range of life options. The dilemma for the Black male was that he was excluded from a long list of occupations and skilled crafts and from trade unions. Black doctors and lawyers were largely restricted to practicing in segregated communities. Black youth were told by their parents that they would have to work twice as hard to get half as far, be twice as good and yet expect to be the last hired and the first fired. Black sharecroppers in the South never knew what to expect when they went in to settle with the White landowner at the end of the harvest season. The landowner could arbitrarily deduct exorbitant prices for seed, fertilizer, food, and clothing from the sharecroppers' potential profits. Rather than earning money, the sharecropper was often in debt at the end of the year because accounts were rigged in favor of the landowner. Protest would bring swift reprisals in the form of beatings, firings, jail, and sometimes fatal assault.

The work ethic double bind for the Black male was that either way, he lost. If he worked hard, he ended up second best in low-status, dead-end jobs and segregated tiers of professions. The fact that he didn't achieve at the level of White males was used as evidence to support the belief that the Black male didn't have the right stuff. If he refused to work in low-status jobs and segregated ranks, he reinforced the self-fulfilling prophecy that Black males were lazy and irresponsible. It was a paradox from which there was no easy escape.

In their book *Black Rage,* William Grier and Price Cobbs, two Black psychiatrists, explain that the paradox of racial oppression in a society committed to justice and fair play creates a permanent condition of rage in the Black male that takes a psychic toll.[29] The dilemma for the Black male is what to do with his rage. Externalizing rage in the form of anger and aggression directed toward acquaintances and family members can destroy loving relationships and friendships. Acting out aggression toward society will lead to incarceration within the criminal justice system, which, in turn, makes it more difficult to obtain employment and support a family. Internalizing rage is likely to raise blood pressure, thereby increasing the risk of stress-related illnesses like strokes, heart attacks, and ulcers. Escape into alcohol and drugs reduces opportunities for a productive life and can ultimately destroy the person.

The psychological dilemmas of Black males were acted out in the civil rights movement and the urban rebellions, the two phases of the Black revolution of the 1960s. On the surface, the revolution was about jobs, open housing, voting rights, and participation in decision making at the local, state, and national levels. At a deeper, more personal level, it was about the right of self-determination and self-definition. The Reverend Martin Luther King, Jr., used terms like "somebodyness" to define the psychological meaning of the revolution. Other terms coined to reinforce this concept were "Black pride," "Black is beautiful," and "Black power." On the eve of Dr. King's assassination in Memphis, in April 1968, striking African-American sanitation workers were carrying signs saying "I am a man." Self-definition from the perspective of one's own experience is the first step in deconstructing the oppressor's negative definitions. In Alex Haley's book *Roots,* his African-American slave ancestor Kunta Kinte refused to accept the name Toby because that was the slave owner's way of defining him as less than a man.

Because Dr. King, the undisputed leader of the civil rights movement, understood the spiritual and psychological rhythms of the Black community, he was able to channel legitimate rage and frustration into nonviolent social protest. He was a product of the Black church, the Black extended family, Black educational institutions, and Black fraternal orders. The civil rights movement under Dr. King's guidance is an applied case study of the Black way of being. Mass protests with singing, marching, and call-response speeches involved the major social institutions of the Black community, the Black aesthetic, and the African-American psychological characteristics of improvisation, resilience, connectedness, spirituality, and the value of direct experience. The movement was a visible display of the power of soul force.[30]

The young African-American males involved in the urban rebellions expressed their pent-up rage and frustration in burning and looting. They rejected Dr. King's call for nonviolence and love of one's oppressor. To them it did not make sense that Euro-American oppressors deserved to be loved or that love would move the oppressor to live up to America's promises of justice and fair play. The heroes of the street Brothers of urban America were Malcolm X, Stokely Carmichael (author of the Black power battle cry), and Huey Newton, cofounder of the Black Panther party. These men believed in the right of Black self-defense against White-on-Black violence and renegade White police. Malcolm X, spokesman for Elijah Muhammad's Lost/Found Nation of Islam, or Black Muslims, profoundly distrusted White society. He felt that the Euro-American abuse of Blacks for more than 350 years represented a quality of inherent evil in Whites. He defended the right of self-defense, preached Black pride, and called for the separation of the races.[31]

By bringing the struggle into the public arena, the Black revolution forced White America to address the dissonance created by the ideals of freedom and equality and the reality of Black oppression. (The genius of Martin Luther King was his ability to generate tension in situations, covered by the mass media, that revealed the contradictions between democratic ideals and persistent racism.) As the revolution progressed, it also became obvious that there was a gap between Black and White definitions of "progress." What Whites considered progress, Blacks defined as tokenism and gradualism. No mechanisms were in place to resolve Black/White differences by engaging in collaborative decision making and a synthesis of opposing views. Conflict resolution based on creative synthesis of differences is not possible when Whites refuse to give up control and a belief that their social construction of reality represents the only valid point of view.

Reminiscent of the Reconstruction period after the Civil War, laws were passed as a consequence of the civil rights movement to ensure Blacks their fundamental rights as American citizens in such areas as public accommodations, jobs, housing, voting rights, and higher education. And, just like Reconstruction, change was more apparent than real. When the dust cleared, Whites, once again, had a monopoly on economic and political power and on the mass media. Today, the Black male is still struggling with issues of identity, values, and inclusion. Early in this century, W. E. B. Du Bois said that the problem of the twentieth century would be the color line. As we approach the end of the twentieth century, that problem is still very much with us.[32]

Part II

CONTEMPORARY IMAGES

AND EXPRESSIVE STYLES

Chapter 4

Contemporary Black Male Images: A One-Sided View

In contemporary America, the distorted images of Black masculinity projected by the media and social scientists are an ongoing phenomenon. Black males are typecast as superathletes, entertainers, and clowns; occasionally, there are superachievers, such as the actor and social commentator Bill Cosby and retired Chairman of the U.S. Armed Forces Joint Chiefs of Staff Colin Powell.

Basketball, the premiere sport in Black urban ghettos, has become a multi-million-dollar sports industry. To build winning teams, which translates into profitable TV contracts, colleges actively recruit in inner-city high schools and playgrounds, and have become training grounds for future professional stars. Inner-city youths who can barely read aspire to be like their superstar heroes; they spend hours on concrete courts practicing steps and moves they hope will get them to the heavenly kingdom of professional basketball.

On the surface, it appears that TV has made considerable progress in projecting Black male images since the early days of the 1950s when Blacks were cast primarily in antique sitcoms like *Amos 'n' Andy*. *Amos 'n' Andy* began as a radio series in 1928, moved to TV in 1951, and continued as a widely popular syndicated series until 1966, when it was finally driven off the air after years of protest by the National Association for the Advancement of Colored People (NAACP) and other Black groups.[1] Built around slapstick humor and buffoonery, it featured both working-class and professional Blacks. The leading men were Andy, easygoing but not very smart; Amos, a softhearted, gentle cab company owner; and King Fish, the show's central character. King Fish, who detested manual labor, was depicted as a shrewd, likable, but not too creative con artist. The men seemed dimwitted, easily befuddled, and spoke in garbled English, using phrases like "be fo I goes," "I sahs," and "dat's right." Following King Fish's direction, they often got caught up in fancy schemes that backfired, or told fibs and exaggerated tales that could not fool elementary school children much less their wives and girlfriends.[2]

The show was written and directed by two White writers, Charles Correll and Freeman Gosden, who played major roles when the series was on the radio and acted in two *Amos 'n' Andy* movies in blackface. The basis of the NAACP protest was that the show was racially demeaning and bigoted; it symbolized White stereotypes of Black males as dishonest, lazy, not too bright, and clowns.

The casting of African-American males primarily in comedy roles continued into the 1970s with the sitcoms *Sanford and Son, Good Times,* and *The Jeffersons*. The breakthrough for Black males in dramatic roles came with the production of the TV miniseries *Roots* in 1977. *Roots* was based on the best-selling novel by Alex Haley, a story tracing his family's history from life as free men in Africa through the end of slavery in the United States. The premiere of *Roots,* on January 23, 1977, captured America's White and Black audiences for five successive nights. It was estimated that half the U.S. population watched the series, with approximately one hundred million people tuning in the final installment. *Roots* still ranks as the third most watched program in the history of television.[3]

Today Black males appear in a variety of roles in front of and behind the camera. There are Black writers, directors, and producers on the major TV networks. Black actors have appeared in supportive roles in a number of popular series, like *Baretta, Welcome Back, Kotter,*

All in the Family, and occasionally *Kojak. The Cosby Show,* a series about a middle-class professional Black family that ran for eight years in the 1980s, was America's prime-time TV show.[4] In 1996–97, Black males had prominent roles in ensemble dramas such as *Chicago Hope, Law and Order, Dangerous Minds, Homicide: Life on the Street, ER,* and *NYPD Blue* as doctors, police officers, detectives, lawyers, and district attorneys. These shows featured well-developed characters—for example, Lieutenant Fancy, the African-American head of detectives in *NYPD Blue,* a tough, serious, no-nonsense man with a somber, edgy demeanor who has moved up fast in the ranks; or Dr. Peter Benton, the intense, self-assured surgeon in *ER,* so devoted to his work that it interferes with his family life and his relationship with his girlfriend.

Despite two decades of apparent progress, a closer examination of TV images indicates that Black males are still cast predominantly in comedy roles. In 1996–97, there wasn't a single one-hour network drama built around a Black male character; there were, however, at least eight sitcoms in which Black males were the featured stars. Many critics feel that these comedy shows do not give a fair representation of Blacks in American life,[5] but instead are only louder, hipper, updated versions of *Amos 'n' Andy,* with sexual innuendoes mixed with a hip-hop style. In one of these, *The Jamie Foxx Show,* the lead character is a bellhop working in a hotel owned by his aunt and uncle. He seems to spend most of his time joking at the expense of a square friend, jiving, and flirting with women. Some critics feel that *The Wayans Bros.* are the worst offenders of all. Much of their comedy is slapstick, loaded with Black slang and buffoonish behavior. This concentration of Black males in comic roles is supplemented by the appearances of Black entertainers like Michael Jackson, the Artist formerly known as Prince, Snoop Doggy Dogg, or the late Biggie Smalls. Periodically, the super-achievers, like Cosby and Powell, are called upon to do social commentary on current issues or discuss major events in their lives. (Many people think that General Powell has the potential to become the first Black president of the United States.) Such appearances are not sufficient, however, to offset the popular, stereotypical images. A foreign visitor watching American TV could easily conclude that all Blacks are natural athletes, can sing and dance, and spend the day making up funny one-liners.

Since the end of World War II, the study of underclass urban Black men has become a cottage industry in the social sciences, particularly in sociology and cultural anthropology. Using ethnographic research methods consisting of street corner interviews, samples of group dialogue, and biographical narratives, social scientists have developed an extensive literature on urban African-American males. In books like Elliot Liebow's *Talley's Corner* (1967), Ulf Hannerz's *Soulside* (1971), and Elijah Anderson's *A Place in the Corner* (1978) and *Streetwise* (1990), inner-city Black males are depicted as having a negative attitude toward hard work, manual labor, thrift, and planning for the future. They are only intermittently employed and spend much of their time hanging out on street corners boasting about sexual exploits and physical toughness. Dress styles are flashy, and verbal styles are characterized by showboating and exaggerated tales about accomplishments, future goals, and women. Small-time hustling, stealing, and selling drugs are acceptable ways to supplement one's income; popular writer Norman Mailer reinforces this image in his 1981 book *Advertisements for Myself* in which he describes Black males as living primarily for Saturday night—a time when they can drop their inhibitions and experience the joys of lust and the sweet sound of music.[6]

The Urban Underclass

Sociologists and social psychologists now include the street Brothers in the larger urban social caste called "the underclass," sometimes also referred to as "the undeserving poor." Underclass Black males in inner-city slums are generally described as chronically jobless high school dropouts who have fathered two or three children whom they don't support, either financially or emotionally. More often than not, they have a criminal record and no visible means of support. Use of drugs and alcohol is excessive. Relationships with women are frequently unstable, hostile, and exploitative.[7]

The underclass actually consists of two groups, decent people, or the deserving poor, and inner-city residents who are part of an oppositional culture or renegade lifestyle. The "decent people," as sociologist Elijah Anderson refers to them, accept mainstream values, are willing to work at minimal jobs when work is available, and value self-reliance and responsibility.[8] They are willing to sacrifice for their children and grandchildren, and retain a certain amount of faith in the promises of American society. They see today's hardships as a test from God and strive to maintain a positive attitude toward life in the future. A number of women in this group are rearing their grandchildren because their sons and daughters have been lost to crime, drugs, and other dangers of street life. In the second group, the undeserving poor, the Black males are alienated from middle-class society and its values. They feel a deep-seated anger and bitterness toward White America because they have not been treated fairly. Rage, combined with frustration, fuels self-destructive behavior in the form of drug and alcohol abuse and criminal behavior. Explosive violence can be easily triggered by day-to-day conflicts and frustrations. Living involves very little long-range planning, setting of priorities, or carefully examining the consequences of high-risk behavior to themselves or others.

Going for Bad

As part of their oppositional cultural identity, many inner-city young African-American males have adopted a code of masculinity known on the streets as "going for bad." Going for bad involves physical and psychological toughness and aggressiveness, even to the point of ruthlessness. Might makes right. Being able to "kick ass" is a virtue that enhances one's rep; quiet, patient, problem solving does not. If people "diss" you (show disrespect), they have to be straightened out. If aggressive talk doesn't work, physical assault must be used. All challenges must be answered, and assaults are met with paybacks of retaliatory violence. One expresses masculine toughness by one's walk, facial expressions and body language, dress, and aggressive talk. It is important to project an image of being in control. The go-for-bad Brothers act as if they are unafraid of death; indeed, many believe they won't have a long life anyway. Prison or threat of imprisonment does not deter them; on the streets, surviving prison can enhance one's reputation for toughness. Gangs are attractive to inner-city young men because they offer opportunities to learn masculine bravery, toughness, aggressiveness, plus street wisdom.[9]

Inner-city Black males who have not internalized the go-for-bad masculine style must master its rules to survive on the streets. Looking capable of defending oneself is a form of self-defense; acting timid and fearful can invite danger. If others don't respect your masculinity, your life and the lives of those close to you could be in peril. The defensive survival rules are straightforward: Protect yourself; if someone messes with you, straighten that person out; don't punk out. In street parlance, a "punk" is a weak, passive, somewhat effeminate male. In prison settings, punks are quickly turned out or turned into passive sexual partners and passed around among the inmates.

In the urban survival game, occasionally the offensive and defensive go-for-bad strategies can get mixed up. The "urban survival syndrome"—the fear inner-city Black men have of other Black men, which leads them to act first—was used in Fort Worth, Texas, in 1994, to gain a deadlocked jury in a case where a Black man shot two other unarmed Black men in a parking lot. The shooter claimed the other men looked menacing, so he went on the offensive in order to defend himself before the victims overtly threatened him. Also, young Black men have been shot by other young Black men because of perceived disrespectful looks or stares.[10]

Two conclusions seem apparent from our review of contemporary images of Black males projected by the media, popular American culture, and the social sciences. First, these images are reminiscent of nineteenth- and early twentieth-century one-dimensional, negative stereotypes. Second, the images of the Black male as a clown, superathlete, entertainer, and hyperaggressive/sexual street corner Brother are often mistaken for authentic representations. Not only do Euro-Americans believe that these caricatures represent the reality of Black male life, but Black male youths may aspire to live up to these images because they are popularized and romanticized.

The Hood and Its Boys

The characterization portrait of young urban Blacks as tough, swaggering, gun-toting Brothers teetering on the edge of gangsterism is reinforced by movies released in the early 1990s. *Menace II Society, Juice,* and *Boyz N the Hood,* for example, all show Black male teenagers and young adults struggling with the mean, unforgiving streets of America's inner cities. Of the three films, *Menace II Society,* filmed in Watts and South-Central Los Angeles, is the most fatalistic and realistic. The violence is unrelenting and devoid of romanticism. Opening with the murder/robbery of a Korean grocery store couple, the story revolves around Caine, the antihero, and his posse. As a child, Caine witnesses his father gun down a man in the family's living room over a disputed card game. Caine and his posse are constantly engaged in a cycle of offensive and defensive violence where payback and retaliation lead to more violence. The message is that Black men are a menace to society. Along the way, a strong Black male teacher tells the boys that being a Black male in American society is not easy; a hunt is on and Black males are the prey. The predators are, too often, other Black men. In the end, Caine is gunned down in a drive-by shooting payback as a small child watches, thus completing the cycle of three generations of violence.

Juice is about four young African-Americans on the brink of delinquency and crime as they negotiate adolescence on the run-down streets of Harlem. The boys live in a self-contained world that is part of the hip-hop/rap culture. They listen to it, dress it, and express it. While their parents think they are in school, the boys roam the streets aimlessly, looking for action and hanging out in a local pool hall. The term "juice," as the film's title, is a metaphor for power: who has it and how to get it. A male without juice commands no respect. The boys try to rise above the peer pressure and criminality of the streets but are slowly swept up into robbery and shootings. In the end, the power of street life is too strong to resist.

Boyz N the Hood is the most hopeful of the three movies. Growing up in South-Central Los Angeles, Tre Styles, the major character, has a chance of overcoming the destruction that crushes too many African-American males. He is still in school, has a strong father figure (Furious), a part-time job in a West Los Angeles shopping mall, and a steady girlfriend. Drugs and violence are all around him, a reflexive part of street life along with masculine bravado and endless hanging out on street corners. A police helicopter is constantly whirling overhead, even as Tre and his girlfriend make love. People feel trapped. Tre's two friends from childhood, who live across the street, do not have the support of a strong male role model. Doughboy, who has spent time in prison, is embittered and angry; his brother, Ricky, has aspirations of playing college football. The overburdened families of all three boys struggle to provide the young men with the tools of survival. In the end, Doughboy and Ricky cannot transcend the violence and destruction. Only Tre is able to land on his feet and keep moving toward a productive adult life.

Spike Lee: A Different Voice

To his credit, filmmaker Spike Lee uses his movies to provide a broad perspective of Black male lifestyles, identity choices, and perceptions of Blackness. His films move beyond one-dimensional characterizations of Black men mired in endless cycles of self-destructive behavior. He presents Black males as a multifaceted, dynamic group with a diversity of personalities representing a wide range of human emotions, abilities, aspirations, and coping styles.

Based on his experiences in the Black community as a resident and participant, Spike Lee uses his insider's knowledge of African-American culture to infuse his films with Black music, Black humor, Black folk expressions, and Black interactive dialogue. His films capture the texture, meanings, and subtle shadings of Black life in familiar community settings. He weaves into his screenplays excerpts from Black oral and written literature—poetry, newspapers, and graffiti—to provide a sense of the totality of the African-American ethos.[11]

Do the Right Thing (1989) is a story about a hot summer day in the life of Black residents in a tense neighborhood in Brooklyn's Bedford Stuyvesant that culminates in a violent racial uprising. The film opens with musical messages of Black resistance: the Negro National Anthem and rap group Public Enemy's song "Fight the Power"—a militant call to action that plays in the background throughout the movie like a Greek chorus. Other symbols of Black rebellion include images of a Black dancer wearing boxing gloves.

The movie has a sharp, clever ring of authenticity. Black male characters, easily recognizable by Black audiences, represent a range of personality types and social styles. Mister Señor Love Daddy, the local disk jockey, spins the platters and appeals to his listeners to wake up and take care of business. Da Mayor, played by Ossie Davis, is a likable local drunk with a keen moral conscience. Buggin' Out is an angry, disgruntled young man with spiked hair. Smiley, who has trouble communicating, is a friendly young man who carries around pictures of Martin Luther King, Jr., and Malcolm X. Radio Raheem moves up and down the street with a huge boom box blasting rap music. Mookie (played by Spike Lee), who emerges as the film's central character, is a pizza deliveryman. He is continuously trying to solve problems with his girlfriend about child support, sex, and the amount of time he spends with her. Their problems, cast in a context of Black humor, elicit smiles and laughter from the audience. Periodically, three middle-aged Black street corner griots appear in the film using Black dialect and ghetto metaphors to comment on sexual prowess, race, money, and the Asian merchants who run a local market. The camera gives life to the sights and sounds of the community: the tenement walls, street pavements, hip street attire, vibrant music, and the rhythms of Black speech.

The major thread woven into the fabric of *Do the Right Thing* is the racial discontent and anger that permeate America's Black inner cities. The film sends a clear message that race relations in America are in terrible shape. Buggin' Out points out to the liberal White owner of the pizza parlor where Mookie works that he has no pictures of Black male or female heroes on the wall. Sal, the owner of Sal's Famous Pizzeria, who has remained in the neighborhood long after other White businesses have departed, only has pictures of White, mostly Italian, icons like Frank Sinatra and Sylvester Stallone. Sal's oldest son is an out-and-out racist; he openly admits that he hates Blacks and encourages his father to move his business out of the neighborhood. At one point, a series of street characters—Koreans, Hispanics, African-Americans, Italians—look directly into the camera and shout a barrage of ethnic slurs and grievances. As the film draws to a close, a racial confrontation explodes, leaving Radio Raheem dead at the hands of the police and Sal's pizza parlor consumed by flames.[12]

Do the Right Thing ends with the pictures and voices of Martin Luther King, Jr., and Malcolm X talking about nonviolence versus the right of self-defense against violence. For most Whites, the differences between Dr. King and Malcolm X appear to be an either-or choice. Most Blacks see beyond this apparent dichotomy and concentrate on the commonality in their philosophies. Both men were interested in eliminating racial oppression, increasing the range of choices for Black people, and building a world where all men and women could aspire to human dignity. The differences between them were about tactics rather than ultimate goals. In the Black ethos, diversity does not freeze debate; it represents sources of strength arising out of the richness of the Black experience.

Do the Right Thing became one of the most talked about movies of the early 1990s. Black movie critic Donald Bogle says that no other film had as great a cultural impact on both Blacks and Whites.[13] The film became a social phenomenon that was debated and discussed all over the country in newspapers, on college and high school campuses, and on talk radio and TV. Spike Lee became a household name, and *Do the Right Thing* moved him to the top ranks of filmmakers. He was nominated for an Academy Award for the Best Original Screenplay, and actor Danny Aiello, as Sal, won an Oscar nomination for Best Supporting Actor. The phrase "do the right thing" has entered

American popular culture as a colloquial expression. When people are struggling with moral conflicts, they are encouraged to "do the right thing."

Spike Lee's *Mo' Better Blues* (1990) is a film about jazz set in an African-American context, viewing the struggle of a performer for artistic expression and romantic fulfillment against the pressures of a dominating career. The sweet background sound of jazz great John Coltrane's "A Love Supreme" triggers feelings of sensuousness and romance. The film's central character, Bleek Gilliam, played by Denzel Washington, is not some drugged-out, doomed hero tormented by despair. He is a young, middle-class, talented trumpet player who is dedicated to his art, confident, controlled, and ambitious. The movie traces Bleek's life from his childhood in Brooklyn to his early success with his jazz quartet. Bleek's major flaw is that his self-absorption makes him insensitive to the needs of others, especially the members of his quartet and the two young women vying for his attention.

A sense of lighthearted humor surrounds Bleek's complicated love life. The film shows his exasperation as he tries to meet the demands of his two lovers: The camera shows him going back and forth as he makes love first with Indigo and then with Clarke, then goes back to Indigo and again to Clarke. At the end of the love scenes, he is bewildered and confused. The style of Black male camaraderie and bonding is captured in the interaction among the members of Bleek's quartet. The spontaneous use of Black language and expressive gestures is a reflection of African-American male cultural identification.

Eventually, Bleek comes to a major crossroads in his life. He must decide whether to concentrate exclusively on his career as a jazz trumpeter or give up music to become the patriarch of his middle-class extended family. After a period of conflict, he yields to the demands of his family and takes on the patriarchal role.[14]

In *Malcolm X* (1992), Spike Lee skillfully chronicles the life of one of Black America's most famous cultural and political heroes. Working from *The Autobiography of Malcolm X* by Malcolm X and Alex Haley, and an unfinished screenplay begun by James Baldwin and Arnold Perl, the film opens with a sequence of words and images. As the audience listens to the words from Malcolm's speeches, images of a burning cross are interspersed with scenes of Rodney King being beaten by Los Angeles police officers.

Denzel Washington gives a creditable performance as Malcolm X, a man whose life was constantly evolving. The film captures the essence and soul not only of the public man but also the private man, as Malcolm works his way through the critical transformations in his life: his family being terrorized in Nebraska when he was a child, his mother's psychological breakdown after the questionable circumstances surrounding his father's death, his White teacher discouraging him from trying to become a lawyer, his street life as "Detroit Red" in Boston and New York, imprisonment, rebirth as a member of the Nation of Islam, his rise to prominence as a Black Muslim minister, his break with the Nation of Islam, and his assassination at the age of thirty-nine in the Audubon Ballroom in New York City.

Spike Lee's films capture the rhythms of Black culture and the creativity of the Black aesthetic. He raises questions about interracial conflicts, intraracial conflicts, sexuality and romance, intergenerational and family conflicts, Black militancy, political choices, and the consequences of actions. Lee's movies do not provide final answers. As a director, he is like the town convener: He calls the meeting and lays out the agenda, but it is up to the audience to make decisions about the important issues he presents. It is up to Blacks themselves to decide the ultimate questions of values, strategies, and future directions. Moving beyond the social pathology of drugs, guns, violence, and criminal behavior, Lee provides a wealth of male images. He acknowledges that social pathology exists in the Black community, but he doesn't get stuck in it. The diversity and range of personalities in his Black male characters, who are alert, bright, articulate, and strong, suggest that constructive identity choices do exist. Black males do not have to try to become White or turn away from the Black experience to find workable solutions to problems and identity conflicts.[15]

Manipulation of Distorted Black Male Images

Since most Euro-Americans do not have close personal relationships with African-American males, they are vulnerable to being influenced by the images of Black masculinity portrayed in the popular media. Even in racially integrated high schools, colleges, work settings, and the armed forces, racial groups separate when it comes time for after-hours socializing. A look at Sunday church services and attendance at weddings and funerals suggests that Blacks and Whites live in separate worlds of social intimacy. Images of Black males as gangsters, urban outlaws, and street hustlers, supplemented by daily newscasts and newspaper stories of urban neighborhoods as crime-prone, crack-plagued, gang-infested, violence-scarred war zones, both influence and reflect Whites' perceptions of Black males. The stories of Willy Horton, Charles Stuart, and Susan Smith—three widely publicized events—illustrate the power of the media to influence and reflect negative stereotypes of Black males.

In 1988, Republican Vice President George Bush was behind in the polls in his race for the presidency when he accused his rival, Democratic candidate Michael Dukakis, of being soft on crime. To back up his claim, Bush's campaign distributed a nationwide TV ad featuring a Black convict, Willy Horton. While on an approved furlough from a Massachusetts state prison, when Dukakis was governor, Horton, who was serving time for murder, assaulted a man and raped his wife. After the Willy Horton ad circulated, Dukakis dropped behind in the polls and was never able to catch up. Bush went on to win the presidency.[16]

In 1989, in Boston, Charles Stuart shot and killed his pregnant wife as they drove home from a childbirth class. The baby also died. Stuart suffered major injuries to his stomach from a self-inflicted gunshot wound. He told the police that he and his pregnant wife were shot by a Black car-jacker. A citywide manhunt for the murder suspect ensued. Before the hoax unraveled, scores of Black men were interrogated by the police. All Black men were suspects; indeed, one man was arrested and charged with murder. When Stuart's story began to fall apart, he committed suicide by jumping to his death into the Boston harbor. It was later revealed that several of his family members knew Stuart's story was not true.[17]

In South Carolina, in October 1994, a distraught twenty-two-year-old White mother named Susan Smith told police that a Black male had forced her out of her car and driven off into the night with her two young sons, ages three and fourteen months, inside. For nine agonizing days, the public prayed, hoped, and worried with the young mother and her estranged husband as she pleaded on nationwide TV for the safe return of the boys. Before finally confessing that she had killed the boys herself by letting her car roll down a boat ramp into a lake with the boys strapped inside, Smith explicitly denied having had anything to do with the disappearance of her children and continued to insist that they were driven off by a Black man.[18]

In each of these cases, the Black man was presented as a symbol of a lurking evil, an evil presence that would rob a loving mother of her children, rape a man's cherished wife, and destroy another man's pregnant wife and unborn child. Scapegoating Black males in America has a long history. It works because Euro-Americans are too willing to believe that Black men are dangerous predators who need to be controlled.

What's Missing in the Contemporary Picture?

The images of Black males as presented by the media, popular culture, and social science omit three vitally important considerations: the role of ordinary Black men, the continuing impact of racism, and a clear explanation of the steps involved for a Black male to become successful in American society.

In every Black community in the United States, there are strong, quiet heroes. These are the men who work hard every day, pay their bills, and meet their responsibilities for their children and the children of legal and quasi-legal extended family members. They are not celebrated by the media, popular culture, or social science research like the upscale superathletes or sensationalized like the street Brothers. This vast, mostly ignored population of Black males has a lot to offer as constructive masculine role models. In some Black neighborhoods, these ordinary men are referred to as "old heads." According to Elijah Anderson in his book *Streetwise,* old heads are men of stable means who believe in the values of hard work and responsibility. They are advocates of the major institutions in the Black community: family, church, education, and civic organizations. The old heads are living examples of the traditional African-American psychological styles expressed in personality characteristics like resilience, improvisation, connectedness to others, spirituality, and the ability to learn from life experiences. In years gone by, the job of the old heads was to teach boys and young adult males their responsibilities with respect to work, family, preparation for the future, and relationships with the community. The old heads were there to direct young men when they strayed too far from acceptable standards of conduct, and they were respected by the young men as wise teachers and surrogate fathers.[19]

In *Slim's Table,* Mitchell Duneier describes a close-knit group of older, ordinary, working-class Black males who gather frequently at Valois Restaurant near the University of Chicago campus. They go to

Valois because they like the companionship and the meals, which taste like home cooking. In his documentary, Duneier lets the men speak for themselves. Slim, the acknowledged leader of the group, is an auto mechanic. As they talk, over a period of months, the men express their views on current affairs, events in their lives, and the younger generation. They value discipline, sincerity, responsibility, and honesty, and believe in following through on commitments. They know how to be strong without being violent, and can show toughness and compassion without being perceived as weak. Their images of self-worth are not derived from boasting and empty words about accomplishments; they believe in telling it like it is. These men have a quiet, sincere style that gets the job done. They admit failures and shortcomings, are open to feedback from others, and are willing to grow from life experiences.[20]

The old heads and the men who gather at Slim's table disagree with the contemporary portrayals of Black men as superathletes, entertainers, street men, and occasional superachievers. They feel that men like themselves have been left out and ignored. The prestige they once had in the Black community because of their commitment to responsibility, decency, and hard work has been lost because of these exaggerated images.

Contemporary stereotypical images of Black males avoid coming to grips with racism as an ongoing factor in American life. Racism today is more complex and subtle than in the past. It is rarely expressed openly. Lynch mobs, with the support of southern law enforcement officials, no longer kill and dismember Black males. Southern politicians and howling mobs no longer stand in front of school buildings to prevent Black youngsters from entering. "Nigger Head" shoe polish is no longer sold in stores. There are a few token Blacks in managerial and staff positions in colleges, trade unions, corporations, factories, and police departments. Black men are big-city mayors, members of Congress, and TV sports and news announcers. Black students attend predominantly White colleges and, yes, more often than not, make up the majority of the players on their basketball teams. The civil rights laws of the 1960s reduced blatant racism but did not end racism's powerful, lingering presence. While many Whites would like to believe that racism is a matter of the past, race is still a potent force in the nation's consciousness. Appearances of change can be deceiving—like the tip of an iceberg which hides the destructive force below.

In his book *Race: How Whites and Blacks Feel About the American Obsession*, veteran social commentator Studs Terkel conducted 100 interviews with Blacks, Whites, Asians, and Latinos. His conclusion was that racism is very much alive. It comes out in talk about crime, welfare, fatherless children, and other social pathologies of urban ghettos. Even well-educated Whites admit to struggling with the sinister forces of racism very deep inside themselves. A cabdriver who is rushing to get to his destination utters racial slurs at Black drivers out of frustration. Black respondents tell Terkel of racial slights: cabdrivers who won't stop for them, teachers who assume that Black children are slow learners, police harassment, and vacant apartments that are suddenly not available when Blacks show up at the rental office.[21]

Supreme Court Justice Clarence Thomas and football star and TV celebrity O. J. Simpson both tried hard to rise above race. They presented themselves as individuals, to be judged solely on their own merits and talents. But when the going got rough, and their futures were in danger, Simpson and Thomas knew that putting race into the game would create powerful emotions that could be used to their advantage. On national TV, Thomas referred to allegations of sexual harassment in his Senate confirmation hearings for the Supreme Court as a "high-tech lynching." By emotionally infusing images of lynching into the debate, Thomas, no doubt, hoped White senators on the confirmation panel would deny their racism by voting for him—and it worked. Simpson, on trial for murdering his White wife and her friend, Ronald Goldman, was defended by his lawyers, who accused the Los Angeles Police Department of planting evidence in a frame-up motivated by racism. The main culprit, allegedly, was Detective Mark Fuhrman, who was accused of resenting Black males being involved with White women and who routinely used the pejorative term "nigger." The defense's strategy apparently worked; Simpson was acquitted.

The two most persistent types of racism in contemporary America are institutional racism and individual racism. Institutional racism involves the recurring ways in which White people dominate Black people in almost every major aspect of public life. It involves patterns of resource allocation, selection, advancement, and expectations that consistently lead to different and more negative status for Blacks than for Whites. In America's success pyramid, Black males are underrepresented in high-status professions, corporate management, tenured university professorships, and high-paying skilled jobs. Black males are overrepresented in prisons, felony arrests, school failure, unemployment, and low-status jobs. Since institutional racial barriers are difficult to detect, unequal outcomes are justified on the basis of racial differences in merit, abilities, and motivation. And this allows the illusion of equal opportunities to be maintained.

Even when Black males meet the criteria for advancement and promotion by displaying the same job-related personality, characteristics, and skills as White males, subtle methods can be used to block their pathway. For example, in a personality assessment study done on police officers in Cleveland in 1979, Black and White police officers were judged differently on the same personality characteristics. A White police officer's performance tended to be rated favorably by his superiors if he was outgoing, freethinking, and heterosexual. A Black officer with the same characteristics was more likely to receive a negative performance evaluation. Conversely, Black policemen who were assessed as nonaggressive, nondominant, and deferential were evaluated favorably, whereas White police officers with the same characteristics were evaluated negatively or neutrally. These evaluations suggest that police officials preferred Blacks who were retiring and unassertive and Whites who were strong and forceful.[22]

Individual racism involves individual acts of discrimination, prejudice, hostility, degradation, and paternalism that grow out of the belief that Blacks are genetically and culturally inferior to Whites. Blacks are considered to be unable to achieve; more interested in fun, sports, and sex; more oriented toward crime; and unlikely to be effective in responsible roles. The following are examples of individual racism, some of which occurred in an institutional context.

In November 1994, Dr. Francis Lawrence, president of Rutgers, New Jersey's prestigious state university, warned the faculty during a two-hour meeting discussing admissions policies that if admissions standards were set too high, fewer Blacks would be admitted because Blacks don't have the genetic/hereditary background to attain high scores on college admissions tests. Lawrence has a reputation as a progressive educator. In his work at Tulane University in New Orleans and at Rutgers, he significantly increased the numbers of Black faculty, staff, and students.[23] A few days later, White students were rooting for Black athletes during a basketball game. When Black students staged a demonstration on the court at half-time to protest Lawrence's remarks, White students jeered and called them niggers.

Al Joyner, a 1984 Olympic gold medal winner whose car has a special Olympic license plate, "LA-TRACK," was pulled over by the police twice in less than an hour in Hollywood in May 1992. In the first incident, which police describe as routine questioning, Joyner was ordered out of his car at gunpoint, handcuffed, and told to kneel on the sidewalk shortly before 11:00 A.M. on a busy stretch of Sunset Boulevard. Only a few minutes after being released and continuing on his way, Joyner was pulled over again, two blocks away, and ordered from his car. In neither instance was Joyner arrested or accused of committing a crime or a traffic violation. The police who pulled him over the second time were backup officers at the scene of the first incident. The second set of officers told Joyner he was being detained as a suspect in a hit-and-run accident before releasing him.[24]

In Orange County, an upscale suburb of Los Angeles, young Black males are routinely followed when they enter many of the stores in shopping malls. Two star high school athletes were warned by their friends, who worked in one of the malls, to be careful when they went into the stores because security police and plainclothes security officers would be watching them. Democratic Senator Ernest Hollings of South Carolina, while attending trade talks in Switzerland in December 1993, jokingly implied that African heads of state were cannibals.[25] In a losing battle in the 1991 Louisiana gubernatorial race, David Duke, former neo-Nazi and Imperial Wizard of the Ku Klux Klan, captured 55 percent of the White vote.[26]

There is a third, subtle type of contemporary racism. It is embedded in the accusation that affirmative action policies are a form of reverse racism. Affirmative action is the general rubric for a series of programs designed to increase the range of educational, economic, and legal opportunities available to Blacks, other minorities, and women by correcting the negative effects of racial and gender discrimination in employment and promotions, government contracts, and university and professional school admissions. To increase minority participation, affirmative action programs use terms like "aggressive outreach," "timetables," "goals," "targets," "objectives," and sometimes "set-asides" and "preferences."

Affirmative action has come under attack by White conservatives, some Black conservatives, and a large group of angry White males. The criticism aimed at affirmative action is that it is no longer a corrective remedy but a form of discrimination—thus, "reverse"—against White males. According to conservative critics, affirmative action is an uncontrolled means of entitlement for racial minorities, particularly Blacks; unqualified Blacks are being spoiled by riding a gravy train of quotas, preferences, and set-asides. Furthermore, affirmative action undermines Blacks' self-esteem and dignity. The debasers of affirmative action preach about fair play and achievement on the basis of merit in a color-blind society. They feel that the debt for centuries of oppression and discrimination was paid in full by the Civil Rights Act of 1964. Notwithstanding the persistent rumors in the Black community that some of Dr. King's conservative critics still refer to him in private as Dr. Martin Luther "Coon" or Dr. Martin "Lucifer Coon," they readily quote his 1963 March on Washington speech in which he said that he hoped the content of one's character would be used as the basis of social judgments rather than the color of one's skin. They consciously omit the parts of Dr. King's philosophy in which he talked about Americans working toward a beloved community where all men and women could live together as sisters and brothers in a land of mutual respect and mutual opportunity.

Despite the cry that they are being discriminated against by the reverse racism inherent in affirmative action programs, White males still have an iron lock on wealth and positions of influence in America. The upper echelons of top corporations remain overwhelmingly White and male. Blacks occupy only 0.6 percent of the top executive jobs.[27] White males make up 39 percent of the nation's population, yet they account for 82.5 percent of the people whose net worth is at least $256 million, 92 percent of the state governors, 77 percent of members of Congress, 70 percent of tenured college faculty, approximately 90 percent of newspaper editors, and 77 percent of TV news directors.[28] The competition for jobs between Black and White males is likely to be most intense in middle-class jobs as, for example, firemen and policemen, jobs that were formerly the exclusive domain of White males.

Using mental jujitsu to project the blame onto Black males for racial problems in employment, university admissions, and government contracts is the latest tactic in a long history of victim-blame. Historically, Whites have relied on the general concept of Black male inferiority, thus avoiding responsibility for the detrimental effects of White racism. Using affirmative action to create a smokescreen of reverse discrimination is a convenient defense mechanism that protects Whites from facing the real problem, which is twofold: the lack of a level playing field for America's Black males and the lack of a long-term programmatic commitment based on mutual agreement between Blacks and Whites to make equal opportunity a reality.

Anger and Rage

Repeated encounters with all forms of racism create a combination of frustration and rage that has a cumulative effect over a lifetime. Every Black male in America has some emotional scar tissue from the psychological toll of racism. In Studs Terkel's account of American race relations, Black interviewees repeatedly tell of racial incidents: A White female clutches her purse and then looks tense when a Black male enters an elevator; a cop hassles a Black man for no reason; a cab refuses to stop, but then pulls up for a White male a few yards away; a vacant apartment suddenly is no longer available; a Black male is told he is overqualified for a job, or he gets the job but his coworkers whisper that he is an underqualified affirmative action hire; a student works hard to write an excellent paper only to be accused by his teacher of plagiarism; a student receives an A on a math paper and his teacher tells him Blacks aren't usually very good in math.[29]

Encounters with racism can keep a person off balance. One never knows when the next incident will pop up, or whether the incident was unintended or was a genuine act of discrimination. Often Whites accuse Blacks of being oversensitive about race and racism. What they don't realize is that each encounter with racism is a part of a larger individual, group, and family history of racism, a history that triggers memories of past racial incidents. Experiences with racism are lodged not only in individual memories, but in family stories and group recollections of Jim Crow, lynch mobs, ironclad discrimination in voting, housing, and employment, redneck southern sheriffs, police brutality in northern cities, and lifetimes of lost opportunity and dreams deferred.[30]

The deep-seated rage in Black males is a potentially destructive force acted out daily in Black-on-Black violence in urban America. There are frequent news reports of fifteen-year-olds killing other teenagers to steal their jackets or sneakers, of homicides and violence resulting from stare-downs or being dissed, of turf wars and random killings. Women are often the victims of violent abuse and sexual exploitation. Periodically, Black male rage coalesces as a group force. The acquittal of the four White officers accused in the Rodney King beating case was the spark that unleashed the most destructive urban rioting in America in the twentieth century. At the end of the carnage in Los Angeles, 51 people were dead, 2,328 injured, and damage was estimated at close to $1 billion.[31] Residents, social activists, clergy, and scholars say the violence had been smoldering since the Watts rebellion twenty-seven years earlier. They felt the violence was the end result of benign neglect; nothing had substantially changed since the urban rebellions of the 1960s. Resentment, frustration, and despair were still there. People were rioting in the streets because they had little hope that America would put forth the effort required to improve race relationships and address the social and physical deterioration of inner-city Black neighborhoods.

Black male anger cuts across all social classes. As a group, middle- and upper-middle-class Black males feel the same rage more readily observable in the alienated street Brothers. In *Rage of a Privileged Class,* Ellis Cose points out that hard work, occupational success, and high achievement do not totally protect Black males from individual racism, institutional racism, or accusations of reverse racism.[32] A Black doctor on his way home from the hospital late at night can easily become another Rodney King. Black male students walking across campus at night at predominantly White universities are routinely stopped and questioned by campus police.

While middle-class and upper-middle-class Blacks are able to more effectively suppress or sublimate their anger, that anger is always present and it eats away at psychological well-being. Black male rage poses a challenge to American society. At the individual level, the challenge is to turn the rage and anger into creative energy, creative energy that can generate resourcefulness and resilience in striving to overcome racial barriers and attitudes. At the larger level, the problem for society is to eradicate the social conditions created by unresolved racial problems. As long as society refuses to change, Black-on-Black violence will continue and large-scale group violence, like the 1992 Los Angeles rebellion, will inevitably erupt again.

Superstars, Muddled Pathways, Broken Dreams

The media and popular culture presentation of Black males does not spell out the steps along the pathway to mainstream success. The most popular role models for young Black males are the superathletes, especially professional basketball players. Basketball is the quintessential inner-city sport. It is an article of faith that the sport is a ticket out of the despair, poverty, and violence that pervade inner-city slums. Professional tennis star Arthur Ashe repeatedly said that ghetto youngsters spend too much time on basketball and other sports and not enough time on classroom work.

Statistics show that the odds against a high school basketball player making it into the pros are astronomical. Fewer than 1 percent of the slightly more than half-million teenagers who play high school basketball will win scholarships at four-year colleges, and many of those who do win basketball scholarships never graduate. Approximately 200 players are drafted annually into the National Basketball Association, and of those 200, about 50 make the teams. The average NBA career lasts about four years, so the top fifty of the millions of youngsters who start playing in grade school will be basketball has-beens by age twenty-six or twenty-seven.

In the 1980s, after the National Collegiate Athletic Association signed a multi-million-dollar TV contract, Congress complained about the low percentage of scholarship athletes graduating from colleges with powerhouse athletic teams. The NCAA responded by passing Proposition 48, which raised eligibility standards for freshmen to be able to play college basketball. To be eligible to play as a college freshmen, under Proposition 48 an athlete would need a 2.0 average in a core high school curriculum and a combined score of at least 700 on the Scholastic Assessment Test, which is about 200 points below the national average for high school seniors. Because of low grades and SAT scores, Black athletes were disproportionately affected by the proposition. According to some reports, 91 percent of the Proposition 48 casualties were Black.[33]

What makes the basketball dream such a cruel hoax is the parallel belief many Black males hold that school success is for White folks. According to this view, pursuing school success is akin to selling out to the enemy by "acting White." It is more important to be "cool and down" with the peer group than to demonstrate academic achievement. In the end, basketball can become an unhappy parody of the traditional American success story. Rather than starting out with nothing and slowly climbing the success ladder, the young Black male ends up with nothing and few future prospects when basketball doesn't work out because his math and reading skills are too low to qualify for high-paying jobs. In contrast, suburban White youths whose basketball dreams don't work out can shift over to the pursuit of skilled trades, technical occupations, and professions because they have hands-on role models and, along the way, have mastered core skills in reading and math. The cardinal sin for many Black males is that they do not have the skills to pursue plan B when the plan A basketball fantasy ends.

The human side of the perilous basketball myth is depicted in Darcy Frey's *The Last Shot* and in the documentary film *Hoop Dreams*. Frey, a young White writer, spent eight months with players from the powerhouse Abraham Lincoln High School basketball team, in Coney Island, on the edge of Brooklyn, New York. He shows how young fatherless Black men living in Coney Island's housing projects get caught up in the big lie that their prowess in basketball will automatically guarantee a college degree, a ticket out of the ghetto, and a pro basketball career. The rejects from past high school teams are all around: Semiliterate former athletes, discarded when their scholarships ran out, are now among urban America's invisible Black men—unemployed, underemployed, in and out of jail, and hustling on the streets. College athletics is a carnivorous machine that psychologically eats Black males alive. Recruiting begins at the elementary school level with street scouts and high school coaches scouring inner-city playgrounds for the best talent. Even when young people follow their part of the contract by staying out of trouble with gangs and drugs, studying hard, and giving their all to basketball, they can be dropped for minor flaws or rerouted to the oblivion of out-of-the-way junior colleges.[34]

Hoop Dreams follows two talented Black fourteen-year-old basketball players from the end of grade school through high school. The boys, William Gates and Arthur Agee, from Chicago's impoverished West Side, are good enough to dream of college stardom and careers in professional basketball. The filmmakers spent four and a half years with the boys, their families, friends, and coaches, acquiring 250 hours of film including shots of actual games. The pressure on the boys is severe as they try to endure the stresses of adolescence, poverty, family conflicts, and the relentless expectations of coaches and recruiters who are ready to cast them aside when they stumble. The boys endure because they believe basketball is their ticket to success.

Ordinary Males and Real Role Models

The real role models for young Black males are not TV stars or superathletes but people in their everyday lives whom they can see, reach out to, and touch. Parents, children, and child psychologists need to distinguish between superstars and everyday role models. Superstars are people who were blessed with a combination of extraordinary talent and luck, the one-in-a-million person like Michael Jordan or Magic Johnson. They often cannot explain how they got from point A to point Z in the achievement of greatness. Children who attempt to duplicate their superachievements have about as much chance of succeeding as they do of winning the lottery.

True role models, on the other hand, are ordinary people who can explain the steps involved in accomplishing goals. True role models are ordinary citizens who live and work in the Black community as recreation directors, teachers, postmen, bus drivers, school principals, grocery clerks, ministers, attorneys, businessmen, and the like. They are the men who pay the bills, take care of their families, and maintain active fathering roles when divorce separates the family. These men know the value of improvisation, resilience, hard work, long-term effort, planning ahead, and sequential, goal-directed steps. They can explain to young people what it takes to be successful in the mainstream. Hands-on role models can help Black youths assimilate those Euro-American values they will need in the world of work, but without compromising their Blackness. They can teach young men how to survive and retain their dignity in job situations and corporate structures where institutional racism and individual discrimination still exist. The old heads and ordinary males can transmit the strengths and vitality of the African-American way of being that have enabled generations of Black males to keep moving forward in the face of adversity.

But the effectiveness of such men as role models is reduced for two reasons. First, in neighborhoods where the social infrastructure built on church, school, family, and fraternal orders has crumbled, there are not enough functional males available to work as role models with the overwhelming number of boys and young men whose fathers are absent. Second, the glitter and glamor of TV superstar athletes overshadow the value of ordinary, hardworking Black males, as the following example illustrates: In a small midwestern city, several Black men started a Saturday morning mentorship group for Black boys between the ages of ten and twelve. The program included field trips, tutoring, ethnic awareness training, career counseling, social skills training, confidence building, problem solving, and goal setting—and some fun and games. At the first meeting, the boys were asked to state their career goals. Of the fifteen boys in the group, thirteen wanted to be professional athletes, one a paramedic, and one an astronaut. During a Saturday meeting on careers, the boys asked about the salaries of their mentors. The mentors were two teachers, a social worker, a postal supervisor, a government engineer, a school guidance counselor, and an assistant principal. Their salary range was from $25,000 to $47,000 per year. The boys laughed. They pointed out that basketball and baseball players were signing multiyear contracts worth $10 million to $15 million. One of the boys said, "Forty grand ain't no kind of money."

Chapter 5

Cool Pose, Rap, Hip–Hop, and the Black Aesthetic

Cool Pose: A Black Masculine Coping and Expressive Style

In a society where lingering manifestations of racism continue to restrict life's options and prevent the achievement of goals, many African-American males have adopted a coping style called "cool pose." A term coined by the psychologist Richard Majors, cool pose refers to a set of related physical postures, clothing styles, social roles and social scripts, behaviors, styles of walk, content and flow of speech, types of dances, handshakes, and attitudes that are used to symbolically express masculinity.[1] Mastering the cool pose is part of the rites of passage in the inner cities of urban America. Here's an example of the cool pose expressive style:

Case Example I

A young Black man strolls down the street in Oakland, California's, African-American community. He is wearing a Chicago Bulls athletic suit with expensive matching sneakers. The sneakers are untied and he walks with a slight limp, leaning just a bit to one side. His arms take turns trailing behind him as he ambles on his way. He knows he is cool and looks good. He follows the popular rap groups and knows all the latest dance steps. Since he lost his job as a stock clerk six months ago, he has been unable to contribute to the support of his two children, who live with his former girlfriend and her mother. Halfway down the block, he runs into a good friend who is similarly dressed. They exchange a variety of low-five and high-five handshakes. Using a combination of Black speech patterns and street terminology, they discuss the latest happenings and exchange ideas about generating some income. The friend works part time as a security guard and is a disk jockey for neighborhood parties. Future employment possibilities for both young men are bleak, since they barely graduated from high school and have reading and math skills at about eighth-grade level. Neither young man lets on to the other that he is worried about the future as they continue strolling and talking nonchalantly in hip ghetto accents.

Cool pose is a form of self-presentation designed to show others that the person is on top of things, that everything is under control. It is an assertion of masculinity that enhances pride, dignity, and a sense of personal power in a society that offers African-American males a limited range of options. To maintain a façade of adequacy and control, feelings that do not correspond to the cool pose image—fear, sadness, tenderness, disappointment, despair—are suppressed.

Cool pose is part of the African-American expressive style displayed in spectacular basketball slam dunks, spontaneous end-zone dancing at football games, and dramatic sermons that make Black churches rock on Sunday mornings. African-American expressive styles are constantly changing as new clothing styles, dance steps, rap styles, and hip-hop fashions emerge. According to Richard Majors, cool pose came about as a response to racial oppression: To combat the negative status and demeaning images in American society, Black males created a symbolic universe of behavior scripts and postures that exude creative self-expression.

As a coping mechanism, cool pose can be adaptive or maladaptive. Obsessive reliance on its symbolism can lead to negative consequences. First, in the long run, exaggerated, ritualistic masculine façades, postures, and poses cannot substitute for real educational and occupational achievement. Looking good can temporarily insulate one from feelings of failure and inadequacy, but it does not alleviate the need for marketable, mainstream competencies and skills. A rigid cool pose masculine style can become a prison that limits rather than expands real-world choices.

In a short poem entitled "We Real Cool," from her *World of Gwendolyn Brooks*, the poet and writer discusses some of the negative consequences that can occur when young Black men spend too much time being cool.

> *We real cool. We*
> *Left school. We*
>
> *Lurk late. We*
> *Strike straight. We*
>
> *Sing sin. We*
> *Thin gin. We*
>
> *Jazz June. We*
> *Die soon.*[2]

Second, the cool pose style of suppressing emotions is likely to be harmful in intimate relationships. Mutual sharing of feelings is essential in close relationships with family members, girlfriends, spouses, children, and significant others. Bottling up powerful emotions over an extended period can lead to pent-up frustration that can explode. In Albert Camus's novel *The Stranger*, the protagonist is sealed off from his emotions to the point where he becomes a stranger to himself; ultimately, he explodes in an act of homicidal violence. In prison, while awaiting his execution for murder, he spends his time struggling to define who he is and what he believes.[3]

Poor, unemployed African-American urban youths are particularly vulnerable to self-destructive involvement in a dysfunctional cool pose masculine style. In a world where they are often stuck at the day-to-day survival level, it is difficult for them to imagine themselves as productive adults who have a realistic chance of achieving their dreams in a larger society. Cornel West sees their nihilistic alienation and despair as a danger not only to the Black community but to America as a whole.[4]

On the positive side, cool pose is likely to be an effective coping strategy when it is part of a multidimensional definition of self and masculinity. A growing body of evidence in mental health research suggests that the best copers use a variety of strategies in a flexible manner.[5] Cool pose can boost morale and invigorate an otherwise bleak life. Creative self-expression not only relieves tension, it is also fun and helps build the self-confidence that young Black males need to take the risk of exploring opportunities for personal growth and development. The Black community offers multiple options for masculine identity, as Jason's story illustrates.

Case Example II

Jason is an eighteen-year-old African-American high school senior. He lives in a working-class neighborhood on the edge of South-Central Los Angeles. His mother is a nurse, and his father works in the Long Beach, California, naval shipyards. Jason's mother and father are separated, but they have a good working relationship as parents. He sees his father two or three times a month; they go out to dinner, attend ball games, and sometimes talk about Jason's future. Jason has a twelve-year-old brother who lives with him and his mom. Jason dresses in a moderate hip-hop style: baggy pants, expensive sneakers, athletic jackets. He avoids red and blue because these are the colors of two notorious Los Angeles street gangs, the Crips and the Bloods. Jason is part of a rap crew that competes in neighborhood and citywide contests. They write their own verses and hold impromptu competitions with other crews at parties and dances. Some of their raps were featured in a radio show. Jason plays football and runs the 200- and 400-meter track events. He has been offered a four-year football scholarship to a Division I school contingent on his grades and SAT scores. He has two part-time jobs, one at a print shop, the other as a referee for elementary school and playground basketball leagues. His uncle, who is a recreation director, plugged him into the referee jobs.

Until two years ago, Jason was a mediocre student. His grades were mostly C's and D's, and his reading and math scores were two to three years below grade level. He and his friends thought that doing well in school was for girls and White folks. Through her church, Jason's mother found out about a male mentorship program jointly sponsored by a Black fraternity and California State University, Los Angeles. She and his father pressured Jason for several weeks until he agreed to give the program a try. In his two years in the program, Jason has been exposed to career planning, study skills, problem solving, social skills development, and life planning; and he meets a number of Black males in different occupations. As part of the mentorship program, he studied the seven principles of *Nguzo Saba*. *Nguzo Saba* was developed by Maulana Karenga, director of the Black Studies Program at California State University, Long Beach, as the basic foundation for a Black value system. The principles, adopted as a guiding philosophy by many African-American organizations, are *Umoja*—unity; *Kujichagulia*—self-determination; *Ujima*—collective work and responsibility; *Ujamaa*—cooperative economics; *Nia*—purpose; *Kuumba*—creativity; and *Imani*—faith.[6]

Since he started the mentorship program, Jason's grades have improved, and he now has a B average. He has attended summer school to make up deficient past grades and bring his reading and math skills up to grade level.

This case study on Jason illustrates how a Black American male who has mastered the basics of cool pose can enhance this coping style by tapping into African-American community networks, extended family relationships, mentorship programs, and African-American value systems.

Rap and Hip-Hop

Despite crime, drugs, violence, and the breakdown of the social, physical, and economic infrastructure of America's inner cities, the Black aesthetic is still very much alive in rap music and the hip-hop culture. Rap is a talking/singing musical style rooted in the African-American oral tradition. Rap is hip Black voices talking, singing, profiling, and styling to the accompaniment of a strong musical beat. The rapper's voice becomes a creative instrument manipulating a flow of words in a rhythmic pattern. Rappers use African-American speaking styles against a musical background of jazz, funk, R&B, and pop.[7]

Modern rap is part of the hip-hop culture. The term "hip-hop" is derived from two words in the African-American idiom: hip, meaning wise, urban, sophisticated, with it; and hop, meaning dance. Hip-hop is a catch-all term for a contemporary, urban-centered, youth lifestyle associated with popular music, break dancing, certain dress and hair styles, graffiti, and street language. Hip-hop culture is energetic, constantly changing, and bears the imprint of youthful rebellion.

Using the storytelling tradition anchored in the African-American experience to present an identity characterized by pride in Blackness, racial militancy, and self-determination, the powerful voices of the rap/hip-hop generation tell young Black men that they can seize the power to transform their lives, take charge of their destinies, and create an optimal range of life choices. A young Black man does not have to turn away from his community to find solutions to existential dilemmas or personal conflicts. Beneath the references to drugs, sex, crime, violence, and teen pregnancies, and the macho posturing, which are prominent in gangsta rap, there is a less visible social reality that contains a reservoir of creative energy, a social reality where romantic interludes, militant social activism, and nonviolent resolutions of Black-on-Black conflict are fostered. Masculine scripts that encourage community building, education, harmonious relationships with others, and responsible sexual behavior are advocated. The social reality created by the dynamic vitality of the rap/hip-hop genre extends far beyond inner-city neighborhoods. With their rapid-fire poetry and dress styles, young Black rappers have created a billion-dollar industry that is not only reflected in American youth culture but has found a niche in radio, TV, movies, advertising, and fashions.

In angry militant tones, accompanied by warrior imagery, rap performers tell society in no uncertain terms that race is a barrier that restricts life's options for Black men. The evils of White racism, police brutality, and poverty cannot be camouflaged by sterile sociological statistics and polite TV discussions between middle-class Whites and Blacks about the merits and pitfalls of affirmative action. If all else fails, revolutionary action and armed conflict will erupt.

Putting together a richly entertaining rap performance requires an effective combination of skills. Rappers are like stage actors. To be successful, they must combine a forceful delivery, a fluency with words, and an ability to portray characters and life situations convincingly while simultaneously keeping vocal rhymes in tune with the music's beat. Rap requires a facility with the Black way of being, knowledge of the latest street happenings, and an awareness of the changing lifestyles in the hip-hop culture.

The Controversy About Rap

Rap music has its critics and supporters. Critics, Black and White, have zeroed in on the message of gangsta rap and the real-life criminal behavior of gangsta rap performers. Former Senate Majority Leader and presidential candidate Robert Dole and many other White and Black politicians think gangsta rappers have crossed the line of decency, and they have urged record companies to be more vigilant in censoring violent and obscene lyrics. C. Delores Tucker of the National Political Congress of Black Women supports the call for a more careful monitoring of rap music. In 1994, the U.S. Congress held hearings on the effects on America's youth of the violent and demeaning lyrics in gangsta rap. The hearings were initiated by two Black congresswomen, Senator Carol Mosley Braun (D–Illinois) and Representative Cardiss Collins (D–Illinois). Such critics are particularly incensed by images and lyrics of Black males threatening to shoot police, freely using drugs, and engaging in wanton sex. "Cop Killer," by Ice T's band Body Count, called for counterviolence against abusive police. He later withdrew the song from commercial sale. The title of Dr. Dre's popular album *The Chronic* is street shorthand for a particularly potent form of marijuana. In his best-selling album *Doggy Style,* Snoop Doggy Dogg tells a girl he and his buddies have a pocketful of condoms and asks what is she going to do.[8] Ice T, in his album *Body Count,* vividly describes bedding down the daughter of the Grand Wizard of the Ku Klux Klan. The cover of Ice T's 1992 album *Home Invasion* depicts hooded Black male intruders attacking a White woman and man.

Rapper Tupac Shakur was sued in Federal District Court in southeast Texas by the widow of a slain state trooper who was allegedly gunned down while his killer, a teenage gang member, was listening to the song "Crooked-ass Nigga" from Tupac's album *2Pacalypse Now.* The song describes a drug dealer on a murderous rampage, who shoots at police officers trying to apprehend him. The convicted killer of the Texas state trooper says Tupac's song was blaring from his car stereo when he snapped. After being pulled over by the trooper, he then loaded his pistol and pulled the trigger.[9]

The exploitation of women and violent behavior by some gangsta rappers in their offstage lives have added fuel to the fire of criticism. Snoop Doggy Dogg was indicted as an accomplice to murder after his bodyguard allegedly shot and killed a man while Snoop was at the wheel of a parked car. Police files in his hometown, Long Beach, California, identify him as a member of the Long Beach Insane Crips, a vicious street gang. Dr. Dre served a five-month jail term in Pasadena, California, after being convicted for breaking another rap producer's jaw. It has been widely rumored in rap circles that Dr. Dre allegedly beat Dee Barnes, hostess of the now defunct rap show *Pump It Up*. Supposedly, Barnes was perceived by Dr. Dre as being too assertive a woman.[10]

Tupac Shakur seemed compelled to live out in his personal life the violence he rapped about in his music. Acquitted of shooting an off-duty police officer in 1993, he was found guilty of sexual abuse in 1994 and sentenced to four and a half years in prison. During the sentencing phase of his sexual abuse trial, Tupac was shot twice by unknown assailants and robbed of $40,000 worth of jewelry as he entered a New York recording studio. Tupac thought the shooting was a contract hit. While out on appeal, he was shot five times on September 7, 1996, in Las Vegas, on his way to a party after watching a Mike Tyson fight. A week later he died at age twenty-five. His life could be summed up by the old Black proverb, "What goes around, comes around."

Case Examples: Tupac Shakur and Biggie Smalls

Tupac Shakur was undeniably one of gangsta rap's biggest stars. Between 1994 and 1996, his recordings grossed an estimated $75 million. His albums *Strictly 4 My NIGGAZ* (1993) and *Thug Life, Volume I* (1994), each sold over a million copies. *Me Against the World*, released in 1995, and *All Eyes on Me*, which hit the stores in 1996, each sold over two million copies. His posthumous CD, *The Don Killuminati: The Seven Day Theory*, which he recorded under the name Makaveli, was an instant best-seller when it was released in November 1996. Tupac was also a talented actor, appearing in movies such as *Juice, Above the Rim, Gridlock'd*, and *Gang Related*. In 1993, he acted opposite Janet Jackson in the movie *Poetic Justice*. Four months after he was gunned down, he was named Favorite Rap/Hip-Hop Artist at the Twenty-fourth Annual American Music Awards in 1997. Although he was capable of expressing empathy with the plight of teenage mothers in the hit song "Brenda's Got a Baby," and longing for a father figure in "Dear Mama," the core message in his rap rhymes was gangsta imagery—guns, violence, shootings, sexual abuse of women, drugs, and paybacks. In *All Eyes on Me*, Tupac bragged with self-centered acclaim about throwing a gangsta party.[11]

Six months after Tupac Shakur's death, Biggie Smalls was shot and killed by an unknown gunman in the early morning hours of Sunday, March 9, 1997. He died in the mid-Wilshire district of Los Angeles after leaving a star-studded industry party hosted by *Vibe* magazine to celebrate the Soul Train Music Awards. The twenty-four-year-old rapper was sitting in his car, moments after the party ended, when the gunman, in a passing car, fired several shots through the passenger side of the vehicle.[12]

In the last three years of his life, Biggie Smalls went from being an unknown Brooklyn drug dealer and small-time criminal to the top of rap music's ratings. Literally bigger than life at six feet three inches tall and weighing over 350 pounds, Biggie took the gangsta rap world by storm. A tenth-grade high school dropout who preferred hanging around drug dealers, pimps, and gamblers to going to school, Biggie had a knack for weaving together narratives about the drugs, sex, guns, and desperation of inner-city streets. Recording for Bad Boy Entertainment in New York City, Biggie's first album, *Ready to Die,* released in 1994, established him as one of gangsta rap's most promising voices. On singles like "Big Papa," "Machine Gun Funk," "Everyday Struggle," "Gimme the Loot," and "Juicy," Biggie described the dangerous Brooklyn streets where he sold drugs, dodged bullets, robbed subway riders, ran games on women, and tried to survive by his wits. In interviews with newspaper and TV reporters, Biggie spoke candidly about his jail time, crack dealing, sexual affairs, and violence on the streets. He said he did what he had to do to survive.[13]

Biggie's life and rap narratives seem to be part of a whole, mutually influencing each other. He could not seem to avoid trouble. Before he became famous, he was arrested in 1989 on weapons possession charges. After being sentenced to five years' probation, he was arrested the next year in Brooklyn on a probation violation. Subsequently, in 1991, Biggie was apprehended again on charges of dealing cocaine in North Carolina. He spent nine months in jail before he could make bail.[14] Trouble continued after he became a gangsta rap superstar. On March 23, 1996, he was arrested outside the Palladium Dance Club in New York after he allegedly chased two autograph seekers and threatened to kill them. According to police reports, Biggie smashed the car windows of the autograph seekers with a baseball bat, then pulled one of the people out of the car and punched him. He pleaded guilty to second-degree harassment and was sentenced to 100 hours of community service. A couple of months later, he was arrested on charges of robbing a friend of a concert promoter and breaking the man's jaw. In the summer of 1996, Biggie was charged with weapons possession; later in the fall, he was charged with drug possession after the police said they caught him smoking marijuana in a car in downtown Brooklyn.[15]

The killings of Tupac Shakur and Biggie Smalls within a six-month period fueled speculation inside and outside the gangsta rap world that an East Coast/West Coast rivalry between competing rap stars and business enterprises had turned deadly. Tupac was one of the leading artists for Marion "Sugar Bear" Knight's Los Angeles–based Death Row Records; Biggie Smalls represented Sean "Puffy" Combs's New York–based Bad Boy Entertainment. In interviews and on recordings for two or three years before their untimely deaths, Biggie and Tupac had been trading insults and playing the dozens. When Tupac was shot and robbed in 1994, he accused Biggie and Combs of setting him up. Shortly thereafter, Biggie released a song entitled "Who Shot Ya," in which he appeared to be taunting Tupac. But he denied any intention to insult Tupac and said the song was not aimed at him. Tupac retaliated by escalating the feud with a 1995 song bragging that he had had sex with Biggie's wife and his mother. He threatened Biggie and Bad Boy Entertainment with payback violence.[16] At the 1995 Soul Train Awards, security forces for Tupac Shakur and Biggie Smalls got into a scuffle at the Shrine Auditorium in Los Angeles; the two camps faced off again in September 1996 at the MTV Awards in New York City, a few days before Tupac's death. At the time of this writing, police in Los Angeles and Las Vegas have no solid evidence linking the killings to a bicoastal rivalry, but this has not stopped ongoing speculation inside and outside the rap world that the murders are related.

Tellin' It Like It Is: Information and Social Protest

While the supporters and defenders of rap music acknowledge the presence of provocative language, especially in gangsta rap, and the less than desirable behavior of some rap artists, they counterattack the critics with convincing arguments regarding rap's positive features. They point out that rap artists see themselves as the voice of the people, informing the world about the joys, sorrows, contradictions, and turbulent conditions of poor, urban Black communities where Black males and females must learn to survive. The rappers say, "Don't shoot the messenger," because the messenger presents a valid description of the conditions in neighborhoods where the family, economic, and educational structures have collapsed. Rap monologues about inner-city life merely reflect, and do not create, the conditions described. Americans get angry with the street language and profanity used by rap artists, but they are telling what's wrong in America; they are among the few groups today who remind us that 400 years of racial oppression are responsible for the social pathologies that exist in inner-city Black communities.

Rap expert Robert Hilburn, a music critic for the *Los Angeles Times*, thinks that if bluesmen and R&B artists like Robert Johnson, Leadbelly, Chuck Berry, and Bo Diddley were starting their careers today, they would be involved in political and socially conscious forms of rap music. The best of the gangsta and the politically and socially conscious rappers—The Fugees, Ice Cube, Chuck D, and Bone thugs-n-harmony—are following in the history of folk singers and bluesmen like Bob Dylan and Leadbelly, who used their music as a form of social protest. In his song "Fuck the Police," Ice Cube articulated underclass hostility toward cops, which can and does explode in violence. Chuck D of Public Enemy addresses questions regarding power, oppression, and race relations in lyrics from "White Heaven . . . Black Hell." Bone thugs-n-harmony acquaint their listeners with the desperation and pain in their inner-city neighborhood of St. Claire and East 99th Street in Cleveland. In their album *The Score,* The Fugees warn young people about the dangers of gang identity.

Master P, a hot new gangsta rapper, expresses the belief prevalent among many urban Black men that the drug trade flourishes in the inner city as a consequence of complicity by the U.S. government and because White society turns its back on the problem. In his song "The Ghetto Won't Change," Master P makes it clear that Black folks do not own the boats, planes, and ships necessary to transport drugs between countries and across continents, and questions how the drugs get to the inner city without the government's knowledge.[17]

The troublesome class and racial problems taken up by rappers are issues White America does not want to face, so it is easier to attack the language and explicit sexual descriptions of the messages rather than for White America to turn inward and examine its social conscience and historical record of brutality against Blacks.

To its followers, rap is like a Black TV station that the Black inner cities have never had. Rapper Chuck D has compared this music to CNN and documentary reportage: Rap tells people what's going on, with an aggressive beat. Like talk radio, its aficionados can tune in to find out what's happening in the hood, including the latest political news, and information on police and community relations, dress and hair styles, and popular hip-hop trends. Before the 1992 Los Angeles riots, which occurred after the acquittal of the police officers involved in the Rodney King beating, rap performers were the only ones who predicted that a violent rebellion would occur. In their recordings, they talked about dead gangbangers and police, shootings, looting, and burning. In October 1991, six months before the Los Angeles riots, Ice Cube, in his album *Death Certificate,* articulated the rage aroused by Rodney King's beating. He pointed out exactly where the flash points of the rebellion would be. After the riot, the angry voices of the rappers sounded like experts.[18]

Emergence of the Entrepreneurial Spirit

Rap supporters point out that by producing and commercializing gangsta rap and other forms of rap music, rap performers are merely following the old adage of America's philosophy of success: "Borrow a dollar and create a better product." Young Black males have taken an innovative mix of authentic Black expressive patterns and hip-hop culture, added a booming beat to the rhythmic verse, and created a lucrative industry.

According to the Recording Industry Association of America, rap music accounted for 8.9 percent of record sales during 1996, or $1.1 billion. Hard-core gangsta rap albums by Tupac Shakur and Snoop Doggy Dogg were among the most successful of the year, and rap/hip-hop recordings accounted for one-fifth of the top 200 albums. Rap music's following is so strong among an active young record-buying audience that albums by superstars can generate $50 million to $75 million in sales.[19] Rap artists who are relatively unknown to the general rap-buying public can quickly break into the national top ten. For example, Snoop Doggy Dogg's backup singers, a group called Tha Dogg Pound, released an album called *Dogg Food* on Halloween in 1995 that became an instant hit.[20] Two rap groups most closely associated with Biggie Smalls, Junior M.A.F.I.A. and Lil Kim, now have albums in their own right.

Unlike their rhythm and blues predecessors, who were often exploited by White-owned recording companies and managers, Black rappers are operating as entrepreneurs. The Brothers own and manage a significant piece of the action. Death Row Records, which features a corporate logo of a hooded man in an electric chair, was founded in 1992 by two young Black men from Compton, California, Dr. Dre and Sugar Bear Knight. It became the most successful rap label in the music business. In its first year, Death Row Records' albums *The Chronic* and *Doggy Style* topped *Billboard* magazine's pop rating charts. In 1993–94, the company grossed $90 million from the sales of CDs, tapes, and other merchandise. In 1996, sales hit the $100 million mark and corporate net worth was estimated at $100 million.[21] Affiliated with recording giants Time-Warner and Interscope Distributors, Death Row Records, located in West Los Angeles, retains artistic and economic control of its products. The company has not forgotten the Brothers in the hood; in 1994 it donated $500,000 to an antigang program in South-Central Los Angeles, and Death Row performers have publicly denounced violence.[22]

Several other companies are owned, operated, or managed by Black men who are part of the emerging Black entrepreneurship. Pioneer rap manager Russell Simmons founded Def Jam Music Group in 1985. Uptown Records, which got started in 1986 under the leadership of Andre Harrel, has been associated with rap and R&B performers including Heavy D, Teddy Riley, Al B. Sure, Jodeci, and Mary J. Blige. Harrel became head of Motown Records in 1995. Puffy Combs started Bad Boy Entertainment, where he launched the career of Biggie Smalls. Hip-hop elder statesman Quincy Jones was a founder of the rap magazine *Vibe* and produced TV's hip-hop-oriented sitcom *The Fresh Prince of Bel-Air* in the 1990s.[23]

Young rap performers are beginning to show a keen interest in the financial side of the enterprise. In director Peter Spierer's 1997 documentary rap film *Rhyme and Reason,* it was enlightening to watch young artists like A Tribe Called Quest, Salt 'N Pepa, Speech, Dr. Dre, LL Cool J, and Kris Kross discuss learning to look out for their money after they had been exploited by record companies eager to cash in on the popularity of rap. The young musicians seemed determined to take control of their own financial destiny and careers no matter what the cost.[24]

Unfortunately, recent troubles surrounding Sugar Bear Knight may derail the skyrocketing financial and artistic success of Death Row

Records. Suge Knight, the driving executive force behind the company, was sentenced to nine years in a California state prison on February 28, 1997, for violating his probation. He was on probation for a 1992 assault on two aspiring young rappers in Hollywood. His parole was revoked after a Los Angeles judge concluded that Knight had been involved in a fight on September 7, 1996, at the MGM Grand Hotel in Las Vegas. Adding to Death Row Records' woes are the departures of Dr. Dre and Snoop Doggy Dogg, a lawsuit by Tupac Shakur's estate, and a federal investigation for racketeering.[25]

Dr. Dre, widely viewed as the creative production genius who forged the distinctive sound of Death Row Records, departed in March 1996. Dr. Dre's productions generated more than $250 million in record sales, including hits such as Snoop Doggy Dogg's "Gin 'N' Juice" and Tupac Shakur's "California Love." Dr. Dre was disenchanted with the gangsta rap scene and was not comfortable with what he perceived as a tense, disorganized negative atmosphere at Death Row Records.[26] A lawsuit filed in 1997 by Tupac Shakur's mother on behalf of the slain rapper's estate contends that Death Row Records and its owner, Marion Knight, ran a criminal enterprise that cheated her son out of millions of dollars. The lawsuit also claims that the handwritten contract Tupac signed with Death Row Records (when Suge Knight paid $1.4 million to bail him out of prison on a sex charge) is invalid because Tupac was unhappy and confused at the time.[27] The FBI is investigating Death Row Records for alleged gang connections, money laundering, drug trafficking, and tax violations.

Despite the troubles surrounding Death Row Records, Sugar Bear Knight remains optimistic about the future. During an interview conducted in California's San Luis Obispo Men's Prison, where he is currently serving time, Knight seems confident that Death Row Records will continue on. He says he is still receiving money from old contracts and has new acts coming out. He is determined to use the time in prison to take a step back from the day-to-day hassles of running his high-pressure business, clear his head, and sort out complex personal and organizational issues. He is convinced that he was taken down by the White establishment because he became too much of a power in the music industry. They didn't want a Black man who was calling the shots and operating on his own terms. Knight claims they had to get rid of him because other Black artists might try to emulate his success and become owners of multi-million-dollar recording and entertainment enterprises rather than contract employees.[28]

Suge Knight is regarded in various ways inside rap circles. Some observers view him as a menacing presence who is not above threatening physical violence to get what he wants. According to court documents, he and a couple of his buddies threatened the late rap star Eazy E with baseball bats and pipes when Dr. Dre wanted to dissolve his contract with Eazy E's Ruthless Records Company and join Death Row Records. Suge has been known to be associated with the Mob Piru Bloods gang in Compton. But he says there is no substance to his menacing image; it is all part of the theater of gangsta rap.[29] Others view Suge as a brilliant executive who saw the potential of gangsta rap as a popular force and made it into a reality. From the start, he was on top of everything at Death Row. He chose the artwork, the promotional materials, the video directors, the singles for albums, the locales of album debut parties, and what performers should wear. Suge was the first to get his rap videos regularly on MTV, at a time when the station had ghettoized rap videos by clumping them together on shows like *Yo! MTV Raps.* Death Row was the first rap label to cross over into pop radio. Suge is often compared to Motown founder Berry Gordy in the way in which he identified, recruited, and carefully shaped the careers and images of talented performers. The perception among young ghetto rap artists is that Suge takes care of his own, his word is his bond. They see him as a godfather who can stand up to White record industry figures, cut through the complications, and bring the loot home.[30]

A cursory look at Hollywood movies and TV productions shows that sex and violence are big sellers. Americans seem to have a voracious appetite for explicit sex, crime, and kick-ass violence. Death Row Records, Bad Boy Entertainment, and other gangsta rap producers are capitalizing on the existing marketplace by doing what moviemakers have done for years. They tell stories that have vulgarity, sex, and violence as themes, and make big bucks doing so. Gangsta rap artists think they are being judged by a double standard. They point out that critics offer praise for Clint Eastwood's movie *Unforgiven,* a film about a character who guns down a bad law officer and dozens of others who are unfortunate enough to be in the vicinity. About the same time, Ice T's song "Cop Killer" was roundly condemned.

There is a widespread belief in rap circles that the criticism of gangsta rap has racial undertones. As long as it was a nickel-and-dime operation reaching a small Black audience, establishment educators, politicians, clergymen, and conservatives made no attempt to criminalize or demonize it. As soon as it became part of a billion-dollar industry, partly controlled by Black males whose customers now included thousands of suburban White youth, the attacks became unrelenting.[31]

In his album *Niggaz4Life,* Dr. Dre discusses the dilemma in the use of vivid street language. He says getting paid fantastic sums of money to use foul or obscene language is better than going to prison for criminal behavior. By using such language as a recording star, he makes more money than most Black doctors, lawyers, and executives. He adds that regardless of what Black men do in America, they are still viewed in negative, stereotypical terms. The album title *Niggaz4Life* is more than a metaphor for how Black men are perceived in America. Almost any Black male, professionals and athletes included, will tell you they fear the experience of being treated like a "nigga" when stopped by the police late at night. At the time of the O. J. Simpson trial, few African-American people were surprised by the fact that the Los Angeles police force had career police officers like Mark Fuhrman who repeatedly used the "N" word in his recorded interviews with screenwriter Laura Hart McKinny.[32]

Rap supporters feel that the critics confuse verbal violence on recording discs with actual, physical violence in the real world. No definitive studies of gangsta rap recordings or videos have shown a direct cause-and-effect relationship between listening to violence or seeing it in videos and actually committing violence. In the lawsuit against Tupac Shakur for allegedly inciting a Texas teenager to murder a state trooper because of Tupac's cop-killing lyrics, his lawyers argued that these verses about inner-city life describe violence but never advocate it. The lawyers added that there were 400,000 people who bought copies of the album and didn't kill police officers. Furthermore, according to Tupac's attorneys, the social message of the album was that violence against Black people is a continuing problem and drug dealing has a destructive effect on the Black community. Rappers maintain that the ultimate causes of mayhem and destruction in the Black community are the intertwined effects of White racism and poverty.[33]

One of the more subtle goals of hard-core rap is to shock America into paying attention to the social problems created by generations of racial oppression. Following the long tradition of parody found in the old, bawdy blues and the serious, social commentary comedy of artists like Richard Pryor, gangsta rap, with its stories of bizarre violence and lewd sexuality, hopes to penetrate White America's repression of unpleasant racial problems. A second goal of the harsh rhetoric and grotesque exaggerations is to educate young people by showing them the folly of such behaviors.

It is fashionable both inside and outside rap circles to see the hard-core masculine images presented in this music as the only authentic version of Black masculinity. Entertainment gets confused with reality. Images and stances are not real flesh and blood. In rap's hard-core masculine view, Black males are violence-prone, disputes are settled with guns, women are denigrated, and sex is without love; getting high on drugs is an ongoing activity. Middle-class life is counterfeit, long-term achievement is devalued, and only rage, macho aggression, and the poverty and suffering of the inner city are real. This message is a repeat of the single-dimensional stereotypes that have plagued Black males in America for generations, to the effect that Black males are sexual brutes, aggressive savages, and incapable of pursuing long-term goals that require patience, vision, discipline, and careful planning. The women-exploiting gangstas of today are reminiscent of the razor-toting, lustful, half-animal/half-child Black male stereotypes that were popular in America's past and the go-for-bad street corner men created by America's social scientists. Ironically, some of the Black male rappers responsible for creating hypermasculine images are middle-class Brothers posing as inner-city representatives. Rapper Suave from the group Onyx apparently grew up in a middle-class neighborhood but claims to have repeatedly seen people shot and murdered. Public Enemy, one of the groups that popularized modern rap, got its start around Adelphi University in suburban Long Island.[34]

Many of the critics fail to see that beneath rap's tough, raw, one-dimensional masculine images, there are old-fashioned, conservative, patriarchal male-oriented social norms. The aggregate voice of young Black male rappers is definitely patriarchal. Male dominance is advocated in gender relationships, and homosexual lifestyles are frowned upon. Aggressive masculinity is encouraged; if intense competition fails to solve problems between males, armed conflict is likely to occur. Rap music does not look to the government for economic handouts. The rappers have followed the conservative principles of economic self-determination. When they could not get their music on the radio, they created mini radio stations in ghetto parks, streets, and basements to play their music. From rap's early beginnings in the South Bronx in the mid-1970s, record companies owned and managed by Blacks have developed into a multi-million-dollar industry. Rap and its spin-offs in the hairstyle and clothing areas provide jobs and a shot of economic testosterone to the feeble economic base of the Black community.[35]

Crossover: Rap Expands Its Audience

The rap/hip-hop genre is no longer confined to inner cities and ethnic neighborhoods. With its crossover appeal, rap music is now popular far beyond its South Bronx origins. Recreation rap, political rap, and hard-core gangsta rap are popular with White suburban teenagers, college students on predominantly White campuses, and upscale young White urban adults. Based on *Billboard* magazine's national sales totals, suburban White male teenagers are rap music's largest buying audience.[36]

The sound, style, slang, and freewheeling poetry of rap/hip-hop provide themes and images for mainstream entertainment, advertisements, fashion, news reports, and, of course, casual social dialogue. McDonald's TV commercials show twin toddlers fashionably attired in baggy urban clothes, happily rapping their way to a sumptuous meal. Bart Simpson hollers out, "Yo!" Disney's record production division has released an album titled *Rappin' Mickey*. Commercialization via MTV was a significant force in expanding the base of rap music's following and increasing its sales revenue. *Yo! MTV Raps* (now titled simply *Yo!*) quickly became one of the most popular programs on the cable music channel after it was launched in 1984.[37]

The world of fashion has adopted the hip-hop look. All over the country kids of both sexes wear oversized jeans and high-priced basketball shoes. The urban preppy styles of Polo Sport, Nautica, and Tommy Hilfiger report sales of over $400 million. Allan Millstein, editor of the *Fashion Network Report Newsletter,* says hip-hop is the biggest single influence on fashion in America today.[38] *Source* and *Vibe,* rap/hip-hop's major magazines, provide fans with the latest on music, news, styles, and rap politics, as well as in-depth profiles on the lives and views of the performers and producers. Despite the fact that these publications are filled with stereotypical images of young Black rappers dressed in fancy brand-name clothing, wearing extravagant jewelry, and sitting in fancy cars, the profiles of the artists are thoughtful, often revealing the tragedies and struggles they have endured en route to success. In the summer of 1997, *Vibe* launched a syndicated TV version of its magazine and hosted its second annual men's music festival, including hip-hop acts at Disney World.[39]

Prior to the advent of modern rap, Black music was softened for crossover White audiences, and sexual and aggressive themes were diluted to become less offensive. Performers like Michael Jackson and Prince tried to perfect a racially ambiguous physical appearance. Rap reversed these trends, and rap artists successfully exploited White America's fears about sex, race, and gender roles and sold them as entertainment. Groups like Public Enemy and N.W.A. adopted styles of bold racial confrontation, swaggering Black male posturing, and language laced with graphic sexual references, macho boasting, and X-rated profanity. Dramatizing racial conflict, Public Enemy marketed its music around the concept of racial warriors; its logo shows a young African-American male in the crosshairs of a rifle sight. N.W.A. pictured authentic male Blackness in the form of gun-blazing, oversexed gangstas. Some critics have accused Public Enemy, N.W.A., and other groups including Biggie Smalls and Tupac Shakur of prostituting a grotesque version of Blackness to make money.[40]

The shift in strategy worked. The harder and more in-your-face the music sounded, the more White audiences it attracted. N.W.A.'s album *Niggaz4Life* became the top-selling pop album in the country within two weeks of its release in the summer of 1991, and Public Enemy's albums *Fear of a Black Planet, The LP Apocalypse 91,* and *The Enemy Strikes Back* recorded huge sales to White audiences as well. White kids in suburbia stood in line to be the first to buy posthumous albums and videos by gangsta rappers Tupac Shakur and Biggie Smalls. Criticism by establishment figures seems to heighten rap's attractiveness. Rather than being offended by the blistering macho styles, Whites are attracted to it.

With rap's pulsating Black rhythms blaring from car stereos and home sound systems, White youth in West Los Angeles and the suburbs of large midwestern and eastern cities are emulating rap and hip-hop styles. They wear the clothes, dance the dances, talk the talk, and try to walk the walk. Calvin Klein and Levi Strauss market clothing lines that feature the baggy, slightly unkempt urban preppy look. White youths seem fascinated by the exotic images of Black males as icons of rebellion, coolness, sexuality, and street life.

Rebellious Whites can experience a sense of power and nonconformity by dressing like gangstas, drinking forty-ounce beers, trying to talk Black, and expressing an "I don't give a damn, don't mess with me" attitude. They can vicariously pick up a slice of what is passed on as authentic Blackness without interacting directly with Black homeboys in the inner city. In their cars, they can hear the blasting rhythms of the Black ghetto without going near it. When suburban White kids grow out of the gangsta style, they can move on to other options in terms of training, education, and lifestyles. Young Black males in the inner city do not have this luxury.

Strength Without Despair: The Challenge Ahead

Using an updated form of *Nommo*—the power and vitality of the spoken word (see Chapter 2)—the strident, sometimes harsh, young Black male rap voices symbolize a strength that has not given in to the despair, hopelessness, and nihilism that Harvard Professor Cornel West describes as pervasive in the poor Black ghettos of America.[41] These alive, high-energy, forceful male voices have the potential to shape values, educate, and influence attitudes, especially among Black youth. Reports indicate that 97 percent of Black youth like rap music and more than 50 percent buy one or more rap albums per month.[42] Since rap sounds are apparently here to stay, the challenge for rap artists is to heighten its potential as an agent of personal discovery and transformation, positive racial identity, social change, and community responsibility. Rap's young men are in a position to come up with creative visions of Black life by encouraging dialogue, political activism, and an attempt to deal with inner-city problems.

A shift toward greater emphasis on social responsibility and personal transformation is already beginning to appear in the work of some rap artists. Public Enemy has been speaking out strongly against Black-on-Black violence and at the same time encouraging positive racial identity, Black consciousness, and political involvement. Rap teacher/performer Gil Scott-Heron, in his 1994 album *Spirits,* encourages rap musicians to chill out on violence, four-letter words, and lack of respect for women. He exhorts his listeners to move toward a more thoughtful vision of life and relationships with others.

Rapper KRS-One, despite the display of guns and gangsta images on the cover of the album *Criminal Minded* (Boogie Down Productions), encourages Blacks to stop the violence against each other. Interspersed in the verses are themes from Black historical struggles and political movements.[43] KRS-One views rap as a combination of education and entertainment, which he refers to as "edutainment." His emphasis on reducing Black-on-Black violence has had at least one dramatic effect:

A few years ago, when a near riot broke out between Blacks at a concert in Detroit, someone in the crowd shouted the refrain from his song "Stop the Violence." Soon the whole crowd picked up the refrain about stopping self-destruction and violence, and the riot was averted.[44]

Some communities have begun to incorporate youthful raps in attempts to solve persistent community problems. In an AIDS-prevention program in San Francisco, teenagers were asked to participate in a rap contest. They wrote raps about the dangers of unprotected sex, needle sharing, and drug abuse. Preliminary rounds of the contest were held in local community centers throughout the city, and the final round, featuring vocal raps, was aired on a popular youth TV show. The participants, ranging in age from seven to twenty-one, came up with innovative and vivid images of the killer disease and how it could be prevented.[45]

It must be remembered that the men of rap are young adults who, no doubt, will mellow and evolve as they get older. For example, Ice Cube, one of the cofounders of gangsta rap with the group N.W.A., has moved away from his gangsta image. As a follower of Minister Louis Farrakhan and the Black Nation of Islam, he is now dedicated to racial pride, Black advancement, and community development through consciousness raising, education, and building economic enterprises. He looks upon his music as a tool for launching a mental revolution to liberate Black youth from the cycle of destructive behavior and awakening them to the value of education and self-determination.[46]

Before his death, Biggie Smalls was struggling to turn his life around. Promising possibilities for his career seemed just over the horizon. He was negotiating for book and movie deals and a TV show, and he was on the verge of becoming rap's biggest star. He told reporters he was tired of his image as a gangsta. According to Biggie, the title of his last album, *Life After Death* (released posthumously), symbolized the changing course of his life.[47] He had a tattoo of a biblical verse on his arm that symbolized his belief in the strength and presence of God in his life:

> *The Lord is my light and my salvation, whom shall I fear?*
> *When the wicked, even my enemies and foes,*
> *Come upon me to bite my flesh,*
> *They stumble and fall.*

Dr. Dre, the creative artistic producer behind the success of Death Row Records' gangsta format, also appears to be transforming the direction of his life and creative energies. After his nonstop profanity and misogyny and references to drugs, guns, and shootings on hits by gangsta rappers Tupac and Snoop, Dr. Dre is departing from the format that made him millions. In a song called "Been There, Done That," on the first album with his new company, Aftermath Entertainment, Dr. Dre renounces the violence of gangsta rap. "Been There, Done That" is part of a 1996 album, *Dr. Dre Presents . . . The Aftermath,* which features a combination of soul singers, jazz, sultry R&B, and non-gangsta rappers. Dr. Dre says he had a wake-up call when he was serving a five-month jail sentence in 1996. With nothing to do in his cell but think, he decided to leave Death Row Records and move his life in another direction.[48]

Elder statesmen in the Black community are joining the performers and producers of rap music in a call for a reappraisal of the role of violence in gangsta rap and in the lives of the rappers themselves. In February 1997, the host of TV's sitcom *The Steve Harvey Show* brought rival figures Snoop Doggy Dogg from Death Row Records and Puffy Combs, executive director of Bad Boy Entertainment, together in a heavily promoted appearance in which they called for an end to the animosity that has cast a shadow over the rap/hip-hop world for the past few years. Snoop and Puffy say it is time to shake hands and give the kids around the world something positive.[49]

That peace effort was followed in early April 1997 by a meeting of several key rap figures, including Snoop Doggy Dogg, convened by Louis Farrakhan. After the meeting, tentative plans were announced for a joint hip-hop peace tour and album. Scheduling conflicts prevented Combs from attending the meeting, but he pledged to support the united peace effort.[50] The 13,000-member National Academy of Recording Arts and Sciences is planning to sponsor a conference of rap/hip-hop executives, managers, producers, and performers to discuss everything from violence to the content of the music. Respected music producer Quincy Jones is one of the spokesmen for the conference.[51]

Two groups that were seminal powers in the beginning of the modern rap era are stepping back into the fray to help their younger Brothers. Having been rediscovered by a new generation of listeners, the Prophets from Watts and the Last Poets from New York are getting together for a unity tour to end the violence.[52]

Part

III

THE AFRICAN-AMERICAN MALE:

MASCULINE ALTERNATIVES

AND PSYCHOLOGICAL CHALLENGES

Chapter 6

Masculine Alternatives:
The African–American Perspective

Because of the toxic psychological and social effects associated with the traditional Euro-American masculine ideal, African-American psychologists have recommended that Black males avoid strict adherence to White norms and seek alternative definitions of maleness.[1] Indeed, the Euro-American masculine ideal has many admirable qualities—an emphasis on logical thinking, organizational skills, and planning ahead to achieve future goals—but there is a definite downside. Excessive emphasis on power, dominance, competitiveness, individualism, and control has resulted in the oppression of ethnic minorities and in sexism. In what appears to be a distortion of human potential, the Euro-American masculine ideal leaves out a wide range of human experiences and feelings. Little or no value is placed on empathy, nurturance, compassion, harmonious relationships, and being in touch with one's feelings.

The social psychologists James Doyle and Michele Paludi, summa-rizing key aspects of Euro-American masculinity, list five factors:[2]

1. *The self-reliant factor.* Real men are in control. They are calm and decisive under pressure.

2. *The success factor.* To demonstrate their masculinity, men should compete and win against other men at work and in sports. Making lots of money, having a high-status job, and driving an expensive car are important.

3. *The aggressive factor.* Men are expected to go after what they want and fight for what they believe is right. Real men defend themselves aggressively against threats and are capable of using physical and verbal violence.

4. *The antifeminine factor.* Real men do not act like soft, gentle, tender females.

5. *The sexual factor.* Men should be the initiators of sexual behavior and control heterosexual interaction. Women are valued as objects of physical beauty and displayed as symbols of conquest.

Since the ideal male is supposed to be in control at all times, pub-lic displays of emotion are taboo. In 1972, when Senator Edmund Muskie wept during his campaign for the Democratic party's presiden-tial nomination, he was roundly criticized. Real men don't cry. The Euro-American masculine paradox, therefore, is that while White males generally have more freedom than women and children and Black males to compete, pursue adventure, seek power, and take risks, they are less free to express their own feelings.

For several reasons it is not psychologically healthy for Black males to follow heedlessly the overly controlled, dominating Euro-American masculine style. First, aggressive individualism and rigid emotional control are likely to be rejected in the African-American community, which values connectedness, interdependence, and emo-tional expressiveness. Second, an extreme emphasis on material suc-cess can be a cause of frustration. Black males have difficulty overcom-ing barriers caused by racism and poverty and becoming part of the good-old-boy corporate and social networks where inside information is passed along and which provide mentoring that enhances the chances for success. Third, acting out frustrated masculine strivings by overcompensating with go-for-bad machismo behaviors, sexual conquests, and violence will inevitably create negative consequences for self and others. The safety net in the inner cities is very thin; slight missteps can lead to poor academic skills and unemployment, unplanned parenthood, prison, or death. Such outcomes unwittingly reinforce negative stereotypes about Black males. Finally, emulating the Euro-American masculine ideal means identifying with a lifestyle that resulted in the enslavement and oppression of African-Americans and created the persistent negative stereotypes of Black males.

As an externally imposed ideal, the norms, values, and dictates of Euro-American masculinity warp the Black males' conception of manhood and prevent new possibilities from emerging. It is difficult, if not impossible, to free oneself psychologically from oppression by identifying with the oppressor and emulating his lifestyle. To free the African-American male from the destructive effects of slavery, segregation, and institutional racism, and to unlock suppressed human potential, a fundamental refocusing of masculine ideology is needed.

Masculinity: The African-American View

Several Black psychologists, including Wade Nobles, Na'im Akbar, Linda Jones Myers, and Asa Hilliard, have convincingly argued that an African-centered ideology represents the greatest potential for transforming the African-American vision of manhood into a psychologically actualizing ideal that will allow Black men to raise themselves above oppression and function as liberated rather than controlled human beings.[3]

Afrocentrism, an African-centered philosophical orientation, value system, and frame of reference, views African values and ideals as the starting place for analyzing such issues as the meaning of masculinity for people of African descent. The Afrocentric worldview incorporates the Black Nationalist tradition of Marcus Garvey, as well as the values represented in African-American expressive forms like dance, literature, art, and drama. Afrocentrism represents an attempt to return to traditional African culture and update it to deal with spiritual, cultural, and psychological change. Rather than anchoring the search for masculine identity and values in a Euro-American perspective, the Afrocentric approach looks within and articulates a point of view that is congruent with the history and culture of African and African-American people.[4]

The Afrocentric View

The Afrocentric view of masculinity places emphasis on spiritual beliefs, the importance of human relationships, and the synthesis of opposites as a way of resolving conflict. Optimal psychological functioning involves incorporating into one's daily life the practice and principles of spirituality, connectedness and interdependent living, harmony with others, and balance.

Spirituality, the first of these basic Afrocentric concepts, is symbolized by a vibrant belief that a spiritual force acts as a connecting link to all life and all beings. Spirituality gives direction, purpose, and energy to all human endeavors. Attunement to and cultivation of spirituality as the core of existence enhances individual and group well-being, healing, and actualization of human potential. Spiritual power enables one to maintain psychological equilibrium during the ups and downs of life. Soul is the essence of human beings; and soul force is fundamental to understanding the African and African-American experience. From soul force come the power, intensity, and will to survive oppression. Soul force is expressed in African and African-American art forms, sports, religion, and relationships. Soul force can provide African-American males with a sense of their own adequacy, power, resilience, and resourcefulness.

People do not exist apart from nature or each other. In Afrocentric reality, there is no separation between spiritual and material, sacred and secular, man and nature. The universe is conceived of as a spiritual totality in which all elements of the system are interconnected: the person, the family, the community, animals, plants, and inanimate objects. With spirituality as the unifying power, the goal is to achieve harmonious relations among interdependent components of the larger system. Rather than dominance and control, the emphasis is on blending in harmoniously with the flow of human and natural events.

Harmony is a central feature of African life and finds expression in all aspects of African culture. The Afrocentric worldview fosters a humanistic conception of life and relationships. The rules of living are geared toward mutual aid, collective survival, and interdependent relationships. The basic human unit is the group or tribe, not the individual person. Individual identity is part of collective identity; the individual does not exist apart from the group. People exist to benefit one another mutually in an altruistic fashion. Because the survival of the group takes precedence over individual survival, cooperative relationships, as opposed to individualism, are encouraged. In Afrocentric philosophy, a high premium is placed on maintaining and enhancing harmonious relationships. Authentic, genuine relationships with people are valued over power, control, or acquiring material possessions. Being true to oneself and others in intimate relationships earns respect and admiration. As part of the Afrocentric masculine ideal, courting harmonious relationships can enhance mutually enriching bonds between men and women, build unity in the Black community, establish a sense of connectedness between Black males, and reduce Black-on-Black crime and violence. In the philosophy of interdependence, we are our brothers' keepers.

Whereas the Euro-American masculine ideal encourages polarities and rigid dichotomies—male/female, Black/White, conservative/liberal, proabortion/antiabortion—Afrocentric values encourage a synthesis of opposites through mediation, conciliation, and dialogue. Thinking and problem solving are based on commonalities of views. Reality involves contradictory forces, which, at the same time, are part of the whole. When Nelson Mandela and his followers took over the government in South Africa, they included their former oppressors in the new government and initiated a movement toward reconciliation. The process of moving beyond either-or thinking in order to achieve unity and completeness is not purely intellectual; harmony, spirituality, and intuition are critical components of problem solving aimed at achieving synthesis of opposites. Sometimes the truth or a workable solution to a complex problem can be sensed or felt before it can be articulated in a rational, logical fashion.

The Afrocentric frame of reference is incorporated in the seven principles of living and guides for conduct outlined in the *Nguzo Saba* value system developed by Maulana Karenga (see Chapter 5). In his *Coming of Age: The African American Male Rites-of-Passage* (1992), Paul Hill recommends that young African-American men go through modern-day rites of passage. In an extended mentorship program conducted in schools, churches, and homes and supervised by teachers, parents, and community elders, young men are taught basic Afrocentric principles, the *Nguzo Saba* value system, and the importance of community service, respect for their elders, leadership and coping skills, health care, and proper conduct in male/female relationships. The rationale for such programs is that boys need hands-on guidance from their elders during the turbulent transition from boyhood to manhood.

For a more extensive discussion of historical interpretations and political connotations associated with the Afrocentric view, the reader should consult Molefi Asante's *The Afrocentric Idea* and Martin Bernal's *Black Athena: The Afroasiatic Roots of Classical Civilization.*

TRIOS: Time, Rhythm, Improvisation, Oral Expression, and Spirituality

A related concept of the African-American heritage of masculinity can be found in the research of the Black social psychologist James Jones.[5] Jones has taken into account five dimensions of human experience: time, rhythm, improvisation, oral expression, and spirituality—TRIOS—which represent basic ways in which individuals and cultures make decisions, organize life, establish beliefs, and derive meaning. The concept of TRIOS emerged from analysis of racial differences in sports performances, personality research in ethnic cultures, psychotherapy research on Black clients, and studies of African religions and philosophies. Jones's findings indicate that African-American males, as compared to Euro-American males, are more spiritual, emotionally expressive, gregarious, flexible, and present-oriented. His findings from TRIOS are supported by the research of other African-American psychologists, including Richard Majors, Robert Staples, and Alfred Pasteur and Ivory Toldson.

Nigrescence: The Process of Becoming Black

Since the late 1960s, African-American psychologists have been examining the development of ethnic awareness as a culturally based empowerment process that reaffirms self-worth and enhances personal efficacy in African-American men. In an African-American context, the essence of ethnic consciousness is captured by the term "Nigrescence." Nigrescence means "to become Black." It is a conversion experience or shift in Black consciousness characterized by movement through a series of psychological stages in which the person becomes more aligned with the African-American way of being. Nigrescence is a new awakening of Black consciousness, a resocialization experience that comes about through a process of discovery and self-examination. It is a process through which a nonaligned Negro becomes a Black.[6]

As a social movement, Black consciousness has been observed in three historical periods in the United States. The Harlem Renaissance of the 1920s, with its concept of the "New Negro," emphasized racial consciousness and pride in literature, art, drama, dance, politics, and psychology. In the 1960s, the cry for Black power, manhood, and self-determination represented the transformation from Negro to Black. In the 1990s, we have the search for Afrocentrism.

Psychologists have discovered five stages of ethnic consciousness, representing an evolution of consciousness of the world shaped by an internalization of ethnic values, lifestyles, and cultural customs. In the first stage, the pre-encounter stage, being Black is not important in a person's life. Stage two, the encounter stage, isolates a powerful event that starts the process of transformation. In stage three, the immersion/emersion stage, a person tries to cast off his old identity and earnestly searches for authentic Blackness. Finally, he internalization and commitment stages represent a period during which the person settles into a new Afrocentric identity and makes long-term commitments in terms of who he is, what he believes, and where he is going with his life.[7]

Let's look at these five stages in more detail, using the life of Malcolm X as a guide.

The Pre-Encounter Stage

The pre-encounter stage is characterized by very little awareness of what it means to be a Black man in America. The lifestyle and the way of experiencing the world of a person at this stage reflect no preference for African-American values. The person could be a fully assimilated Black who believes that upward mobility in the corporate structure depends solely on a combination of hard work, organizational skills, intelligence, careful planning, and people skills. He just happens to be Black, but believes he will ultimately be judged on his own merit. The pre-encounter Black man could be a gang member or a drug-using street hustler who is too busy exploiting other Blacks to think about the destructive effects on himself and others. He could be a suburban Black teenager with streaks of red and green in his mohawk haircut who hangs out with punk rockers. In an extreme case, a pre-encounter Black male could harbor anti-Black attitudes; he accepts the White racist view that Blacks are inferior and the conservative view that all major Black social problems would be resolved if Blacks adopted the White American work ethic and puritanical attitudes toward sex.

The pre-encounter view of the world, shaped in a person's youth by events in the family, community, neighborhood, and school, is difficult to change. Malcolm X's pre-encounter view of the world, for example, was formed by the assassination of his father in Lansing, Michigan, by local Whites, by the breakup of his family after his mother was committed to a mental hospital, and by the racist advice from a White teacher that Black boys should not aspire to become lawyers.

The Encounter Stage

In the encounter stage, a person experiences an event that calls into question his existing belief system. The event usually catches him off guard and raises questions about what one's life and values are all about. An assimilated corporate executive who has tried hard to be the right kind of Negro is turned down for a well-deserved promotion to senior management. Insider friends tell him, off the record, that the company is not ready for a Black in senior management; the stockholders would be uneasy. A college biology professor who has published extensively and has an excellent teaching record is turned down for tenure and promotion to full professor. A young Black punk rocker goes to college and is ridiculed by other Black students as a "weird-acting White boy." A street hustler is busted, convicted, and sent to prison, where he is confronted by Black Nationalist inmates who criticize his lifestyle.

The encounter stage has two steps: The person must consciously experience an event and his life must be profoundly affected by the event. The event can take place in the public or private arena but is ultimately personalized. Martin Luther King, Jr.'s, assassination was a public event that had a profound emotional impact on many Black men. The assault on Rodney King in 1991 was a public event that evoked deep personal feelings of anger in most Black men. Although the encounter experience is generally negative, it need not be. The Million Man March on Washington in October 1995, sponsored by Louis Farrakhan, elicited feelings of pride and affirmation for Black males who were there as well as those who watched the event on television.

The encounter experience generates a wide range of emotions, which can be energizing. The assimilated Black man may feel anger for having trusted the White man. At the same time, he may feel guilty for having abandoned the Black struggle. The street Brother may feel guilt for exploiting his people and for dishonesty in his relationships with women. A Black man who has witnessed a police assault or had a family member or friend assaulted by the police may experience a sense of outrage and righteous anger. The psychic energy provided by rage and guilt triggers the motivation to start the search for a new identity. Old ideals are reexamined and new questions are asked.

Malcolm X started through the encounter experience when he was arrested and imprisoned in his youth. He was convinced that he received a longer sentence than usual because two members of his burglary gang were White females. His early years in prison were filled with unfocused anger at his guards and fellow inmates. He fought, refused to work, and spent time in solitary confinement. Gradually, his rage settled and he began to ask questions about the role of race, power, economics, and history as they affect the life of a Black man in America. Malcolm started to examine the White racism underlying the events that shaped his life and how his reactions to these events had landed him in prison. He realized, slowly and painfully, that his lifestyle was wrong in the sense that it was self-destructive and dysfunctional. His search for answers pointed him in the direction of Nigrescence.

The Immersion/Emersion Stage

The real work of the Negro-to-Black transition takes place in the immersion/emersion stage. This third stage is an in-between state where the old belief system is cast off and the new one has not fully formed. The social psychologist William Cross, one of the leading experts on Nigrescence, describes the immersion/emersion stage as the vortex of the identity-change process.[8] In the immersion phase, a person gets caught up in a furor of emotions and activities as he desperately searches for just the right kind of Black identity. He joins Black-oriented groups, shifts his reading preferences to African-American literature, and wears African-style clothes to social events and sometimes to work. He may take on an African name and give his children African names like Zaire, Kenya, or Tambusi.

His life becomes a sea of Blackness; everything he does must be related to Blackness. He engages friends and relatives in endless debates and confrontations about the correct Black point of view in religion, art, politics, education, economics, and family life. He constantly worries about being the right kind of Black man and projecting the appropriate Black image. His friends and relatives covertly refer to him as being "Blacker than thou." In his attempts to cast off his old Negro identity and liberate himself from any trace of Whiteness, his thinking becomes either-or: Everything Black is good; everything White is bad. As part of self-imposed purification rites, he withdraws from everything White. He has romantic visions of how quickly Blacks can achieve political and economic power through revolutionary action. This immersion into Blackness is akin to religious fervor; the person expresses an undying commitment to Blackness and love for his people.

Gradually, the person enters the emersion phase, a leveling-off period during which he can gain control over the emotional intensity and frantic pace of activity accompanying the desperate search for the most authentic interpretation of Blackness and the African-American way of being. In a calm, reflective manner, he can now sort out, integrate, and consolidate the process of identity change. The person is now ready to internalize a sense of self.

In his immersion/emersion phase, Malcolm X read widely, joined the prison inmates' debating team, and held extensive conversations with his fellow prisoners about existential, political, and racial matters. He toned down his impulsive, rebellious behavior, started working toward parole, and reestablished contact with family members. He examined seriously the Black Nationalist philosophy to which he was introduced by his brother, who was a member of the Nation of Islam, the Black Muslims. And he began correspondence with the Honorable Elijah Muhammad, leader of the Nation of Islam.

The Internalization Stage

During the internalization stage, stage four, the dissonance between the old self and the emerging African-American consciousness is resolved. The man fully integrates a Black frame of reference into his daily life. His life is now calmer and more relaxed; a quiet inner peace and strength are achieved. The person no longer has to prove constantly he is Black enough or has to confront others about the correctness of their views on Black issues. His definition of Blackness is more open and sophisticated. Simplistic either-or definitions are now inadequate. Defensiveness fades, and there is a willingness to consider different points of view. The person feels revitalized and changed. The new sense of Blackness is grounded in affiliations with African-American professional and community groups working constructively for social change. The person's values and cultural style are deeply rooted in the African-American heritage. He feels connected spiritually and psychologically.

Once internalization is achieved, there is no longer a need to rely on supermacho behavior, womanizing, drug use, or other forms of maladaptive coping to deal with the frustrations of institutional racism. Blackness provides a buffer against the psychological effects of racism. A psychological protective strategy emerges that involves an awareness that racism is part of American life, that no Black man is so special that he cannot be a target of racism. When confronted with institutional or individual acts of racism, the person is able to employ a flexible set of coping mechanisms. He knows when to confront, assert, negotiate, or engage in diplomatic problem solving and when to withdraw and fight another day. He is better able to decide when the system is to blame as opposed to when a setback is due to his own irresponsible behavior. If a college student receives a poor grade because he did not study, he cannot put the blame on the instructor. If the course was about urban political science and didn't contain a section on politics in the Black community, rather than flunk the course because of quiet resentment, the student, along with other Black classmates, could approach the instructor and negotiate changes to include coverage of Black politics. In the internalization stage, a spiritual orientation becomes part of coping strategies. Spirituality reduces the tendency to get caught up in bitterness, rage, and unproductive demonizing of all White people.

According to Bailey Jackson, as a person begins to feel more secure in the internalization stage, he can sort out those features of Euro-American culture and masculinity that are acceptable and those that are unacceptable. Rather than condemning all aspects of Euro-American culture, he can reject sexism, racism, oppressive poverty, and imperialism, while at the same time accepting hard work, responsibility, logical thinking, and planning ahead. These values are combined with an Afrocentric emphasis on spirituality, harmonious relationships, synthesis of opposites, and interdependence. Integrating the positive aspects of Euro-American society with Afrocentric values fosters a bicultural orientation that allows the person to work constructively with Whites.[9]

The Internalization-Commitment Stage

The internalization-commitment stage is a long-term extension of the psychological transformation. The person is now secure enough in his commitment to the African-American way of being to become involved in long-term efforts to change the system and help others. Personal identity is complete, and he can pursue concrete actions individually and through organizations to create a more humanistic society. A multicultural orientation develops as the person begins to see similarities between the struggles of Blacks, women, and other groups.

During his internalization stage, Malcolm X came under the tutelage of Elijah Muhammad and joined the Muslim faith. After his discharge from prison in 1952, he became a minister in charge of the Muslim mosque in Detroit. Subsequently, he was given a prized assignment as minister of New York's Harlem mosque, where he became the national spokesperson for the Nation of Islam. He was often quoted in newspapers, spoke at colleges and universities across the country, and appeared on TV news shows and debate programs. Mike Wallace's exposé on the Black Muslims, entitled *The Hate That Hate Produced,* featured Malcolm X as the organization's prime mover. After a break with Elijah Muhammad, and a trip to Mecca during the last year of his life, Malcolm X renounced Black separatism and the blind hatred of all Whites as devils and was moving in a multicultural direction.

Recycling

Thomas Parham, a brilliant young Black psychologist, has added the concept of "recycling" to Nigrescence.[10] As new challenges and crises emerge during adult life, a person who has already achieved Black consciousness may recycle through one or more of the stages of Nigrescence. New issues can trigger a reexamination and a refocusing of values, leading to a deeper involvement in one or more elements of the African-American experience. The rise, fall, and resurrection of Marion Barry is a case in point.

Case Example: The Fall and Resurrection of Marion Barry

Marion Barry was born in 1936 to a family of Black sharecroppers in Itta Beta, Mississippi. As an infant, his mother carried him in a sack as she picked cotton. His father was not in the picture during his childhood. Barry attended a predominantly Black college in Tennessee, where he became involved in the civil rights movement. A brilliant student, he gave up an opportunity to earn a doctorate in chemistry in the 1960s at the University of Kansas. Instead, he chose to continue working with the movement as chairman and fundraiser for the Student Nonviolent Coordinating Committee (SNCC). In the 1970s, he worked as a community activist in low-income neighborhoods in Washington, D.C. Subsequently, he was elected to the city council and thereafter served three terms as mayor.[11] In 1990, he was driven from office in an FBI sting operation that showed videotapes of Barry in a hotel room with a woman other than his wife and lighting up a crack cocaine pipe. After a brief prison term, he surprised his critics by being reelected to his old city council seat, and in 1994, he was reelected mayor.

Somewhere along the line as an adult, Barry fell into a pattern of dysfunctional masculinity that involved alcoholism, drug use, and womanizing, behavior that was well known in both Black and White circles in Washington. When confronted about his behavior, he engaged in denial or accused newspaper reporters and TV commentators of racist bias. When he was arrested and imprisoned, he was forced to reexamine his beliefs and behaviors. During his recovery phase, he discovered a deeper level of spiritual redemption within. He remembered the voices from small Black churches in Itta Beta saying that redemptive suffering could be cleansing: "If a man falls by the side of God, he shall rise again. . . . I have never seen the righteous forsaken nor his seed beg bread. . . . Amazing Grace, how sweet the sound . . . I once was lost, but now I'm found." Whites castigated the Black community for reelecting a man of his vices. What they failed to understand was the redemptive power of the African-American ethos: Any man may fall but the test of life is whether he will seek spiritual redemption and, with the Grace of God, grow and mature through suffering.

Marion Barry's rise, fall, and redemption illustrate that life is like going up and down a spiral staircase that we traverse again and again at different elevations. We retrace many areas we have already traveled. New challenges and crises make us question who we are, questions that need to be resolved by reviewing, reorganizing, and renewing our identity.

Euro-American Masculinity: New Perspectives

In the wake of the harsh portrayal of the Euro-American masculine ideal as fostering blind ambition, destructive competition, sexism, and psychological isolation from self and others, White men are being encouraged to expand the meaning of masculinity. Three major ideas for redefining the Euro-American masculine ideal emerge in the writings and speeches of social psychologists, gender experts, and leaders of the men's movement—a loosely affiliated network of predominantly Euro-Americans.

First, the positive features of traditional Euro-American masculinity should be retained. Logical thinking, leadership, assertiveness, responsibility, and decision making are psychologically healthful, admirable strengths. Second, the excessive power seeking, competition, individualism, and domination of others that have led to oppression, in the form of racism, sexism, and male-dominated patriarchal hierarchies, should be eliminated. Third, the meaning of masculinity needs to be expanded to include expressive behaviors and spirituality. Men need to tune in to the inner self and learn to feel comfortable with expressive human characteristics like nurturance, affection, intimacy, empathy, compassion, and affiliation. Comfort with expressing and receiving compassion can become the basis of the long process of resolving conflicts with ethnic minorities. Finally, Euro-American men need to learn to turn to each other for emotional support, understanding, counsel, and spiritual affirmation.

The men's movement encourages men to move toward definitions of masculinity that allow access to such expressive traits. Groups associated with the movement, such as NOMAS (National Organization for Men Against Sexism), the Texas Men's Center, and the Sons of Orpheus, coordinate activities and dispense information. NOMAS encourages men to work not just to change themselves and other men but also to change social, political, and economic institutions that create unequal distributions of power across racial and gender lines.[12]

Hundreds of men's groups around the country—in 1991 there were 163 in the Northeast alone—sponsor conferences, workshops, retreats, and gatherings devoted to men's issues.[13] The men's movement issues a newsletter and two national quarterlies. The newsletter, *Man's Awareness Network,* is a regularly updated directory of publications, activities, and organizations prepared by a rotating group of men's centers. *Wingspan* (a free publication) and *Man* are the quarterlies, with circulations of 125,000 and 3,500, respectively. Some of the popular authors associated with the men's movement and their books are listed below:

Goldberg, Herb. (1980). *The New Male: From Self-Destruction to Self-Care.* New York: New American Library.

Farrell, Warren. (1986). *Why Men Are the Way They Are: The Male/Female Dynamic.* New York: McGraw-Hill.

Goldberg, Herb. (1987). *The Inner Male: Overcoming Roadblocks to Intimacy.* New York: New American Library.

Bly, Robert. (1990). *Iron John: A Book About Men.* New York: Addison-Wesley.

Keen, Sam. (1991). *Fire in the Belly: On Being a Man.* New York: Bantam.

Farrell, Warren. (1993). *The Myth of Male Power.* New York: Simon & Schuster.

Hicks, Robert. (1993). *The Masculine Journey: Understanding the Six Stages of Manhood.* Colorado Springs, CO: Nav Press Books.

Connell, Robert. (1995). *Masculinities.* Berkeley: University of California Press.

Levant, Ronald, and Pollack, William, eds. (1995). *A New Psychology of Men.* New York: Basic Books.

Kimmel, Michael, and Messner, Michael, eds. (1998). *Men's Lives,* 4th ed. Boston: Allyn & Bacon.

Pollack, William. (1998). *Real Boys: Rescuing Our Sons from the Myths of Boyhood.* New York: Random House.

In men-only conferences, workshops, retreats, psychological growth groups, and other gatherings sponsored by organizations affiliated with the movement, White males are struggling to get in touch with their lives and reach out to other men to build relationships based on sharing, empathy, and mutual support. Using a mix of ancient rituals and modern psychological growth tools, they are trying to

overcome cultural taboos against revealing emotions and showing vulnerabilities. In the chanting, hollering, drumming, dancing, and pray-
ing that goes on at weekend retreats and camp outings, many men experience an emotional catharsis that frees them from the loneliness
and spiritual alienation of modern life. In face-to-face groups men
learn to replace verbal one-upmanship and verbal competition with
active listening techniques such as paraphrasing, summarizing, and
clarifying. They are encouraged to talk about feelings and relationships rather than sexual conquests, athletics, cars, or occupational
achievements. The underlying assumption guiding these groups is that
men can only learn to be men and experience the awareness of what it
means to be a male by being in touch with other men. Through genuine sharing, honoring, acclamation, and reassurance, one can sort
out what it means to be an emotionally healthy man in the postmod-
ern era.[14] Indeed, in trying to discover new dimensions of masculinity
and to expand their consciousness of what it means to be a whole
human being, perhaps Euro-American males should take a look at the
Afrocentric masculine ideal.

Chapter 7

The Black Male:
Major Psychological Challenges

As Black males move through the developmental periods of childhood and adolescence and on into adulthood, they are faced with four major psychological and social challenges: constructing an identity and defining themselves as persons; developing and maintaining close relationships with others; coping with racism; and discovering adaptive possibilities within the African-American way of being. Identity, definition of self, and close relationships with others are concerns with which all American males must come to grips. Coping with racism and discovering adaptive possibilities within the African-American way of being are psychological challenges unique to the African-American male because of his novel heritage, which combines African and American traditions within a context of nearly 400 years of living under oppressive conditions in American society.

Identity and Definition of Self

Identity has three major components: establishing a conception of who one is, commonly known as self-concept; establishing goals and strategies to achieve goals; and fashioning a set of standards and values that can be used as guidelines for behavior and living. In short, identity refers to the process of answering such questions as Who am I?, Where am I going with my life?, How am I going to get there?, and What do I believe in terms of personal standards and values? At the core of the identity process is the definition of oneself as a person, as a man, and as a sexual being. Can the Black male learn to believe in himself as a competent, worthwhile person who can become his own man, reasonably control his destiny in a society dominated by White power, maintain hope for the future, and accomplish his goals? Can he dream a dream of what he wants to become and develop a plan to achieve that dream? To achieve control over his destiny and move beyond mere day-to-day survival, the African-American male must be willing to risk commitment to long-range goals, forgo short-term hedonistic pleasures, and learn to implement strategies to achieve realistic goals.

In defining themselves as males, African-American men are likely to choose from among three clusters of personality and social traits: the traditional Euro-American, those related to the African-American heritage, and those from the renegade street culture. Endless permutations and combinations of these three clusters of masculine traits can be found in the daily lives of Black men. For example, how women are defined and related to are key components of one's masculine style. Are women viewed as "bitches" and "hoes" who exist primarily for sexual pleasure, or are women persons to be honored, respected, and with whom to build complementary relationships? Personal values and standards for behavior determine how we treat others. Commitment to respect of others and fair play increases the possibility of mutually enhancing relationships with males and females. On the other hand, values based on self-centeredness lead to exploitation and dominance of others.

A central feature of masculine identity for both Euro-American and African-American males is productive work. Any conversation among African-American males will eventually come around to the world of work. Work is more than a source of income; it can enhance self-esteem by providing opportunities for mastery, recognition, and developing skills that are highly valued. Too often, structural barriers prevent Black males from receiving the kind of education, job training, and work experience they need to obtain jobs that enhance self-esteem, efficacy, and productivity. It is impossible to fulfill the male role of family provider or co-provider without a job that pays decent wages. When given the opportunity to succeed in a line of productive work, most Black males will work hard to actualize their potential, as David's story illustrates.

Case Example: Opportunity Facilitates Mastery

David is a twenty-six-year-old Black male, a high school dropout who has been working for a data processing company for the past eight years in a medium-sized midwestern city. Early in his employment with the company, he demonstrated a special knack for helping the repairman fix machines that had broken down. His boss encouraged him. The company gave David time off and paid his tuition to attend a trade school to increase his skills. At the same time, David studied for his high school equivalency exam, which he passed on the first try. When he finished the trade school program, he was assigned to the repairman as an assistant and given a pay raise. With support from his boss and his boss's boss, the general manager of the company, David started attending a community college at night to study computer technology. After he finished the degree program, his boss, the general manager, and the owner of the company started a subsidiary business repairing data processing equipment and advising other firms on how to update their equipment. They hired David as a crew chief, and later he was promoted to assistant manager of the subsidiary company. The new business expanded rapidly, and David was allowed to become a part-owner by investing some of his wages in it. David now travels around the Midwest advising companies with technical problems and updating their equipment. He plans to enroll in a four-year college to work toward a degree in engineering and computer science. He feels proud of his educational and work accomplishments, and is able to support his three children: a nine-year-old son from a high school relationship that didn't work out and two children who live with David and his wife.

Intimacy

From birth to death, close relationships are a fundamental part of the life cycle, beginning in the family circle with parents, siblings, extended kin, and family friends. As children move outside the family circle, they form networks of peer relationships at school, on the playground, and in youth activities. Three additional types of close relationships are found in late adolescence and adulthood. First are friendships based on likability and companionship. Most Black males have at least one close male friend—often called "Cuz," "Running Buddy," "Ace Boon Coon," "Cut Buddy," "Road Dog," "Homeboy," or "Main Man." Then there are intimate, romantic relationships. In the ideal case, special romantic re-lationships can lead to long-term marriages and children. The third type of close relationship involves a mentoring process in which the psychological and social growth of the young male is facilitated by the guidance and nurturance of an older adult male.

Family relationships, peer relationships, friendships, mentoring, and special intimate relationships provide affirmation and an interper-sonal context in which one can try out social roles and explore defini-tions of identity. Black men who cannot build and sustain long-term close relationships are likely to experience an increasing sense of lone-liness and isolation as they move through life.

Coping with Racism

Overcoming the debilitating effects of racism in a way that allows him to actualize his potential is a challenge the Black male faces as he tries to fashion an optimal identity and live out his dream. As Black men at-tempt to define who they are, build relationships, and carve out a place for themselves in the work world, they cannot avoid coming to grips with racial discrimination as an ongoing occurrence in American society. The historical and continuing significance of racism in the lives of African-American men represents a contradiction at the heart of Euro-American values. Black men are told that the United States be-lieves in fair play, justice, and equal opportunity, yet all around them they can see that this is not the case. In relating to America, Black males experience a duality, or double consciousness. They are part of America, yet apart from it; in it, but not of it; visible, yet invisible. After four centuries, the Black/White color line is still a divisive factor in American life. Long before they can articulate it in sociological terms, Black youths become aware of the fact that there is a pervasive, often subtle force that prevents them from taking advantage of the full range of opportunities life in America offers its other citizens.

As discussed earlier, racism operates at structural, institutional, and individual levels. Structural racism stems from the fact that White people, especially White males, control the political, economic, and legal power bases of society. White power ultimately decides where low-income and moderate-income housing projects will be built, where jobs will be located, where urban transportation will be routed, and what policies the federal government will advocate in terms of job training, urban renewal, social services, medical care, and criminal justice. A Black male who lives in a rundown inner-city housing project with inadequate public transportation to where the new jobs are located in the suburbs is at a definite disadvantage. Different prison terms are mandated by White legislators for possession of crack cocaine, preferred by inner-city Blacks, than for white powder cocaine, preferred by suburban Whites. This difference has resulted in large numbers of Black men serving lengthy jail terms.

Structural sociological changes resulting in the loss of jobs and businesses have devastated the economic vitality of Black inner-city neighborhoods. Between 1967 and 1985, cities with large Black populations—New York, Detroit, Philadelphia, and Chicago—lost more than half of their manufacturing jobs.[1] For instance, in the predominantly Black neighborhood of Woodlawn, on Chicago's South Side, there were more than 800 commercial and industrial establishments in 1950. In 1996, estimates indicated that only about 100 were still there. Two large factories that served as the employment anchor of North Lawndale, a Black neighborhood on Chicago's West Side, are no longer operating: Hawthorne's Western Electric Plant, which employed 43,000 workers, and the International Harvester Plant, which employed 14,000 workers. A twenty-nine-year-old unemployed Black man, interviewed for a story on Black unemployment, said that there were no jobs anywhere around. He went on to say that people want to work but can't find anything. In the Black Belt neighborhood of Washington Park, on Chicago's South Side, a majority of adults had jobs in 1950; by 1990, only one in three worked in a typical week.[2]

The loss of work for large groups of Black men due to structural racism can have devastating psychological and economic effects. Work is an integral part of male identity in America. More than just making a living, it also constitutes a framework for organizing daily behavior and developing discipline. If a man has a regular job, he knows where he is going to be and when he is going to be there. If he values his job, he organizes his time and plans ahead. In the absence of regular employment, life becomes less structured. Time is not well organized and often is spent hanging out, which can interfere with family life and building a long-term family plan for economic and social development. Many sociologists argue that today's problems in inner-city neighborhoods are fundamentally a consequence of the disappearance of work.

Institutional racism exists where Whites restrict equal access to jobs and promotions, to business and housing loans, and the like. White bankers and mortgage companies can secretly collaborate to redline a neighborhood so that such loans are nearly impossible to obtain. White senior faculty members in predominantly White universities (public and private) determine who gets promoted to tenured faculty positions. A young African-American teacher in an all-White psychology department places himself at risk if his research area is in African-American psychology. His senior colleagues may not consider his area legitimate and may not understand what he is writing about. Indeed, they may consider African-American psychology as not the "real study of psychology." Good-old-boys' clubs in the corporate structure determine who will be mentored and guided through the promotional mine fields; Black males are often excluded from such informal insider networks.

The case involving Texaco is a textbook example of racism at work in America's corporate system. In its public posture, Texaco was a model of equal opportunity and racial equity. Written antidiscrimination policies and channels for discrimination complaints were in place. Anonymous surveys were conducted to provide management with information about areas that needed improvement. As part of an effort to recruit employees from ethnic minority groups, Texaco set up equal opportunity programs and defined standards of company conduct. Glossy brochures with pictures of cheerful groups of multiethnic employees proclaimed the company's commitment to diversity and its promise of a work environment that would provide respect and dignity regardless of race or gender.[3]

It was demonstrated in court that behind the scenes, however, Texaco was a hornet's nest of covert bigotry and blocked pathways for Black employees. It was a company that said all the right things but did little to ensure that its words were carried out in reality. Using diplomatic company channels, Black employees tried for years to voice their complaints about a racially hostile work environment and stalled promotions. After a series of discussions that reached dead ends, in June 1994 six Black employees filed a racial discrimination lawsuit on behalf of themselves and at least 1,500 African-Americans who had worked for the company from 1991 to 1994.[4]

The lawsuit charged that Black employees were systematically denied chances for advancement and opportunities to attend seminars and to travel abroad, while less qualified Whites (sometimes trained by Blacks) moved ahead. Secret lists from which Blacks were excluded were used to fast-track White employees who were thought to have the potential for senior management. Statistical evidence presented as part of the lawsuit indicated that at Texaco fewer than 1 percent of 873 executives making more than $106,000 a year were Black, and not one of the highest paid executives was Black. While the number of Texaco executives in the highest paid echelon grew by 44 percent in the four years preceding the lawsuit, not a single Black person held such a job.[5]

Affidavits collected from Black workers cited the use of racial epithets and racial harassment in the workplace. Black employees reported having their tires slashed and "KKK" printed on their cars. They were asked to caddy golf games and called monkeys. A pregnant Black woman was given a birthday cake decorated with a crude caricature of a Black woman with a huge belly and an exaggerated Afro hairdo, and a printed suggestion that she ate too many watermelon seeds. Many Black employees did not report racial incidents for fear of losing their jobs.

Texaco flatly denied any systematic overt or covert bias. It steadfastly maintained that it was a color-blind company that valued diversity, treated everyone with dignity, and promoted employees without regard to race. The legal battle between Texaco and the Black plaintiffs might have continued indefinitely had not a disgruntled White executive who had lost his job in a corporate downsizing move leaked some audiotapes to the plaintiffs' lawyers.[6]

On the audiotapes, top company executives, one a former treasurer, can be heard sneering and laughing at Black employees, making negative references to Kwanzaa, a Black holiday festival, and referring to Blacks as jelly beans stuck at the bottom of the bag. They go on to mock the African-American National Anthem, "Lift Every Voice and Sing." The executives can also be heard threatening to destroy damaging evidence in the case. Early in November 1996, the tapes were released to the press, and excerpts were printed in the *New York Times* and played on national network evening news programs.[7]

Reactions to the tapes created a wave of negative publicity for Texaco. Federal prosecutors immediately opened a grand jury investigation into whether documents had been destroyed. Civil rights organizations threatened a national boycott of Texaco and its products. A group of San Diego ministers urged customers to destroy their Texaco credit cards. Texaco's stock fell $3 a share in the first days after the tapes were released, a loss of roughly $1 billion to the shareholders.[8]

The specter of economic retaliation, boycotts, disgruntled stockholders, and public censure set the stage for the company to move quickly for an out-of-court settlement. Less than two weeks after the tapes were released, Texaco's chairman, Peter Bijur, who previously had claimed that racial discrimination had never occurred in his thirty years at the company, apologized to the African-American community and to Texaco's Black employees for the company's discriminatory practices. He denounced the remarks on the tapes as a clear violation of the company's policies and agreed to what some say is the largest financial settlement ever made in a discrimination case.[9] (The largest previous settlement in a race discrimination case occurred in 1992 when a $132 million award was given to a group of African-American employees of Shoney's restaurant chain who had been denied jobs other than cooks.)

On November 15, 1996, Texaco agreed to pay out a total of $176.1 million to settle the lawsuit: $115 million to be paid in cash to the 1,500 current and former Black workers who sued; $26 million to be disbursed in pay raises over five years; and $35 million to be used for diversity and sensitivity training programs for Texaco staff. The agreement required Texaco to create an Equality and Tolerance Task Force to monitor changes in employment policies and report twice a year to the company's board of directors. The task force is at work. If Texaco fails to comply with the task force's recommendations, it will have to explain its reasons to the courts.

Frank Cronin, an Irvine, California, attorney who specializes in labor and employment law, feels Texaco had no choice but to settle the case. In his view, a jury listening to the tapes, affidavits, and statistical evidence would have awarded massive punitive damages, and in addition Texaco would have suffered damage from continuing negative publicity, boycotts, and stockholders threatening to revolt.[10]

It would be naive to think that Texaco is one of only a very few organizations in the United States saturated with institutional racial discrimination and bigotry. The kind of reprehensible behavior that went on at Texaco persists in far too many offices, law firms, universities, factories, and businesses. The tendency on the part of most organizations is to deny that racism exists until they are caught in a legally compromising situation. Why is it so hard for Black people to be taken seriously when they complain about institutional racism? Why did it take the leak of an incriminating audiotape to get Texaco to fulfill the commitments to equal opportunity promised in its brochures? Why does a pattern of denial and minimization persist when it is obvious that institutional racism is still a problem? Why do many Whites continue to believe that the war on institutional racism has been won, when fresh evidence that racism is alive and well pops up all the time? If equal opportunity is going to become a reality in the workplace, these are questions America must continue to struggle with.

Individual acts of racism, prejudice, and discrimination range along a continuum from mildly annoying frustrations to acts of physical violence directed at Blacks by Whites. Most Black males know how difficult it is to catch a taxicab in New York City and other major urban centers; some cab drivers routinely pass up well-dressed Black males in favor of White passengers. Some White females, fearful of Black males, clutch their purses and avoid eye contact when a Black male enters an elevator. On a lightly traveled Chicago street in the early evening, a White couple crosses in the middle of the street to avoid walking by a Black male approaching from the opposite direction. A Black male executive dressed in a shirt, tie, and dark trousers is having lunch in an upscale restaurant with two White clients. As he returns to his table after making a phone call, a White man at an adjacent table snaps his fingers, signaling the Black executive to refill his wine glass. To the chagrin of the maitre d', and of his clients, the Brother obliges.

Nigger jokes are told by White machine shop workers in hearing distance of Black employees in the lunchroom and on the floor of the plant. The supervisor refuses to intervene when Black workers complain. In suburban shopping centers, security guards and the police keep Black males under surveillance. In a suburban Buffalo, New York, mall, African-American males are referred to as Units, an acronym for "unwanted niggers in town."[11] The police in Beverly Hills, California, are accused of frequently questioning Black males driving through the community, walking along city streets, or merely sitting on benches at bus stops.

In many cases, reporting racial hostilities to supervisors at work does little good. It may even cause matters to get worse, as the following incident illustrates. Beginning in the mid-1980s, Black men working as civilian employees for the U.S. Army Corps of Engineers along the rivers of western Pennsylvania in the Corps' Pittsburgh district were subject to ten years or more of racial harassment, name calling, and even being threatened with physical violence. Some Black workers were draped in chains and had shackles put on them so White coworkers could take pictures they considered hilarious. A life-sized poster of four armed Ku Klux Klansmen surrounding a Black man with a noose around his neck was placed in the locker room. When a Black employee complained about the harassment and being called a nigger, a coworker threatened to shoot him. Human feces were placed in his work boots and someone broke into his locker and poured acid over his clothing. When the Black employee reported what happened, his supervisor suggested that he keep quiet about the incidents. Finally, in 1990, Stanton Greenwood, a long-time Black employee, contacted a lawyer and brought a class action discrimination suit against the Army. In January 1997, after fighting the lawsuit for years in court, the Army finally worked out a settlement.[12]

African-American couples and single African-American males are routinely harassed by neo-Nazi skinheads in Huntington Beach, California, where a Black male was severely beaten and stabbed. Lenard Clark, a thirteen-year-old Black boy, was beaten into a coma in March 1997 by three White teenagers in Chicago's Bridgeport neighborhood, home of Chicago's legendary mayor, Richard M. Daley. According to police, young Lenard was on his way home from playing a pickup basketball game when he was attacked. He and his friends ran but Lenard was caught in an alleyway. He was hit with a flurry of punches, repeatedly kicked, and his head was shoved into the wall of a house. Afterward, according to the residents of Bridgeport, the three White teenagers bragged about beating up a nigger.

The three White teenagers who were arrested for attempted murder and hate crimes attended a South Side Catholic high school, the same one from which Daley graduated. Despite requests from the Cook County prosecutor that bail be set at $1 million, the judge reduced the bail to $150,000 and $100,000 and the youths were quickly released. Two weeks prior to the beating of Lenard Clark, White youths at another Bridgeport Catholic high school taunted visiting Black students and players, calling them "Buckwheat" and other racial epithets. In 1966, Martin Luther King, Jr., was harassed when he marched through Bridgeport to protest segregated housing. Have racial attitudes undergone any significant changes in Bridgeport in thirty years?[13]

Five days before Christmas in 1986, three Black men whose car had broken down in Howard Beach, a predominantly White Queens, New York, community, stopped at a pizza parlor to phone for help. As they chatted with the counterman and waited for a pizza order, a hostile crowd gathered outside and started shouting racial epithets. When the Black men left the restaurant, they were beaten and chased by the crowd. One of the Black men, after unsuccessfully pleading to a bystander for help, tried to escape the menacing crowd by running onto the highway, where he was killed by an oncoming car. White residents of the community, defending the actions of the crowd, told reporters the crowd probably thought the three Black men had come into the community to cause trouble.[14]

In December 1996, at Fort Bragg, North Carolina, a Black couple walking home from a social event was killed, allegedly by three White men with neo-Nazi skinhead affiliations; the three White men had been members of the U.S. Army's elite 82nd Airborne Parachute Division. The following spring, two of the ex-paratroopers were convicted in separate trials of first-degree murder and conspiracy to commit murder on the testimony of the third ex-paratrooper, who was present at the killings. The two convicted murderers, former Private James Burmeister and former Private Malcolm Wright, Jr., were devotees of Nazi ideology and skinhead teachings. The case promoted a worldwide Army inquiry into racism in the ranks. The inquiry, completed in March 1996, found that 3.5 percent of the 7,600 soldiers interviewed had been asked to join one extremist group or another since joining the Army.[15]

The continuing presence of racism creates powerful emotions and uncertainty in the lives of African-American men. Over the long haul, prejudice and discrimination can generate rage, anger, frustration, bitterness, resentment, grief, despair, or any combination of these emotions. Contending with racism can be energy consuming and keeps one on constant guard. Uncertainty comes from not knowing when racist events will happen or whether prejudice was the cause of an event. Will a man be stopped by police when he passes through a White neighborhood? Will he be forced to lie on the ground in his freshly cleaned suit? Will he be beaten or arrested? Did someone else get the job he sought or the promotion he deserved because that person was better qualified, or was it because of subtle institutional racism? Whites rarely understand how powerfully racism can affect the lives of Black men. They tend to see incidents of racism as isolated events rather than as signals that racial oppression is still a major problem in America.[16]

Some writers refer to Black males as an endangered species, a class of individuals in peril.[17] Stresses experienced in repeated exposure to racial discrimination can trigger high blood pressure. Medical researchers and social scientists have long known that African-Americans are more likely than Whites to die of diseases related to hypertension. The higher rate of Blacks succumbing to strokes, heart attacks, and organ damage was formerly believed to be genetic or due to a combination of heredity, poor diet, lack of exercise, and being overweight. Now researchers have evidence to suggest that some hypertension-related problems in African-Americans are traceable to racial hostility and discrimination.[18]

A study of racial discrimination and blood pressure involving 4,000 Black and White men and women, reported in the October 1996 issue of the *American Journal of Public Health,* indicated that racial discrimination and reactions to it made a substantial contribution to differences in blood pressure between Blacks and Whites. Blood pressure was highest for working-class Blacks who experienced two or more instances of racial discrimination or hostility at work, when looking for a job, or when looking for housing. Professional Blacks, who were conscious of discrimination and who challenged racial discrimination, were at a lower risk for elevated blood pressure. The researchers speculated that working-class Blacks may be more likely to accept racial discrimination as a fact of life or to try to ignore it because they feel they have very little power to challenge racial discrimination successfully.[19]

White males have constructed a society in which they have empowered themselves in positions of wealth, decision making, and prestige. They exercise controlling vetoes over aspirations and choices in most of the political, economic, and legal areas of American life. In empowering themselves, they have reduced the opportunities and choices of Black males.

Resolving the deprivation of power/empowerment dilemma is a recurring existential problem confronting Black males as individuals and as a group. Life in a society controlled by Whites is unfair and unjust. The existential struggle involves the decision to overcome or be overcome. Does one cave in to the inhumanity of oppression of

American society or actively struggle to transcend anger and despair and try to become as whole as possible in a broken world? Does one seek a safe haven, eke out a survival existence, or actively try to change the society for oneself and others, and in doing so, risk being destroyed? How the Black male copes with these dilemmas is a key factor in determining the significance of his life, the meaning of his identity, and who will control his destiny.

Coping with racism can be viewed as a quest for empowerment, a strategy for increasing options, and a way of protecting oneself from harm. Historically, Black men in America have used a variety of coping mechanisms including conformity, rebellion, retreat, and separation. The conformist accepts mainstream values and the means for achieving them without protest; the philosophy of the conformist is that half a loaf is better than none. Rebellion occurs inside and outside the system. The civil rights movement of the 1960s was an innovative rebellion that sought to increase opportunities within the system. Gang youth and street hustlers are rebelling against society and seeking empowerment by establishing their own norms and values. Withdrawal, retreat, and escapism are motivated by despair. African-American men who are addicted to drugs or who exist homeless on the margins of society may no longer believe that success within the mainstream is possible.[20]

Coping with racism involves both feeling and thinking. The raw emotions it generates can be acted out or sublimated into constructive energy. In the machismo culture of Black urban gangs, anger, rage, and frustration are acted out inappropriately in explosive violence directed toward other Blacks. Writers like Richard Wright and James Baldwin, on the other hand, turned their rage into eloquent literary expressions. In his best-selling novel, *Native Son,* Wright expressed his anger and rage through the protagonist, Bigger Thomas.[21] In *Notes of a Native Son,* an autobiographical essay, Baldwin described his attempts to deal with his rage by seeking sanctuary in religion as an adolescent preacher when he was growing up in Harlem in the 1930s.[22]

At the cognitive level, coping involves trying to understand the meaning of events, setting goals, and developing plans to achieve them. A fifteen-year-old Black adolescent living in a high-rise inner-city project wants to attend college, stay out of gangs, avoid drugs, and not become a teenage father. To accomplish his goals, he must devise a strategy that allows him to study, take college prep courses, establish peaceful coexistence with gang members who live in the projects, stay away from situations where drugs are used, and practice safe sex. His best friend, who believes the only way to ensure your safety is to have a group to back you up, joins a gang and drifts into drugs and street crime. The friend is subsequently arrested in a gang-related homicide and sentenced to five years in prison.

Coping with troublesome situations can be adaptive or maladaptive.[23] Adaptive coping empowers the person by extending the range of options. There is no single solution to complex social and personal problems, and the best copers use a variety of coping mechanisms. Problems such as staying out of a gang while remaining on peaceful terms with gang members will most likely require a combination of interpersonal conflict-resolution skills, backup support from others, knowing who to stay away from, what parties to avoid, how to dress, and who not to date. Effective coping facilitates the development of mastery, allows a competent course of action to develop, and keeps powerful emotions from becoming too overwhelming. Solutions to perplexing problems caused by racism, identity conflicts, and masculinity choices do not occur instantly. A person must be willing to persist, keep the faith, improvise, learn from mistakes, and recover from setbacks.

Maintaining dignity and self-esteem is essential when pathways are blocked because of discrimination and structural racial barriers. Whether the Black male is in college or the work world, or is unemployed or in prison, it takes inner strength to continue the journey of growth and personal development. Adult life is about having choices and being able to visualize those choices. When seeking empowerment, the young Black male must be able to think beyond the immediate moment. He must be able to dream the dream of possibilities not yet visible and evolve a plan to make the dream a reality. When an individual can conceptualize a dream of what he wants to be in the future and lay out a plan for achieving his objectives, he has acquired a major organizing principle, which gives direction and purpose to his actions.

One of the major psychological traps preventing Black males from actualizing their dreams is getting caught up in the web of dichotomous thinking that arises from polarities generated by living under White oppression: the inclusion/exclusion dilemma, acceptance versus rejection of mainstream norms and goals, Black versus White lifestyles, acquiescence versus assertive confrontation, macho toughness versus authentic caring, and so on. To move beyond such either-or thinking requires a logical reasoning system that can envision multiple possibilities, a system of thinking that can assimilate new information and synthesize opposites to form novel possibilities for resolving identity issues.

That fifteen-year-old boy who wants to go to college will have to plan ahead, be alert for opportunities for financial aid and part-time employment, and seek out people who can provide him with emotional support, constructive guidance, and mentoring. As he seriously pursues college preparatory studies in a ghetto school with a high dropout rate, especially among the male students, he will probably be accused by his peers of acting White and not being a real Brother. In defining his identity, he will have to resolve the "twoness dilemma." Does he assimilate both the Black and White worlds into his identity, or does he ultimately choose one over the other? Finally, if he succeeds in accomplishing his educational goals, he will still have to develop adaptive coping mechanisms to deal with potential racial barriers as he moves through his work career.

Maladaptive coping, in the long run, decreases options, makes the original problem worse, and blocks the innovative thinking necessary to overcome troublesome dilemmas. By engaging in dysfunctional coping behaviors—dropping out of school, fathering children out of wedlock, abusing drugs, street hustling, indulging in indiscriminate outbursts of rage, or adopting a go-for-bad attitude—Black males ultimately decrease their power by increasing the risk of unemployment, arrest, and alienation from active participation in family and community life. They become unwitting allies in their own destruction. Maladaptive coping reinforces Euro-American stereotypes of Black males as lacking the maturity, commitment, and discipline to follow through on adult responsibilities.

The paradox of maladaptive coping can be illustrated by the example of the boy's friend who joins the gang for protection. Protection is a legitimate human need; the gang also offers status, recognition, and adventure. As a consequence of becoming involved in a homicide, the boy is convicted of a felony and sent to prison. A felony record makes employment harder to obtain and increases the risk that the boy will turn to illegitimate street activities when he returns to the community. Continued involvement with criminal activities will, no doubt, lead to further incarceration. Once initiated, a vicious cycle of arrests and incarceration is difficult to turn around. What started out as an attempt to fill a legitimate need for protection ends up being self-destructive.

Discovering Adaptive Possibilities

Black males must find adaptive possibilities within the African-American way of being. From one stage of life to the next, the ideas, values, and styles of behavior rooted in African-American social and religious institutions, psychology, and culture can provide alternative definitions of masculinity, new possibilities for resolving identity dilemmas, and constructive approaches for coping with racism. Following the African-American way of being, Black males can learn how to experience life, organize their world, make decisions, resolve contradictions, and derive meaning from life events. Internalizing this way of being can help them move beyond street images of tough guy, player of women, and hustler and the negative Euro-American masculine images based on dominance, individualism, and excessive competition.[24]

Adopting a frame of reference rooted in African-American values makes life understandable and provides guidelines for decision making and adaptive coping. Essential to sound decision-making strategy is a conscious understanding of the issues involved, as well as deliberately thinking through the consequences of choices. Under the oppressive conditions of American society, too many Black men find themselves in situations where they internalize masculine scripts, definitions of self, and coping styles without exploring the contribution that Afrocentric principles can make to their lives. Awareness of the African-American way of being allows the Black man to experience himself as part of a larger group history with a unique set of cultural norms and traditions. The African-American heritage fills in the missing identity pieces and allows the Black man to develop a sense of self that is grounded in his own soul and is not simply a reaction to White racism or to stereotypical roles he is expected to act out.

Aligning themselves with the African-American way of being poses special conflict for Black gay men. They must negotiate a complex matrix of challenges comprising their ethnic identity on the one hand and their sexual identity on the other, seeking validation in the predominantly White American gay community and in the African-American community and attempting to integrate both their gay and African-American identities.

In their discussion of the dichotomies between ethnicity and sexuality, Samuel Delaney and Joseph Beam explain that an African-American gay man must attempt to integrate and reconcile himself into two worlds simultaneously. As a Black man, he is in the White and Black worlds; as a gay man, he straddles the straight and gay worlds. Some gay Black men may give priority to their ethnic identity, while others consider their sexual orientation to be the more salient aspect of their identity. Black gay men are likely to feel caught in a double bind. Emphasizing their gay orientation can trigger hostility from the Black community, which wants them to assume an African-American identity; on the other hand, placing a priority on their African-American heritage can trigger a negative reaction in the gay community. Many Black men feel that they must deny their race and culture to fit into the White gay world or risk rejection in the gay community. The presence of racism in White gay culture forces African-American gays to return to their African-American communities for support, only to confront hostility.[25]

There is a pervasive view held by a number of African-American social scientists that homosexual desires and actions are either nonexistent in African and African-American societies or, when they do occur, are simply contaminants of European societies or are merely among the secondary products of oppression. Such writers discount homosexual activities engaged in by Black men as social aberrations, which occur mostly in prison, or as instances of rape or prostitution. Homosexual relationships between Black and White men are generally classified as dysfunctional by-products of the cultural and economic domination of White Americans over Black men. Some Black investigators confuse homosexuality with cross-gender behavior, effeminacy, or weakness. Others cite religious passages to justify their opposition to a gay identity as a valid option for African-American men. Many African-American women seem to condemn gay lifestyles because of their belief that homosexuality exacerbates the emerging problem of a decreasing pool of available Black males—already lessened by interracial dating and marriages, racially disproportionate rates of incarceration, and the relatively high rates of premature death among Black males from heart disease, cancer, AIDS, substance abuse, and violence.[26]

Because many African-American gays perceive themselves as African-American first and gay second, the need for support from the African-American community becomes very important to them. The perceived lack of support from both the White gay and the heterosexual African-American cultures frustrates the successful achievement of a well-integrated identity.[27]

The Role of Mentors

Older African-American males play a critical role as facilitators in teaching younger men how to sort out identity dilemmas, chose styles of masculinity, cope with racism, and discover adaptive possibilities within the African-American way of being. The African-American heritage is passed on from one generation to the next by the old heads in the community. In their roles as mentors, they are interpreters of their life experiences in a society where Euro-Americans control political, economic, and legal power. Because they have walked the walk, lived the life, and accumulated the wisdom of experience, the old heads can provide insight, in terms of how to navigate oppressive racial barriers and the dangers of inner-city environments. They can be instrumental in hooking up young people to support systems and services in churches, fraternal orders, educational institutions, job training, and employment. From the tribal elders, young African-American males can learn how to maintain hope, keep the faith, and move forward despite obstacles. The old heads understand and can share the qualities of improvisation, resilience, connectedness to others, and spirituality embedded in African-American psychology. Through them, younger African-American males can see the continuity of life experiences as each generation attempts to cope with the dynamics of racism and existential choices. The younger men can see that they are not alone, that others have found ways to transcend oppression and maintain their dignity.

Mentoring does not always have to come from only one or two people. Alert, resourceful young people can pick up bits and pieces of positive behavior and coping skills from a variety of older adults they observe in community, educational, employment, religious, and extended family settings. The African-American way of being is not a static process. Each generation adds new ideas and refashions cultural and masculine styles to fit changing conditions.[28]

Case Example: Guiding the Dream

According to the psychologist Daniel Levinson and his associates, a young man formulates a dream, establishes a set of occupational goals, and forms a relationship with a mentor. The dream has two parts. Part one is a vision of what the young man wants to become. It includes not only occupational, marriage, and family goals but also images of one's self as a powerful, special, heroic person who is respected in the world of adults. The second part of the dream is a plan for actualizing it—the bridge between the dream and reality. As the young man moves from late adolescence into adulthood, the dream and the plan are fine-tuned until a fit is established between what the person wishes to become and what options are available or can be created.[29] The dream provides motivation and energy for the young man to strive toward fulfillment of his goals.

The mentor is an older man who functions as the young man's guide, facilitator, or adviser. The mentor believes in the young man's dream and has confidence that he can achieve it. The young man looks up to the mentor and draws strength and confidence from him. According to Levinson's theory, the mentoring relationship lasts two to eight years. The high school and early adulthood years of the *Newsweek* writer Vest Monroe illustrate how this relationship with a mentor helps a young man to define his identity and achieve his dream.

Monroe's dream was to become a writer. The dream gave him hope. As a teenager, his literary hero was F. Scott Fitzgerald and he went so far as to sign his name S. Vest Monroe. Fortunately, Vest found a powerful mentor in his ninth-grade English teacher, Mr. Lovelace. Lovelace was a tough taskmaster who pushed Vest to excel. He believed that despite the gang-infested corridors, drugs, poverty, and teen pregnancies in Chicago's inner-city high schools, there were students like Vest who had the potential and wanted to learn. Lovelace had overcome obstacles in his own life and believed his students could do the same. He had grown up amid the poverty and racism of rural Alabama during the Great Depression of the 1930s. His mother, who had no formal education to speak of, instilled a love of learning in her children. Lovelace graduated from Hope College in Michigan, a church-affiliated school. He knew he could not save all his students, so he concentrated on those who had the talent, motivation, and willingness to persist in spite of the hardships all around them.

The teacher's honors class was a blend of precision, work, discipline, and tough love. Life was an uphill fight for poor Black kids like Vest Monroe, so Lovelace taught survival skills by pushing the students from class bell to class bell and assigning two to three hours of homework a day. Missing a class or an assignment could result in failure. Vest blossomed in the class. Subsequently,

Lovelace opened up opportunities for Vest to attend a private prep school and an Ivy League university where he could get the kind of training and internships he needed to start his career as a writer. Vest married a young woman from the projects who believed in his dream and provided the emotional support and companionship he needed while striving to fulfill his dream.[30]

Cyclical Development

Answers to the challenges involving identity, masculinity, and intimacy, coping with racism, and discovering adaptive possibilities within the African-American way of being are not found once and for all at any particular stage of the life cycle. There is no one period at which a person gets it right and then puts it to rest. New situations emerge that require new strategies, redefinitions, and alterations in old solutions and values. Human development is like a spiral staircase where at each turn the person comes to a deeper level of understanding and effectiveness. As he comes to turning points and decision-making junctures in the cyclical course of psychological development, the Black male must articulate and reformulate the dream of becoming, revise plans for achieving goals, try out new behaviors, hook up with mentors, search for a niche where he can become his own man, and build intimate relationships.

The intimacy issues for a sixteen-year-old experiencing his first romantic relationship differ from those faced by a thirty-five-year-old man with two young children who is trying to revive feelings of vitality and exuberance in a long-term marriage that has flattened out emotionally. The mentoring issues vary for a sixty-three-year-old grandfather who is counseling his thirteen-year-old grandson, teetering on the verge of gang involvement, and his thirty-seven-year-old son, going through a painful marriage breakup. An eight-year-old African-American boy in a predominantly White school is being harassed and called names by his classmates; he doesn't want to tell his teacher or his parents because he thinks being labeled a snitch will make the situation worse. He wants to resolve the situation himself. Coming up with a workable solution will test his resilience, resourcefulness, and problem-solving skills. A seventeen-year-old star athlete's girlfriend is pregnant and she refuses to get an abortion. He wants to fulfill his responsibilities to his child and girlfriend, but he is worried that becoming a father will interfere with his dreams of going on to college and professional sports or to a career in marketing. Finding a workable solution will force him to examine his values and what it means to be a father. A forty-two-year-old Black junior executive is approaching the corporate glass ceiling; he has been unable to break into the insider network within his corporate structure to get the mentoring and sponsorship he needs to move up. Should he confront the corporate hierarchy and risk becoming labeled as an angry Black man with a chip on his shoulder? Should he quietly persist? Or should he consider career alternatives outside the corporate structure?

As we discuss in subsequent chapters, many Black males encounter three somewhat distinct lifestyle choices and cultural patterns with respect to identity, masculinity, coping, and values as they move through cycles of transition and decision making. The street culture offers the lure of excitement, adventure, and recognition. Extended family networks and social and religious institutions in the Black community provide an opportunity to connect to an African-American way of being that emphasizes harmonious relationships, expressiveness, persistence in the face of obstacles, spirituality, and conflict resolution by synthesis of opposites. Within the context of education, employment, and correctional institutions controlled by Euro-Americans, Black males are faced with demands to conform to authority and not speak out against injustices or push for social change. How Black males balance these choices, opportunities, demands, and expectations affects their mental health, physical well-being, productivity, and life chances.

Chapter 8

Biographical Memoirs I
Boyz 'n the Hood: The Macho Identity

This chapter and the next are devoted to the memoirs of a group of Black males who grew up in different sections of the country during the 1950s, 1960s, 1970s, and 1980s. Their stories—although they do not represent the entire spectrum of lifestyles in the African-American male community—illustrate the psychosocial challenges that Black men commonly encounter. They provide a candid view of how these men handled the challenges involving identity, intimacy, coping with racism, and discovering adaptive possibilities within the African-American way of being.

The profiles of Monster Kody and Nathan McCall demonstrate the power of the African-American ethos to trigger a psychological rebirth or identity transformation in young Black men who are caught up in a vortex of gang activity, street behavior, and go-for-bad masculine patterns. Kody and McCall, bright, sensitive, multitalented young men, were temporarily derailed by a combination of overt and covert racism, restricted opportunity, rage, peer group reinforcement of macho behaviors, and the excitement of the streets.

Monster Kody

In his book *Monster: The Autobiography of an L. A. Gang Member,* Kody Scott, a.k.a. Sanyika Shakur, provides us with a first-person, insider's account of life in a Los Angeles gang set. Kody grew up near the intersection of Normandie and Florence in South-Central Los Angeles, the flash point of the 1992 rebellion after the acquittal of the White policemen in the first Rodney King beating trial. Kody's gang set is the Eight-Tray Crips, a subgroup of the notorious Crips gang that controls hundreds of city blocks in L. A. Kody joins the gang at age eleven in 1975 on the night of his graduation from the sixth grade. After he passes the initiation rites, which consist of fighting several fellow gang members at once, stealing a car, and going on a raid with blazing guns to attack an enemy gang, the Eight-Tray Crips gang becomes the center of his life. Kody's gang moniker, Monster, comes from an assault on a victim when he was thirteen. While Kody was trying to rob a man, the victim fought back. Kody stomped him for twenty minutes, leaving him unconscious in an alley. The man, who was disfigured by the beating, later lapsed into a coma. The police who investigated the case said that whoever had committed this brutal act must be a monster.[1]

For the next six years after being jumped into the gang, Monster Kody's identity as a gang warrior is a seemingly endless series of assaults, drive-by shootings, homicides, funerals for homeboys killed in battle, and time spent in and out of locked detention facilities. His dream, which he achieves, is to become an "O.G." In L. A. street parlance, an O.G. is an original gangster, the baddest homeboy on the set, a true hero who epitomizes daring, courage, risk taking, raw machismo, loyalty to his friends, and ruthlessness to his enemies. An O.G.'s reputation is known throughout the community—and within California correctional institutions.

As a teenager, Monster Kody is totally committed to gang life. Nothing outside his Eight-Tray Crips set seems to matter. Kody has the drive, motivation, resourcefulness, and organizational skills to become a leader and mentor for younger members of the gang set. The Eight-Tray Crips become a mirror through which he defines himself and his life. Within the gang structure, his tough masculine persona is reinforced and affirmed by his public posture. The gang provides him with adventure, excitement, meaning, and a chance to test himself against danger. Kody describes the adventure and excitement of gang life as something akin to an addictive drug rush.

In the early days of his involvement with the Eight-Tray Crips, the gang operated somewhat like an extended family social club; they held picnics, parties, and backyard barbecues. But as a series of disputes with a rival Crips gang escalated, Kody and his road dogs changed from a social group into urban warriors. The Eight-Trays took on the structure of a military machine. Retaliation killings and preemptive assaults seemed to be the only way to satisfy their rage and anger.

Psychologically, two features stand out regarding Monster Kody's adolescent lifestyle as a gangbanger. First, no older adult males seem to be closely involved in his life as confidants, mentors, or guides. His close relationships take place predominantly within the gang structure. He has occasional arguments about his lifestyle with his mother, but no ongoing contacts with his stepfather or legal father, who he later finds out is not his biological father. His biological father is a famous former Los Angeles Rams football star who has never acknowledged Kody as his offspring. Second, he makes major life choices, starting at age eleven to join the Eight-Tray Crips, without giving serious consideration to alternatives or to the disastrous consequences of his choices to himself, his victims, and those he cares about.

Monster Kody and his Crips homeboys know that prison is an inevitable consequence of gangbanging and jacking. "Jacking" is a street term that refers to robbery, burglary, car theft, and other illegal means of making a living; true gangbangers don't work. Prison is viewed as a test of masculinity and part of the gangster's dues paying. The trail to prison is like fate; it is going to happen. The goal is to survive prison and voluntarily come back to the hood with new ideas about how to get over on the streets and protect the gang set. Rehabilitation is considered a joke; prison is a place where gangbangers can learn new criminal techniques and hustling skills from other inmates. The danger of putting youths in prison is that their associating with older, more hardened prisoners reinforces perceptions youths have of themselves as criminals and gangsters. Surviving prison enhances one's reputation as an O.G. The street gang rivalries and hierarchies are replicated in California prisons and juvenile incarceration systems. Kody and his associates have friends and foes in all of California's correctional institutions.

In his gangbanging days, Monster Kody doesn't understand or acknowledge the role of structural and institutional racism as a major factor in producing poverty, unemployment, substandard health care, and underemployment in the Black community. His enemies are not White folks or the racist structures they created, but other Blacks in rival Crips sets and other gangs. Kody and his cohorts don't know how to fight the system; they take out their anger and frustration on each other. His way of resolving conflicts is based on physical aggression carried out in the form of retaliation, payback, and preemptive strikes. In addition to his gang orientation, Kody's philosophy is influenced by TV shows and movies that feature powerful males, such as westerns and movies about war or crime. He admires *The Godfather,* but doesn't understand that the Corleone family had economic and political goals. They weren't killing each other only to gain respect or to protect a turf they didn't own. Kody's thinking is based on either-or logic. Outside his family and gang set, everyone else is fair game. There is no middle ground. As a schoolchild, before he joined the Crips, Kody was beaten up and his lunch money was taken. He learned quickly that there were victims and victimizers. He chose to be the latter. Non–gang members, or hooks, as Kody calls them, are vulnerable to attack because they have no backup or respect.

Periodically, Monster Kody wants to open up and share with his mother or his girlfriend the vulnerabilities he secretly harbors beneath his masculine warrior persona. His girlfriend is worried that Kody is becoming so totally committed to gang warfare that nothing else matters, including their relationship. Kody is afraid to reveal himself because facing his fears and guilt for harming others may force him to question his lifestyle. In the code of the gang, admitting to fears and vulnerabilities is a sign of weakness that is not tolerated. He suppresses his feelings by acting out or drowning his worries with alcohol and drugs as he confronts the never-ending gang tests of manhood.

Kody and his Crips gang set exist outside the African-American way of being and mainstream American society. They seem unaffected by the Black consciousness movement, the powerful Black religious and civic organizations in South-Central Los Angeles, or the fact that L. A. has a Black mayor and the neighborhood schools have Black teachers and administrators. Kody is only nominally involved in school and is not concerned with developing skills that will lead to employment in the mainstream economy.

In prison, Kody begins a spiritual and psychological rebirth into Black consciousness. He discovers adaptive possibilities within the African-American way of being. Kody becomes Sanyika Shakur, a leader in the New Afrikan Independence Movement. His name, Sanyika, means a unifier, a gatherer of one's people. His rebirth is triggered by his relationship with Muhammad, a Black Muslim minister he meets while incarcerated in a youth facility who continues working with Sanyika after he is discharged. Minister Muhammad is the first strong male in Kody's life who is not affiliated with gangs or street life; he embodies a combination of spirituality, Black consciousness, masculine strength, firm tenderness, and moral principles. Minister Muhammad introduces Kody to Black Nationalist philosophy and acquaints him with the writings of Malcolm X and the Black Panther party. Kody admires Malcolm X and the Panthers for their masculine strength; they preach active resistance to racial oppression and do not turn the other cheek when attacked. Under the mentorship of Minister Muhammad, Kody begins to understand that by killing and maiming other young Black males he is helping the oppressor to destroy the building blocks of African-American liberation. It becomes crystal clear to Kody that without any mainstream skills, the only way he can make a living is by returning to criminal activities, which will inevitably lead to being locked up, locked down, and locked out of a productive adult role.

The spiritual rebirth of Kody Scott to Sanyika Shakur does not occur all at once; the psychological recycling process takes several years. Back on the streets at the beginning of his conversion, Sanyika Shakur slips back into Monster Kody and starts using and selling drugs. Work is still not something he feels comfortable with. He is arrested and returned to prison for allegedly participating in a gang assault. In solitary confinement, he becomes determined to consolidate his rebirth. Back on the streets again, he starts to become a mentor for young males who are falling into the trap of gangbanging. His New Afrikan Independence philosophy stresses spiritual and cultural awareness of one's self, one's people, and one's heritage without denying the humanity of other groups. He becomes a caring husband and an active father to his children.

Sanyika Shakur's goals are derailed when he administers street justice to a drug dealer who refuses to stop selling drugs in the community. When the drug dealer refuses to heed repeated warnings, Sanyika beats the man up and confiscates his car. The drug dealer happens to be a police informant, which does not help Sanyika when he is arrested and taken to court. Sanyika is given a seven-year sentence and placed in solitary confinement when he is returned to the California prison system. Sanyika was released in 1997 and is working to redirect Black gang members into a more productive life.

The transformation of Kody Scott is a remarkable story of the triumph of the human spirit over destructive internal and external forces. The key to his change seems to be in the discovery of creative forces within the African way of being that occurred under the mentorship of Minister Muhammad. Young African-American males roaming the streets of urban America cannot make the spiritual and psychological transitions necessary to become productive adults without the guidance of older African-American males. Left on their own, the archetypical anger and rage in these young people can easily turn into the brutality that creates monsters like Kody Scott. To channel rage into self-actualizing energy, boys need strong men to help them sort out alternatives and find nondestructive definitions of masculinity and responsibility.

Nathan McCall

Nathan McCall is a journalist with the *Washington Post,* one of America's most prestigious newspapers. He has also worked as a reporter for the *Virginia Pilot/Ledger Star* and the *Atlanta Journal Constitution.* He is currently working on a biography of Louis Farrakhan, the controversial leader of the Black Muslim Nation of Islam. McCall outlines the events surrounding his fall, imprisonment, and resurrection in his memoir *Makes Me Wanna Holler: A Young Black Man in America* (the title comes from a song by the late Marvin Gaye).[2]

McCall's descent into a maelstrom of gang violence, drugs, armed robbery, and gang rape defies conventional explanations of Black male social pathology as a product of deteriorating inner-city neighborhoods and crime-infested housing projects. He grew up in Cavalier Manor, a Black middle-class neighborhood in Portsmouth, Virginia, as part of an intact family. Cavalier Manor, a community of homeowners built in the 1960s, had large houses, well-manicured lawns, two-car garages, and streets named after famous African-Americans: Horne Avenue, Belafonte Drive, Basie Crescent. Fathers were present in most of the families. Nathan's stepfather, a retired Navy man, worked as a guard at the naval shipyards and ran a gardening business on weekends; the rest of the family consisted of four brothers, his mom, and his grand-mother. Cavalier Manor was a supportive community where neighbors looked after each other's children, went to church, and attended community meetings. Working-class Blacks, civil servants, schoolteachers, and small business owners mixed easily. Nathan describes a pleasant childhood during which he played cowboys and Indians, skinny-dipped in a nearby lake, and did odd jobs to earn spending money.

As a young adolescent, Nathan starts drifting toward a go-for-bad street definition of masculinity and identity. By his midteens, he is fully aligned with a peer group that has turned into a gang. Beginning with petty theft, Nathan and his cohorts escalate into burglary, armed robbery, drug using, drug dealing, beatings and assaults, shoot-outs, drive-bys, and gang rapes. His life is a constant search for ecstasy, excitement, adventure, and danger. Respect, power, and reputation are the themes that guide his identity. Respect is built by becoming known as a bad Brother, a "crazy nigger" who will not back down from a challenge or allow anyone to diss him without swift retaliation. Nathan literally believes in the dictum that power grows out of the barrel of a gun. The gun is the great equalizer; it can take life or allow life to continue. Nathan shoots a young Black man in the chest at point-blank range for insulting his girlfriend. The victim lives and Nathan is convicted of felonious assault. The shooting made Nathan feel powerful and enhanced his reputation as a bad Brother who was not to be messed with.

In Nathan's teenage macho world, women are objects of pleasure and sex is a source of release of tension. His initiation into sex at age thirteen is through a gang rape, referred to in street language as "running a train." Nathan and his peers lure unsuspecting neighborhood girls into vulnerable situations and rape them. Gang rape consolidates the group's identity. Nathan and his cohorts separate girls into two groups: mothers and sisters and "bitches" and "hoes." Bitches and hoes are sex objects to be conquered by macho power or by manipulation and cunning. There is no room in the gang philosophy for love. Love means weakness and being controlled by women. The object of relationships with women is to get sex without falling in love, but making the woman believe you are in love. In his senior year in high school, Nathan does fall in love. He and his girlfriend conceive a child. He wants to be responsible, cares for his girlfriend and infant son, but is not ready for responsibility. His girlfriend's parents provide financial support and medical care for the baby.

Nathan is consumed by feelings of rage, anger, and hatred toward White society. His rage is triggered by a combination of specific racial events and general perceptions of how Whites control power and opportunity. He was beaten up and called names by White boys in a newly integrated junior high school. White youths in passing cars routinely shouted racial epithets, which complicated the daily humiliations Black men suffered growing up in the South in the 1960s. Furthermore, his grandmother compares him unfavorably to the well-mannered White children she sees in homes where she works as a maid, and his mother repeatedly tells him not to act like ill-mannered or low-class Black folks. As a bright, perceptive child who watched Whites on TV and who accompanied his father on his lawn-mowing rounds in the White community, Nathan quickly figured out that there were two worlds. One was Black, with limited opportunities and economic and political power; the other was White, with endless opportunities and economic and political power. Needless to say, White power controlled the Black community.

As a teenager, Nathan did not fully realize the irony of his actions. By openly defying society's standards of conduct, he was delivering himself into the hands of the oppressor who would imprison him. During his period of adolescent lawlessness, a quiet inner voice of conscience tells Nathan he is destroying himself and hurting others. He wants to open up and share his feelings, but expressing doubt goes against the macho code. His family teaches by examples of hard work and responsibility, but there is no communication, which is what Nathan desperately needs. His parents tried hard to protect him from the street life he embraced, but they didn't talk about critical issues like work, sex, drugs, and the future. His attempts to talk out his doubts and confusion with his girlfriend, Liz, are unsuccessful. Despite his rejection of middle-class standards, Nathan manages to finish high school and one year of college with a B average before he goes to prison. In high school, he starts to show promise as a writer but has trouble following through because he can't connect with the teachers.

As an adolescent, Nathan does not see any adaptive possibilities in the African-American way of being. The working-class fathers in his neighborhood seem to be beaten down by the system and consigned to roles in which they are subservient to White power. Even when White people try to be kind—like the mayor's wife, who was one of Nathan's stepfather's lawn service customers—Nathan detects a condescending tone. As he sees it, older Black men have lost their ability to protest, seem resigned to economic and social injustices, and spend their off time on the weekends drowning their frustrations in alcohol. To Nathan, a working father in the home cannot serve as a positive male role model if he is oppressed, frustrated, and defeated. Nathan quits a summer job in construction because he refuses to take orders from a White boss.

Nathan cannot relate to Black professional middle-class people because he perceives them as pretentious, bourgeois, and phony. Nathan and his homeboys seem unaffected by the civil rights movement and the Black revolution of the 1960s and 1970s; they know how to do the Black power salute but don't seriously consider the emphasis on Black pride, Black power, Black unity, spirituality and love, and the creative power of the Black struggle for liberation and social justice. Nathan doesn't comprehend the power of Black social, political, and religious networks, the resilience of Black psychology, the creativity of the Black aesthetic, or the alternative definitions of masculinity embodied in the Afrocentric frame of reference.

Nathan's life of crime ended when he was convicted of armed robbery and sentenced to twelve years in prison on April 11, 1975. He was twenty years old when he joined the legions of Black men who are under control of the courts and the prison system in the United States. For Nathan, who earlier had served only four weekends in jail for shooting and nearly killing a Black man, the message was crystal clear: Black life is not important, but White property is, and Black men will be severely punished if they mess with a White man or his property.

While incarcerated, Nathan goes through a time of self-reflection that leads to a spiritual, mental, and emotional rebirth. His metamorphosis is guided by older inmates, strong Black males who teach a mix of Black Nationalism, Black consciousness, Black revolution, Black Muslim religion, and the practical psychology that Black men need to know to avoid self-destructive behavior. His prison mentors are the unofficial source of rehabilitation for many younger Black inmates. These men command respect by their seriousness, responsible character, and knowledge of the world, rather than by an ass-kicking machismo persona. They teach Nathan in unequivocal terms that actions have consequences that can be anticipated just as surely as night follows day. If he abuses drugs and acts out indiscriminately by engaging in robbery, assaults, burglary, and gang rapes, he will deliver himself into the hands of the White authorities he despises. His mentors tell him that life is like a chess game; he should anticipate the consequences of his moves, develop strategies and flexible contingency plans, and not back himself into corners. Nathan listens to his mentors because he respects them and because they believe that he has the potential to move forward in life.

Nathan establishes a daily routine of prayer, meditation, relaxation techniques, and reading. Journal writing reduces fear and apprehension; once he writes something down, it loses its terrifying power. He engages in periods of fasting. Black literature has a profound influence on Nathan's transformation. In *Native Son,* Nathan can identify with the rages, frustration, and anger that Bigger Thomas feels toward White America. Na'im Akbar's African-American psychology book *Natural Psychology and Human Transformation* gives Nathan a frame of reference for understanding his past behavior and the level of self-actualization he is moving toward. Akbar explains that some people remain stuck at the lower instinctual levels where they focus on satisfying hunger, thirst, pleasure, and sexual drives; others move toward higher peaks of creativity and spirituality. The teachings of Malcolm X convince Nathan that he too can move from being a dope-dealing street gangster to a more advanced level of spirituality and Black consciousness. He embraces Malcolm's philosophy that you can change your behavior if you change your self-perception.

Because he wants an early parole, Nathan avoids the prison gangs and the go-for-bad games that are rampant in the prison system. He also has to protect himself from sexual predators who are out to expand their reputations as studs by "turning out" heterosexual males. When prisoners gang-rape another inmate, Nathan begins to understand how the girls in his neighborhood must have felt when he and his peers sexually abused them. Nathan develops a two-part plan to gain parole. He successfully completes a series of courses in the printing trade taught by a friendly civilian instructor at the prison. And he applies to the journalism program at his old college, Norfolk State. Nathan explained that he was incarcerated and that he was determined to make a new start. The head of the journalism department asked Nathan to write an essay explaining why he wanted to be a journalist. Nathan wrote the paper and won a tuition scholarship. He was released on parole in February 1978 after serving three years of a twelve-year sentence.

As Nathan reflected on his journey of discovery, rediscovery, and transformation, several adaptive features of the African-American way of being became apparent to him that he could not fully appreciate before his incarceration. Black spirituality helped him achieve an optimal level of psychological and emotional functioning. African-American psychology helped him understand himself and his existential struggle. Black Nationalist mentors provided him with a frame of reference by which to distinguish between adaptive and maladaptive coping. His family stood by him during his struggle to change, and he learned to appreciate their quiet dignity, respect for hard work, sense of responsibility, and willingness to keep the faith and stay the course. Finally, it was a Black college that not only took a chance on him as an ex-con but gave him a scholarship.

The first major decision Nathan makes after winning his freedom is not to hang out with his old friends. The downfall of many young Black parolees is returning to the same social environment and former acquaintances. Before they realize what's happening, they get caught up in the illegal activities that, inevitably, lead back to prison. Nathan works his way through Norfolk State College, delivering the campus newspaper and then landing a job with his former prison teacher, who has opened up a printing business. Nathan enrolls in Na'im Akbar's graduate class in African-American psychology, joins the American Muslim Mission, which Akbar leads, and marries his girlfriend, Yvette, in the Muslim faith. He eventually outgrows the ritualistic orientation of the local Muslim group but continues his goals of journalistic excellence, personal responsibility, and spiritual growth.

Nathan graduates from Norfolk State College with honors in 1981 and starts a search for a newspaper job. He is a twenty-six-year-old Black male ex-convict. The quandary he faces in the job search is what to say about his prison record. There is a three-year gap in his résumé. Nathan is interviewed all over the country. As a finalist for a position at the *Louisville Courier/Journal,* he decides to tell them about his incarceration. Nathan doesn't get the job. From that point on, he decides to say nothing about his prison record. Nathan becomes a reporter with a local newspaper, the *Virginia Pilot/Ledger Star.* They know about his prison term and know something about his abilities as a journalist because he interned there as a journalism student. He starts his way up the ladder, moving to the *Atlanta Journal Constitution* in 1983 and from there, eventually, to the *Washington Post.* In Atlanta, he rubs shoulders with powerful Black politicians and heroes of the civil rights movement such as Mayors Andrew Young and Maynard Jackson, Congressman John Lewis, Julian Bond, and Coretta Scott King. He does an award-winning story on ambulance chasing. Along the way, he loses out on his first try with the *Post* because he fails to tell them about his prison record; they find out and decide not to hire him. A

Black reporter with the *Post* who has a brother in jail encourages Nathan not to get discouraged. He tells him to keep the faith, to continue proving his excellence, and he will get a shot at the big time. The advice is sound and Nathan gets his chance. D.C. Mayor Marion Barry welcomes him to the big leagues in 1989 at a press conference.

As Nathan approaches midlife at the end of his memoir, he grapples with several ongoing dilemmas. He has been unable to sustain a mutually enhancing long-term relationship with a special woman in his life. Liz, the mother of his first son, Monroe, drifts away when Nathan is in prison. He and his wife, Yvette, break up after a few years. He didn't love his second wife, Debbie, but married her to be a father to their two children. In male/female relationships, Nathan seems unable to see validity in a point of view that differs from his own. He gets stuck battling opposing ideas rather than moving toward a conflict resolution style that reconciles opposing beliefs with a creative synthesis. He can spot psychological weaknesses in his wife and girlfriends, but he has trouble identifying and building on their strengths.

He is perplexed about his role as an absent father. For a long time, his oldest son, Monroe, lived in California with Liz and her husband. Nathan builds a relationship with him when Liz sends Monroe to live with Nathan. In California, Monroe, who is now in his middle teens, was challenging parental authority and starting to engage in delinquent behavior. Remembering the absence of communication in his own family, Nathan works at building a two-way dialogue with Monroe. They talk about sex, race, street life, masculine styles, education, goal setting, and the like. He instructs Monroe on how to survive in the streets. He tells Monroe that if someone tries to take his jacket, give it to him. Life is more important than a jacket; you can always buy another jacket. He moves from Washington to an apartment in Arlington, Virginia, to get Monroe away from gang influence. Monroe stays out of trouble, graduates from high school, and starts college.

Nathan is struggling with how to create a balance between the toughness and freedom of the street culture, the richness of the African-American way of being, and the Euro-American interpersonal relationship strategies and conflict resolution styles operating in the workplace. How can he be an authentic Black man while working in a world controlled by Whites? It's hard for Nathan to give up the street culture. During a frustrating period in his and Debbie's marriage, he uses drugs, drinks excessively, and experiments with smoking crack. He thinks about leaving the hassles and confinements of middle-class life and selling drugs for a living. He longs for the freedom of the streets and the days when he could vent his frustrations by beating up White boys or threatening someone with a gun.

Nathan has trouble understanding the political environment and the mixed interpersonal signals in the newsroom. On the streets, he knew the rules and the interpersonal codes; he knew when to fight or when to back down. In the newsroom, which he finds in many ways to be more treacherous than the streets, it's hard to figure out where White folks are coming from. He never knows when he is being set up for failure by friendly condescension, paternalism, and subtle power games. He gets double-bind messages about assertive behavior. Blacks who speak up are pigeonholed as having an aggressive negative attitude; those who operate in a low-keyed manner are viewed as passive and meek. He is also confronted with the insider/outsider dilemma. He is included at some levels in peer dialogue, excluded at others. Nathan avoids socializing with his White coworkers because he distrusts Whites and because he finds Euro-American social activities stifling and boring. When Blacks get together to party after work, the speech is lively; they dance, clap hands, and throw down. Whites stand around, debate and discuss and play subtle one-upmanship games. Nathan's distrust of all White people eases a bit after he builds a close relationship with Danny, a White colleague. Danny encourages him to be less hostile and defensive and to build positive work relationships with his colleagues.

Finally, Nathan does not see any quick solution to the internal and external forces destroying the Black men of his generation. When he visits his family in Portsmouth, he comes face-to-face with the destruction of his former adolescent peers. Most of his old gang and acquaintances are in jail, strung out on drugs, unemployed, or dead or dying. What's happening with the younger generation is even more frightening. They seem even more alienated, more violent, less afraid of dying or prison, and quick to escalate the slightest sign of disrespect into a life-and-death battle. Nathan thinks the answer lies somewhere in how people perceive, invent, and act on choices. Many Black males get stuck trying to find workable choices that will allow them to maintain their dignity as they seek productive adult lives.

Two Lessons

Two major lessons arise from the profiles of Monster Kody and Nathan McCall. First, when young Black men perceive a limited range of options for gaining respect, recognition, and mastery, they are vulnerable to becoming locked into a destructive course of action characterized by a go-for-bad macho identity. They can mistakenly conclude that pursuing the excitement of the streets provides the only authentic Black identity, especially when their actions are reinforced by peer pressure in the absence of hands-on guidance from older, mature African-American males. Deciding on an identity pattern in early adolescence, before examining a range of choices, can temporarily, or in some cases permanently, seal off other options. As teenagers, Kody and McCall followed courses of action that led to incarceration, which ultimately made their struggle for a productive lifestyle more difficult. Prior to imprisonment, they did not seriously consider alternatives that would have reduced their chances of being locked down by the criminal justice system.

Second, their stories illustrate the cyclic nature of the psychological challenges facing Black men as they confront existential dilemmas. Initial choices can be reversed through a mentoring process conducted by respected, older African-American males that exposes younger Black men to the richness of the African-American heritage. Empowered by the strength of the African-American ethos, young Black men can gain the confidence needed to dream new dreams, build constructive relationships, generate more life options, and devise strategies to achieve their goals.

Identity choices are based on one's perception of social reality. Young Black men are left less likely to make destructive life choices if guidance is available to enable them to discover opportunities and assist their efforts to gain recognition, respect, and mastery. On the other hand, if perceived opportunities for personal empowerment are restricted by overt or covert racism and economic barriers, anger and frustration can erupt, which in turn may lead to the acting out that inhibits the development of effective coping behaviors.

In many Black men, such as Nathan McCall, there is a subconscious inner voice, internalized from family experiences, which is at odds with their overt self-presentation or persona. This inner voice needs to be reactivated as they make decisions about the course of their adult life. For example, during his period of acting out, Nathan privately worried that he was destroying himself and others. When he seriously examined the message from his inner voice, he came to a deeper understanding of himself, his core values, and what he wanted his life to represent.

Chapter 9

Biographical Memoirs II
Searchers and Achievers

Brent Staples and Henry Louis Gates, Jr., two of the "searchers and achievers" profiled in this chapter, are alike in several respects. As adolescents they explored a variety of options for identity, building and maintaining close relationships, coping with racism, and finding adaptive possibilities in the African-American way of being before making final decisions as adults. Along the way they were alert to opportunities to expand their horizons and discover new options that, at first glance, were only dimly visible. Explorations into politics, debates and discussions, literature, drama, writing, and social activism enabled them to meet a variety of people and develop skills and competencies that in turn opened up opportunities for mentorship and multiple educational opportunities and career choices.

As they evolved through adolescence and young adulthood, Brent Staples and Skip Gates developed flexible strategies to cope with racial conflicts and other dilemmas that Black men face. At one time or another, they utilized coping strategies involving confrontation, negotiation, debate and discussion, social activism, and revolutionary dialogue. Flexible coping strategies enabled them to avoid blind alleys and destructive acting out, and they were able to shift gears when a course of action proved no longer productive. Incorporating the African-American ethos into their personal values enhanced their resilience and served as a foundation for identity.

Staples and Gates were bicultural. They were able to function effectively in both predominantly African-American and Euro-American social environments. Greg Bronson, however, turned his back on White corporate America and decided to strike out on his own after several years of a frustrating bicultural existence.

Brent Staples: The Searcher

Brent Staples is a Black man with high credentials. He holds a Ph.D. in psychology from the University of Chicago and is a writer and editor for the *New York Times.* In his memoir, *Parallel Time,* he tells the story of growing up in the 1950s and 1960s in Chester, Pennsylvania.[1] His story continues as a young adult attending graduate school at the University of Chicago in the 1970s, and it concludes with his becoming a writer in the late 1970s and early 1980s. Brent's memoir begins and ends with the events surrounding the murder of his younger brother, Blake. Blake, ten years younger than Brent, was killed by a former drug customer in February 1984.

As Brent moves through childhood, adolescence, and adulthood, the most striking feature about his unfolding personality is his perpetual searching. By examining the world within and keenly observing the world without, Brent is constantly on the alert for opportunities to extend the boundaries of his identity and life experiences. Along the way, he weaves together bits and pieces of experiences to create opportunities to attend college, enter graduate school, earn his doctorate, and ultimately choose a career as a writer.

The Chester, Pennsylvania, where Brent grew up was a blue-collar town with a strong economy. It had a large Ukrainian and Polish population, with a sprinkling of Blacks who initially lived in segregated neighborhoods. Brent was the oldest male in a family of nine children. His childhood was marred by the chaos and instability that engulfed his family. His parents would argue, fight, break up, and reconcile, only to repeat the process. The family was constantly moving. Brent had eight different addresses before he completed the eighth grade and at least three more before he graduated from high school. His father had a good income as a truck driver, but wasted his salary on alcohol. His mother never had enough money to run the household or keep the children in clothing and shoes. She was a good Christian who believed in helping others in need. Even though the family was often in dire straits financially because of the father's drinking, Geneva Staples took in stray people who needed a home. In many cases, they were single, pregnant girls who had no place to go.

As the oldest boy, Brent became a surrogate parent. He helped the younger children get ready for school and he bathed, diapered, and fed the infants. He negotiated extensions on overdue bills at local markets and the utility companies. It seemed to Brent that his father was a more active, concerned parent when he was not living with the family; he would come by and take the children on outings and trips to visit relatives in Virginia. Brent craved his father's attention, but was afraid of him and didn't know how to get close to him.

Brent experienced subtle and overt racism when his family moved into a neighborhood where the racial mix was slowly changing. Since the racial rules were ambiguous in Chester, Brent never knew quite what to expect. Before the 1960s, the shipyards had separate Black and White work crews. Brent also experienced, firsthand, how cultural styles change as the ethnic makeup of a neighborhood changes. Andy's Musical Bar, on the corner from the house where Brent lived, featured Ukrainian and Polish polkas on the jukebox. When Black owners took over the bar, the polkas were replaced with rhythm and blues tunes.

Four events occurred during Brent's high school years that would profoundly affect his identity and the course of his life. First, on his sixteenth birthday, his father gave him a black eye in response to some adolescent sassing. At that moment, Brent vowed to detach himself from his family. He remained living with them physically until he went to college, but he distanced himself psychologically. A rupture had occurred that would never be repaired. Brent stayed out of the house as much as possible after the fight with his father, spending his time wandering the city seeking new experiences. It was almost as if he sensed unconsciously that the chaos and instability of his family would drag him under. His older sister was already a long-term runaway. The only way to save himself was to create distance. The black eye was a catalyst that brought to the surface a separation process that had started much earlier. The psychological separation, coupled with the constant moving from house to house, left a permanent psychological scar. As an adult, he would discard friends and lovers without warning, leave boxes unpacked when he moved to a new residence, and not subscribe to magazines because he was uncertain how long he would remain at any address.

Second, Brent took a business/commercial concentration in high school. He was eligible for the college prep academic track, but passed it up because of fears of failure. Occupational options included working in a local factory or trying to get a job as a secretary in the steno pool at IBM, where his teacher said he would get royal treatment because he was a male. His high school courses were a utilitarian mix of shorthand, typing, business machines, and basic math. However, in his English class, he discovered a love for writing, which grew as he progressed through adolescence and young adulthood.

Brent's high school was 70 percent Black. The most popular male students were the athletes, fashionable dressers, and boys who could talk to the girls. On the football field, Brent spent more time thinking than executing plays. Until he started working at the shipyards in the summer, he was too poor to afford fashionable clothes. His "rap" with the girls did not put him in the top tier socially, and he had very little to brag about sexually.

The third event was that Brent reached out to a series of religious, cultural, and intellectual experiences that increased his self-confidence and verbal skills, exposed him to a range of human diversity, and broadened his awareness of what was happening in the world beyond his neighborhood. He joined the Black church across the street from his house, which had just been purchased from a White congregation. Two White women who had stayed behind from the old church congregation to help the Black church get started introduced Brent to the Chester Repertory Theater Group, a racially integrated local drama group. A small part in a biblical play, *Gideon,* led to starring roles in two other plays, Edward Albee's *The Death of Bessie Smith* and his *Happy Ending.* Brent's acting career culminated in a leading role in his high school senior class play, *A Raisin in the Sun.* He imagined he was Sidney Poitier. For the tryouts, he made up a monologue about a man whose job in a bottling factory is watching a machine put caps on bottles all day long. This was Brent's persistent nightmare: that a monotonous, meaningless future was waiting for him.

In his midteens, Brent started hanging out in a community center, the Friends of Chester Project House, run by the Quakers. He participated in a weeklong retreat with other young people held at a Quaker boarding school. They discussed serious current events such as civil rights and the Vietnam War. He reassessed his desire to join the military after listening to debates about the antiwar movement. At the Friends of Chester Project House, Brent met Black students from nearby Swarthmore College. Impressed with the intellectual sophistication of the students, their future goals, and their commitment to social change, he visited the college often. He liked the beauty of the campus and the surrounding community, and he enjoyed the parties and social events. Although he could not keep up with the college students intellectually or socially, he blended in by teaching them the latest dance steps. It was a relief to get away from neighborhood parties and dances, which were starting to turn violent.

One of his sisters introduced him to the office manager at the local office of the League of Women Voters, an older Black man everybody called "Dumb-Dumb." Brent hung around the League office because he liked the doughnuts and coffee and the conversation. Dumb-Dumb introduced him to Eugene Sparrow, a Black sociology professor at a local college, P.M.C. College. Sparrow encouraged Brent to think about going to college rather than going into the factories or the military, and connected him to an educational outreach program for high-risk minority students at P.M.C. College.

Finally, there was the Black revolution of the late 1960s. Brent admired the posture of groups like the Black Panthers. He read the Nation of Islam's newspaper, *Muhammad Speaks,* after one of his brothers became a subscriber. His friends at Swarthmore formed a Black activist student group and were pressing the administration to admit more Black students, hire more Black professors, and start a Black studies program. At Chester High School, Brent came under the influence of a fellow student named Josephine. She was a personification of militant young Black people in the late 1960s, a symbol of courage and defiance dedicated to Black consciousness and revolutionary social change. Brent was smitten with Josephine, but she was more interested in the Black revolution.

In the summer of 1969, Brent was admitted to P.M.C. College. Since he had not planned to attend college, he had not taken the

Scholastic Assessment Test (SAT), nor had he filled out any financial aid forms. He worked his way around the SAT and, with some creative arithmetic, managed to obtain financial aid. He was required to attend a special summer program, called Project Prepare, with twenty-three other high-risk Black students. The program was designed to get them ready for the rigors of college life and improve their skills in math, science, literature, and writing. The *Philadelphia Inquirer,* reporting on Project Prepare, said it should be carefully watched; Brent and his fellow Black students felt that they were under a microscope. Two dozen new Black students in a school that traditionally enrolled only a handful of Blacks were very noticeable.

Brent's ability to function effectively in diverse environments served him well in college. He was elected class president without actively campaigning, instead lying low while his White supporters engineered his victory. He helped White fraternity students who were pushing the administration to relax its ban on overnight coeducational visits in the dorm and on alcoholic beverages. Brent threatened to bring the street Brothers from the community to tear up the campus if the administration didn't relent. The administration caved in and the White students got their sex and alcohol. Brent and his cousin, who was a Black Muslim, formed a Black student activist group that demanded concessions from the administration.

Brent started a rumor that he was a captain in the Black Panther party. He would later find out that his group had been under surveillance by the FBI, and that he was on the list of radical revolutionaries to be rounded up and detained in case of a national Black insurrection. As a college student, Brent, who in high school had been careful about drugs, alcohol, and sex, went through a period of sexual promiscuity and alcohol and drug abuse.

Brent's academic performance in college was outstanding. As a behavioral science major with a concentration in psychology, he excelled in statistics, writing, and German. By the time he was a senior, he was consistently making the dean's honor roll. One semester, he had a perfect A average. He was elected to Alpha Chi, the national scholarship honor society. Encouraged by his professors to apply to graduate school, he chose psychology for graduate study with the possibility of becoming a college professor. He was admitted to the doctoral program in psychology at the University of Chicago and was awarded prestigious five-year fellowships from the Danforth and Ford foundations.

As an undergraduate, Brent further distanced himself from his family. With the dean's permission, he was allowed to stay on campus year-round, including Christmas and Easter vacations. He would only visit his family briefly on holidays and then return to the solitude of the empty campus. Drinking was beginning to jeopardize his father's job, siblings and peers were using hard drugs, and young people in the neighborhood were being shot in violent disputes. Going to graduate school a thousand miles away was a way of escaping friends and family. Leaving, rather than engaging in serious interpersonal conflict resolution, was a style that was becoming a pattern in Brent's life; by his own admission, leaving was the only way he knew how to change things. He was really not that interested in going to graduate school; his primary motivation was to escape.

Brent left Chester in the fall of 1973 to begin graduate studies in Chicago. He described the university as a place of magic architectural beauty located on the edge of Chicago's Black ghetto of Woodlawn. Knowing how to work the system, Brent tapped into the university's Black secretarial network to obtain a nice apartment and good on-campus office space. He got in touch with the Brothers in the community by joining a basketball league, which took him deep into Black Chicago's South and West sides. He augmented his studies in psychology and behavioral sciences with philosophy, literature, and writing. Despite his credentials as a member of Alpha Chi, he experienced subtle racism from some faculty members. Petitioning to take a course with a well-known psychoanalyst, he was told by the professor, in Viennese-accented English, that because Black people suffer from the effects of oppression, it would take him a little longer to get his Ph.D.

Brent's anger toward White racism began to surface in a private game he called "scatter the pigeons." He noticed that, despite his attempts to smile or display a friendly face, White people tensed up and avoided his eyes when he passed by. Sometimes they would cross the street when they saw him coming. Women walking ahead of him would increase their pace or start to run when they looked back and saw him. One day, Brent decided to change his friendly demeanor; he is not sure why. He saw a couple walking toward him. When they stiffened, Brent walked straight toward them. He kept walking toward them until the man and the woman parted so he could glide between them. He suppressed the urge to scream, but laughed after the couple passed. In his "scatter the pigeons" game, Brent would walk the dark streets at night looking for victims. Once he had tried to appear harmless and friendly, but now he enjoyed scaring White people with his Black face, six-foot frame, and peacoat with the collar pulled up. A Black man was frightening by his very existence; White folks made him terrifying and now Brent would show them how terrifying he could be.

Back home in Chester, things are getting worse. Brent's father loses his job because of alcoholism; his older sister is serving time in a federal prison on a felony drug charge; and a fifteen-year-old sister, who showed considerable academic promise, is derailed by an unplanned pregnancy. Two of his brothers are abusing drugs, and friends are being shot, killed, and sent to jail. The industrial base of Chester is deteriorating; factories are closing and the large shipyard shuts down. His parents make a final separation, and his mother moves back to her native Roanoke, Virginia, with the younger children.

After finishing his Ph.D. with a dissertation on statistical probabilities in decision making, Brent decides on a career in writing. The academic market is glutted with new Ph.D.'s and Brent doesn't get a call from a university in the Ivy League class. He writes and writes: short stories, book reviews, and articles on science, agriculture, politics, and current events. While working as a reporter for the *Chicago Sun Times,* he is contacted for a job interview by the *Washington Post.* Brent has impeccable academic credentials and experience as a writer for the tenth largest newspaper in the United States. The first interviews go well; Brent thinks the job is in the bag. In his final interview with the senior editor, however, things fall apart. The editor wants Brent to answer two troublesome questions. First, is he an authentic Black man from the streets or a bourgeois Negro who hasn't paid his dues? Second, how can Brent explain his survival when so many Black men fill the jails, morgues, unemployment lines, homeless shelters, and drug rehabilitation centers? The questions trigger a sense of anger. He feels that he was being asked to explain his existence and answer questions for which no one really has the answers. From Brent's perspective, the only answer is life itself.

Brent's usual answer to such questions was that through a chance encounter with Eugene Sparrow, the Black professor at P.M.C. College, he was connected to an outreach program for high-risk minority students. The rest unfolded from there. The answer that chance was responsible for his turnaround from a nonacademic high school student to a Ph.D. psychologist/writer is not good enough for many White folks. They want to hear a logical explanation based on American values of hard work, planning, determination, up by the bootstraps, rags to riches. Such an explanation reinforces the belief that the American dream is alive and well and that other Black men could also make it if they tried harder. The answer is not in resolving racism and poverty, but in making sure that Black men learn to accept responsibility and the work ethic. Brent didn't get the *Washington Post* job. His answers to the senior editor's questions were, apparently, unsatisfactory. In an interview with the *New York Times* several months later, he avoided similar questions by making up excuses to end the interview early. He got the job.

At the end of his memoir, Brent Staples examines a portrait of his family taken after his brother Blake's funeral. Brent, who did not attend the funeral, is not in the portrait. As he examines the family photograph, he feels alone, apart, and somewhat remorseful—remorseful because he has not been reconciled with his family or been there when they needed him. He is alone and apart because he is either unwilling or unable to bond closely with others. He has paid a high price for his success in White America.

Skip Gates: The Prince

In his memoir, *Colored People,* Henry Louis "Skip" Gates, Jr., describes what it was like growing up in the segregated community of Piedmont, West Virginia, in the 1950s and 1960s.[2] Gates, a literary critic, is currently a professor of English and director of African-American Studies at Harvard University. He received his B.A. from Yale and his Ph.D. in English from Cambridge. Before joining the faculty at Harvard, he was a London correspondent for *Time* magazine. He has published several books on literary theory and writes frequently for magazines and newspapers such as the *New York Times, Harper's, The New Yorker,* and the *Village Voice.*

Skip was born in Piedmont in 1950. The town, situated on the side of a hill in the Allegheny Mountains, is two and a half hours by car from Washington, D.C., to the northeast, and from Pittsburgh, to the southeast. Its population in 1950 was 2,565 Whites and 350 Blacks—or Colored people as they were called then. Between childhood and young adulthood, Skip would experience a Black-consciousness transformation from Colored to Negro to Black. The White folks in Piedmont were mostly descendants of Italian and Irish immigrants, with a smattering of WASPs. The economic life of the community revolved around the paper mill, which was the primary employer.

In 1950, Blacks in Piedmont lived in an enclosed space where they felt confident, secure, and in charge. They went to Colored schools, Colored churches, and Colored social activities. They ate Colored food, listened to Colored music, danced Colored dances, and clapped their hands to Colored gospel music. They answered back in the call-response style to Colored preachers and went to Colored barbershops and beauty parlors. When they died, Colored ministers delivered farewell sermons, and they were buried in Colored cemeteries. When White people intruded on their world, it upset the rhythms. White folks who came into their space were referred to privately by occupational titles, such as Mr. Insurance Man, Mr. Milkman, Mr. Repairman, and Mr. Meter Reader Man.

Despite the Jim Crow segregation, Colored folks in Piedmont never thought of themselves as second-class citizens. Segregation was viewed as an inconvenience, a condition of existence they had learned to live with. Colored people could not own property, sit down at lunch counters, try on clothes in stores, or use certain restrooms. Colored men were not allowed to join the skilled-trade union at the mill; they were restricted to jobs on the loading dock. Skip's father and uncles worked as loaders at the mill. His father also had a part-time job from 4:30 to 7:30 in the evenings as a janitor at the local phone company. Because he picked up take-out food orders for the telephone operators, Skip's dad was the only Colored person allowed to sit at the counter of the drugstore to eat. The owner did not want to lose the operators' business. Although Colored folks did not openly protest segregation, beneath the quiet surface of their community there were signs of suppressed rage. Some men drank too much, others womanized excessively, and still others ignored high blood pressure warnings while they continued to eat high-cholesterol foods.

When the effects of the civil rights movement were finally felt in Piedmont, Colored people, who were now in the Colored-to-Negro-to-Black transition, experienced a distressing combination of opportunity and loss. They welcomed the opportunity to move up to the skilled trades in the mills. They no longer had to stand to eat at the lunch counters, and they could buy property and try on clothes in stores. However, newly desegregated Piedmont Blacks lost some of their cherished institutions. The Black school, which had nurtured students with a first-rate education, was closed down. Because of possible civil rights violations, the mill's annual Colored picnic—the biggest annual event in the Colored community—was ended in 1970.

Skip spent his early years in a family that engendered a sense of personal worth and self-confidence by providing support, affection, and encouragement. He was taught values of achievement, self-reliance, and excellence through hard work. His nuclear family was surrounded by a large, tight-knit, extended family that lived within walking distance. Close relationships with his brother, Rocky, five years older, and with his uncles provided Skip with multiple male role models. With his two jobs, Skip's father had steady employment and a good income. His mom, Pauline, could stretch a dollar so the family had what they needed.

Pauline Gates was a strong, capable woman who was active in community affairs. She was the first Black secretary of the Parent-Teacher Association when the schools integrated, and she encouraged other Black women to join. Pauline delivered eulogies that were objects of beauty. She made downtrodden Black folks who had been defeated in life sound like saints and angels. She tried to focus on what people wanted to become rather than what the world had made them become. Pauline admired Malcolm X. When she saw him in 1959 on TV commentator Mike Wallace's show, *The Hate That Hate Produced,* Pauline answered "Amen" to Malcolm's depiction of White folks as devils.

The legal walls of segregation in Piedmont started to crumble as Skip moved into adolescence. Without protest from either Blacks or Whites, the schools integrated in 1955, the year before he started first grade. Skip was marked as the academic "prince" from the beginning. His mother had taught him how to read and write before he entered school. He scored high on the pre-first-grade academic readiness test. Since his mother was active in the P.T.A. and his brother was at the top of his sixth-grade class, the teachers, no doubt, sensed that Skip was from a family that valued education. A positive, self-fulfilling prophecy was set in motion. For the next twelve years, Skip excelled. He was popular socially, elected president of his class four times, and was the top student academically every year through high school. He was valedictorian of his high school senior class.

Within the integrated school setting, there were cultural collisions and unwritten rules governing social contact between the races. There was no interracial dating, dancing, or hand-holding. At school-sponsored operettas and musicals, if the racial mix of boys and girls was uneven, then boys of the same race or girls of the same race would dance with each other. In elementary school there was one Colored teacher, and in high school one Colored cheerleader. The basketball coach was encouraged not to start too many Black players. Most of the Black students in the high school were in the vocational track. Black students and their parents were encouraged to abide by the rules so that the system would work; "go along to get along" was the byword. School authorities meted out corporal punishment to Black students who violated the rules.

The contributions of Black Americans to the vitality of American life were invisible within the school curriculum. Two hundred and fifty years of slavery were passed over lightly. The major theme in discussing Blacks historically was that White folks freed Black folks from the primitive jungles in Africa and civilized them under benevolent, paternalistic guidance in America.

Skip's older brother bore the brunt of the treachery of White racism. Five years ahead of Skip, Rocky was the pathfinder who showed him how to work around some of the pitfalls and dangers of racism. But Rocky was denied the award of a prestigious scholastic prize he had won fair and square. He was one of the apparent winners of the Golden Horseshoe Award, West Virginia's most coveted academic prize for eighth graders. The winners were written up in the newspaper and got a trip to the state capital to meet the governor. As Skip's family found out later, the White judges denied Rocky the prize by falsely claiming that he had misspelled a word. He would have been the first Black student to win the award. Something died in him when he found out that Whites didn't really mean what they said about hard work, excellence, and fair play. Rocky learned that White folks can use subterfuge to cut Black folks down whenever they choose. They have the power, and as the old folks used to say, they will not let a Black man rise too high. Rocky ran into a similar situation in the eleventh grade. He was selected by his school to participate in Boys' State, a high school leadership program sponsored by the American Legion. The White representative of the American Legion informed Rocky's principal that they preferred a White boy, but the principal refused to back down and told them that they would take Rocky or nobody.

Although Rocky continued to be an outstanding student, and went on to become an oral surgeon, he was never the same. He knew that excellence was no guarantee of success. Racism, always lurking in the shadows, could leap out and destroy one's dreams at any given moment. Angered by the injustice, Skip set out to win the Golden Horseshoe Award five years later. This time the judges played it straight and Skip won the award.

Between childhood and young adulthood, Skip encountered a series of turning points and major decision-making junctures as he struggled to define himself, build intimate relationships with the opposite sex, cope with racism, and discover adaptive possibilities within the African-American way of being.

Between the ages of twelve and fourteen, Skip experienced a religious crisis brought on by a combination of adolescent turmoil and his mother's severe episodes of depression. As a child, he was drawn to the Black church. He liked the animated sermons, jubilant and sad songs, foot stomping, head nodding, and the call-response dialogue. He enjoyed the fervor of camp meetings and revivals. Although he felt secure within the atmosphere of belonging, closeness, and intimacy created by the church, he was also afraid of the powers of the Holiness Church. He witnessed the power of the Holy Ghost to take over the lives of his friends when they became engulfed in the righteousness of the church. They stopped playing cards, dancing, smoking, partying, and chasing after girls.

While Skip was in the process of deciding whether to devote his life to Jesus Christ, a nearly lethal mix of depression, phobias, obsessions, and compulsions took over his mother's life. Pauline had been a strong, confident, energetic woman. Now she experienced periods of deep depression during which she cried excessively and talked constantly about death. Memories of scarcity in her childhood triggered hoarding and pack rat behavior. The house was cluttered with canned goods, huge amounts of cloth, and other items that she would collect. In the midst of the clutter, Pauline was obsessed with cleaning. She spent a good portion of each day dusting and vacuuming over and over again. Once fearless, she became afraid of dogs; her weight ballooned.

Skip, who was closely bonded to his mom, felt powerless, devastated, and afraid. He invented a variety of compulsive rituals to ward off what he thought was punishment from God for his sins. For instance, he would walk around the kitchen table only from right to left or approach a chair only from the left side. One Sunday, out of defiance, Skip decided to tempt fate by refusing to perform the rituals. That same Sunday his mother had an emotional breakdown that necessitated a brief psychiatric hospitalization. Psychotropic medication was prescribed, which eased the depression a bit, but Pauline never regained her confidence, strength, and vitality.

Skip, afraid that he was responsible for his mother's emotional breakdown, prayed to God, promising that he would devote his life to

Jesus Christ if his mother's life was spared. When she didn't die, Skip followed through on his promise. He joined the Evangelical Methodist Church and made a public commitment to accept Jesus Christ as his personal Savior. The minister, who saw Skip as his heir apparent, welcomed him into the church in a formal ceremony. For the next two years, Skip's life revolved around school, religion, and helping his mom with cooking and household chores. He gave up dancing, card playing, smoking, partying, and experimenting with sex and tried not to have lustful thoughts about young women. As he moved toward his midteens, Skip began to pull away from his rigid fundamentalist religious beliefs. He could no longer find answers to complex existential questions in this belief system. He also sensed that he was hiding in religion because he was afraid to face life. Conversations with a liberal Episcopal minister helped release him and convince him that he could have a spiritual life without being imprisoned by it. He could be a good Christian and still date girls, dance, and party.

Skip's two-year journey into religious fundamentalism provided him with a much needed holding space between the end of childhood and middle adolescence. Religion protected him from guilt and worries. Not only was Skip worried about what was happening to himself and his mother, he was also worried about the threat of nuclear war generated by the Cuban missile crisis of 1962 and America's growing involvement in Vietnam. The solitude provided by religion gave Skip a chance to slow down, control his emerging libido, and reflect on how he wanted to define himself in the future.

As he moved into his middle and late teens, he became deeply involved in the immersion/emersion stage of Black consciousness. His consciousness developed, based on a solid foundation in the African-American way of being. Skip was part of a Black extended family, attended Black churches, and socialized with Black peers. He listened to Black music and danced the latest Black dances. His extended family could trace their roots back to slavery. In line with the oral tradition, Skip's father told him about different Black lifestyles and different cultural mixes he had observed when he served in an all-Black Army unit at Fort Lee, Virginia, during World War II.

While Skip watched the standard run of TV shows in the 1950s and 1960s, he also stayed up late to hear rhythm and blues and gospel music beamed in on the radio from *Randy's Record Shop* in Gallatin, Tennessee. He read *Jet* and *Ebony* magazines and ordered Black recordings from a record club. On his own, he started compiling a list of facts on African-American life and history. He saw the civil rights movement unfold on TV. His family had a cable hookup that allowed them to get stations and news updates from Washington. In 1957, he witnessed Black youths integrate Central High School in Little Rock, Arkansas, guarded by U.S. Army paratroopers while White students and community people jeered and hurled racial epithets. He saw Malcolm X call White people devils on Mike Wallace's 1959 TV show. He witnessed southern governors in Alabama, Georgia, and Mississippi attempt to defy court orders to allow the admission of Black students to state universities.

His awareness of what it means to be Black in America shifted to a higher level of consciousness in the summer of 1965, during the Watts rebellion in Los Angeles. At that time, Skip was attending a racially integrated, coeducational summer camp sponsored by the Episcopal Church. The camp provided an opportunity for young people from different racial and cultural backgrounds to get together and discuss religion, values, and current events like civil rights and Vietnam. Skip and his idealistic fellow campers were bewildered by the rage and violence they saw on TV as Watts burned for five days. His feelings of bewilderment were mixed with feelings of pride and power. The Brothers had stood up to "the man," and Skip was proud of them. A counselor gave him James Baldwin's *Notes of a Native Son* to read. For Skip, Baldwin's book captured the essence of America's racial dynamics. From that point on, Blackness was a central part of Skip's identity.

The following summer, in 1966, Stokely Carmichael shouted the words "Black power" as a psychological call to arms during his march through the segregationist stronghold of Mississippi. Changes in Skip and his friends appeared both outwardly and inwardly. Outwardly, young people started wearing dashikis to social events. People who had spent hours applying conks and pomade to make their hair look wavy now turned to cotton-candy naturals. Friends and acquaintances greeted each other with a variety of Black power fist salutes and handshakes. Whereas light skin had been a status symbol in the past, now Black skin was a badge of honor. People were proud to be Black, the Blacker the better. Inwardly, Skip and his friends seethed with rage toward White oppression and were determined to end it by any means necessary. Self-determination and self-definition became their mantras. Searching for meaning in Blackness, they read books by Richard Wright, James Baldwin, and Eldridge Cleaver. Skip's uncles jokingly referred to him as "Malcolm" and "Stokely." For a while, the world seemed to be turned upside down. Blackness, which had once been avoided, was now a symbol of pride. "If you're White, you're right" was no longer the in-phrase.

Two days after the Reverend Martin Luther King, Jr., was assassinated in 1968, Skip and his fellow students staged a walkout at their high school in Piedmont. In his graduation valedictory address, Skip gave an unauthorized speech about civil rights, abortion rights, and the Vietnam War. The next year, in 1969, he and three of his friends, referred to as "the Fearsome Foursome," challenged a local dance hall that refused to admit Blacks. During the protest, the owner of the hall assaulted one of Skip's friends, and some of the young White patrons called them racial names. The owner said he would close the dance hall before he let Blacks in. Skip took him at his word and filed a complaint with the state's Human Rights Commission. The owner refused the Commission's order to integrate, so they shut him down. In his personal statement for his application to Yale, Skip described his Colored-to-Negro-to-Black transition. He wrote that his grandfather was a Colored man, his father defined himself as a Negro, and now was Skip's time to be Black. His destiny was in the hands of Whites on Yale's admissions committee. They admitted him.

Piedmont's Black elders were uneasy about the militancy of Skip and his friends. They felt comfortable within the old boundaries. They were afraid that a White backlash might result in harm to both young and old. The younger generation, however, was undeterred. They believed in Black self-determination and saw confrontation as a challenge to White power. One of the by-products of his involvement with the Black consciousness movement was that it served as a point of contact between Skip and his father. With his father on the "go slow" side and Skip on the "radical change" side, they had endless debates about Black consciousness and Black power. The debates, while not producing much agreement, nonetheless brought them closer together.

Romance, love, and sex eluded Skip until his late teens. His secret love was his childhood soul mate and intellectual peer, Linda Hoffman. They were paired together from the first grade as the two brightest students in the school. If Skip was the academic prince of the school, Linda was the princess. As a child, Skip adored her. But his adoration would never blossom into a full-blown romance. As a White female, Linda was the forbidden fruit of race relations in the South. When they entered adolescence, Skip and Linda grew apart. They were socially conditioned to follow the rules that forbade interracial dating and romances. While Skip publicly denied his love for Linda, privately he pined for her.

Beyond Linda, Skip was unsuccessful in his attempts to connect romantically with other girls. He prayed to God to send him a girlfriend. He was popular and likable. Older women thought of him as a charming boy, but he couldn't get past the friendship stage with his female acquaintances. To make matters worse, other boys had girlfriends. When his male peers talked about their romantic and sexual experiences, Skip felt more alone and rejected. In the Black Piedmont barbershop, part of the male rites of passage was talk about sex, sex, and more sex, reinforced by explicit pictures in girlie magazines. In the sleepy hollows of West Virginia, sex was a prime-time activity. Everybody was doing it with their wives or girlfriends or with someone else's wife or girlfriend.

As a freshman at nearby Potomac State College, Skip's romantic life changed for the better. He started dating Maura Gibson, a White coed from Keyser, a town not far from Piedmont. Initially, Maura felt Skip was too obsessed with talking about race. In time, however, their relationship progressed from the discussion/debate level to dating, to lovers' lane visits, and finally, to overnights in motels where they would talk, listen to music, eat oysters, and, no doubt, do what young lovers all over America do when they spend the night together.

It didn't take long for Skip and Maura to become an item of gossip on and off campus. The elders of both races disapproved. White students at Potomac State shouted insults out of dorm windows when the interracial couple walked by. Maura's father, Bama, did not approve of the relationship but tolerated it. In the midst of their relationship, Bama decided to run for mayor of Keyser. No one thought he could win. Employed as a postal worker, he was a political neophyte running against a former college president. Plus, his daughter was creating a racial scandal. To complicate matters further, the election occurred about the time Skip was involved in the racial protest at the dance hall. To everyone's surprise, Bama won the election; the good White folks of Keyser did not want to be labeled as bedrock racists. They voted for him to prove that they would not disown him because his daughter was dating a Black man. After the election, Bama found out that the West Virginia state police had a file on Skip. He was to be picked up and detained if racial rebellions or riots occurred.

Skip's choice of a career in literature, writing, and teaching grew out of his enchantment with words and ideas, his superior mental abilities, and encouragement from teachers. As a child, he was a voracious reader, infinitely curious, and always motivated to stretch his abilities to the next level. He listened to recordings of Shakespeare's plays at the local library. He wrote essays and news stories for the school paper.

When he started his first year of college at Potomac State, one of his friends suggested that he look up Professor Duke Anthony Whitmore, a gifted teacher of English and American literature. Whitmore and Skip hit it off instantly, and he became Skip's mentor. In class, they would debate Emerson, Thoreau, and the hot issues of the day. Whitmore would read passages from poems or a play and demand rapid-fire identification of the source. Words, sentences, and ideas came alive in their discussions. Impressed by Skip's talent and intellectual curiosity, Whitmore suggested that he transfer to an Ivy League school to complete his undergraduate education.

It is interesting to contrast how self-fulfilling prophecies operated in the lives of Malcolm X and Skip Gates. As a junior high school student in Lansing, Michigan, Malcolm X was at the top of his class and a member of the basketball team and he had a part-time job. As a seventh grader, he was class president. When his eighth-grade teacher told him to give up his ambition to become a lawyer because Black boys couldn't achieve that goal, Malcolm was crushed. Shortly thereafter, he dropped out of school, moved to Boston, and drifted into street life. In Lansing, he had had no strong base of psychological support. His father had been assassinated, his mother was confined to a mental hospital, he was living with White foster parents, and his brothers and sisters were scattered about in various foster homes and with relatives.

Skip Gates, on the other hand, had multiple support systems. He had a strong family, several extended family male role models, and the power of the Black church. He was part of a well-defined Black community where people teasingly called him "Professor" even before he started college. Whites and Blacks alike recognized his superior talent and encouraged Skip to push himself to be the best. When a White doctor, who misdiagnosed Skip's disconnected hip joint as a case of psychosomatic hysteria brought on by the stresses of overachievement, tried to discourage him from pursuing high academic goals, such as a career in medicine, Skip didn't miss a beat. He had the self-confidence and support he needed to keep on pushing. While he ultimately decided on a career in literature rather than medicine, it was not because he could not have made it as a doctor.

Death of loved ones was the final marker in Skip's passage into adulthood. His grandmother, who lived up the hill, was the first to go. Big Mom, or Biggie, as she was called, was the undisputed head of his mother's side of Skip's extended family. Biggie's children and grand-children revered her and catered to her. Family celebrations, reunions, and holiday dinners were always held at her home. Next to go was his favorite uncle, Nemo. Nemo taught Skip the ways of the world and the powers of the spirits. His mother lingered on for many years, suf-fering recurring bouts of depression and despair. In her last years she withdrew from life, unable to shake her preoccupation with death and dying. By the time she died, Pauline was alienated from her family and friends.

Pauline's funeral was a brief service, and she was buried in a racially integrated cemetery. During Pauline's short, emotionally con-tained funeral, Skip missed the powerful funerals of his childhood when the dead were borne away with powerful preaching and sad songs. He missed the old Black services where the saints and sinners hollered, shouted, and literally collapsed in public displays of grief in small, crowded, hot churches. He missed the call-response sermons, in which the preachers would talk about God meeting the deceased in Paradise that day to help God set the welcome table or sing a special part of a song. He missed the old segregated graveyard with its uncut grass, where departed souls hung about in the shadows waiting for God to swoop them up in His arms on Judgment Day. In the old tradi-tion, African-Americans knew how to work with death and grief. They were ever on the alert for the man "going 'round taking names." They knew how to touch sadness, knew how to help people cry and shout until the grief started to work its way through the human emotional labyrinth.

Greg Bronson: Yuppie by Day/Revolutionary by Night

Greg Bronson, one of the Black men from Chicago's Trey-Nine housing project profiled in Vest Monroe's book *Brothers,* coped with the anger, alienation, disappointment, and disillusion associated with the middle-class blues by developing different at-work and after-work personali-ties. As a sales and marketing manager in the daytime, Bronson was a picture-perfect Black yuppie. His body was slimmed down and hard-ened by playing competitive tennis. He wore a dark suit, white shirt, conservative tie, and tassel loafers. His attitude was positive and low-keyed, a Black embodiment of Norman Vincent Peale's positive thinking. He was an expert in sales. He took pleasure in smiling, talking about golf and tennis, and sharing tidbits of stories from *Forbes* magazine and the *Wall Street Journal* with customers as he moved through the sales process of assessing needs, addressing the needs, reviewing it all, and closing the deal. Sales to Greg were like athletic contests, where he was the prime competitor who took pride in demonstrating his mastery of the game.

At night, Greg's personality was that of an angry Black Nationalist. After work, he dropped all pretenses of coexistence with the White world. Kaumau Akil, his nighttime alter ego, was a warrior in the Republic of New Africa (RNA). The RNA is an underground Black revolutionary separatist organization that believes in armed struggle. Since the 1960s, they have unsuccessfully tried to create a Black secessionist state in the American South. It was not that Greg hated all White people; he had just come to a point in his life where he needed a refuge from White control and dominance. He didn't have the time or the energy to separate the "good" Whites from the closet racists.[3]

Greg's anger toward and hatred of Whites was a product of two generations of experience. Before the civil rights movement, his father, a college graduate, could only find work in Chicago as a truck loader for an insurance company. Greg watched him suffer in silence and would hear his father crying when he was alone at night in his bedroom. His father was a living example of America's racial injustice. In the work world, Greg found himself thwarted by several instances of institutional racism. He was repeatedly turned down for jobs for which his expertise qualified him. Once a bank vice president refused a deal Greg offered him that would save the bank $40,000 a year in photocopy costs. The V.P. denied he was turning down the offer because Greg was Black. Greg went around him, contacted the president of the bank, and got the sale. More and more, Greg began to feel that the system was designed to make Black men, except for a token few, fail.

No matter how well a Black man assimilated or learned to play the game, he never arrived at the top of the mountain. Greg finally could no longer work with White people because they were committed to his destruction and that of other Black men. He could no longer surrender, even in the daytime, so he declared his independence by starting his own company.

The Middle-Class Blues: Cracks in the Dream

Achieving middle-class economic, occupational, and social success through education, hard work, and planning ahead has been held out as the ideal for Black males to pursue. Lately, though, some cracks have appeared in the success ideal. Many of the best and brightest Black males who have achieved the symbols of success are expressing disillusionment. Black men who blazed a pathway in industry, corporate structures, and government organizations are having second thoughts. Writers like Ellis Cose and Sam Fulwood talk about the rage and despair of middle-class Blacks.[4, 5] What is happening? Why are Black men who have worked so hard for success now questioning its validity? Why are men like Brent Staples and Nathan McCall frustrated, angry, and disappointed despite the fact that they achieved their goals of becoming writers and journalists? Why did Greg Bronson turn his back on his goal of success in the White corporate structure? The answers are complex, but several themes appear again and again in discussions with successful Black males.

Much of the anger and disappointment stems from the subtle racism Black managers and executives encounter in corporate structures and bureaucratic organizations. They feel this racism in two ways. First, in most major organizations controlled by Whites, there is a glass ceiling for Black males. They seldom end up in powerful roles as chief executive officers, senior managers, or vice presidents of substantive programs. Second, Black men feel excluded from the informal insiders' clubs where on-the-rise White colleagues receive the mentoring they need to keep moving up into higher positions.

Nathan McCall thinks it is difficult for Black males within organizational structures to decipher double messages about assertive leadership behavior. If they speak out forcefully, especially about racism, they run the risk of being labeled as having a negative attitude. White coworkers tend to describe them as angry, belligerent, pushy, overly sensitive, abrasive, and hard to work with. Getting a reputation as a pushy, angry Black man can be a kiss of death for a Brother trying to move up into senior management. On the other hand, if the Brother doesn't speak up, he runs the risk of being labeled as weak and passive.

To avoid being seen as a troublemaker and to survive within White-dominated, mainstream organizational structures, many Black males develop an institutional self or organizational personality. On the job, they display a calm, low-keyed, nonthreatening, professional façade. They become what the psychologist Ken Hardy calls GEMMs: good, effective, mainstream, model minorities. Whites generally approve of GEMMs and wonder why all Black males can't act that way. Beneath the double messages, the rules are very clear for Black males: Be like Whites, act like Whites, talk like Whites, walk like Whites, dress like Whites, and don't openly challenge Whites in authority. Don't display intense emotions, especially anger. Defer to Whites in authority and don't be too assertive; don't make yourself scary to Whites. Stay in your place and you will be promoted until you reach the glass ceiling. The bottom line is that White folks are in charge and they make the rules.[6]

Many Black managers and executives feel a double sense of alienation and loneliness. They are not closely connected to their White colleagues at work, where their real selves, concealed by an organizational personality façade, are invisible. They are separated from the day-to-day rhythms of the African-American way of being. They live in a psychological cocoon that is separated from genuine involvement in either Euro-American or African-American lifestyles.

What is surprising to researchers is the perceptual gap between middle-class Blacks and Whites. One would expect that middle-class Blacks who are successful economically and educationally would hold views on racial issues similar to Whites. The reverse appears to be true. Polls show that as education and income increase, Blacks are more likely to respect controversial Black figures and to entertain conspiracy theories of White racism. According to several polls cited by *Newsweek* correspondent Joe Klein in a 1995 article, 40 percent of middle-class Blacks believe AIDS in their community is a White plot. Sixty-seven percent believe that the U.S. government makes drugs available in the Black community; 84 percent believe there is a concerted effort on the part of the government and law enforcement agencies to destroy elected Black officials. In a 1995 CBS poll, approval of Louis Farrakhan increased with education: Farrakhan had a 5 percent approval rating among Blacks with less than a high school degree, a 25 percent approval rating among high school graduates, and a 47 percent approval rating among college graduates.[7]

Among Blacks as a whole, according to a 1994 *Time/CNN* poll of 504 African-Americans, 73 percent of those surveyed were familiar with Farrakhan, more than with any other Black figures except Jesse Jackson and Supreme Court Justice Clarence Thomas. Two-thirds of those familiar with Farrakhan viewed him favorably; 62 percent said he was good for the Black community, 63 percent said he spoke the truth, and 67 percent said he was an effective leader. Only one-fifth of the sample thought he was anti-Semitic. When asked to name the most important Black leader today, 9 percent volunteered Farrakhan's name, more than any one else except Jesse Jackson and three times as many as Nelson Mandela.[8]

As a controversial figure, Minister Farrakhan is respected by middle-class Black males because they believe that he tells it like it is. While other Black leaders may seem timid and ineffectual, the Brothers perceive him as a strong Black man, not beholden to the White power structure. Black men think Farrakhan is America's just reward; the White power structure wouldn't give up any victories, listen to Martin Luther King, or deal with men like Jesse Jackson, so Minister Farrakhan stepped into the leadership vacuum. The fact that he is so outrageous toward Whites makes him more attractive to Black men. The more Whites denounce him, the more Blacks seem to listen to him; Blacks resent being told by Whites what to do, what to think, and whom to follow. They figure that if the White man is denouncing a Black man, the Brother must be saying something.

The controversy surrounding Farrakhan seems to be related to his in-your-face public speaking style and commentary, especially his provocative comments directed at Jews, other Whites, and even some non-Whites. He has allegedly called Jews and other non-Blacks "bloodsuckers," referred to Judaism as a "dirty religion," suggested that the U.S. government is deliberately encouraging the spread of drug abuse and AIDS in the Black community, and accused White liberals of being insincere about their commitment to resolve racial conflicts that hamper the progress of Black males.[9]

The Brothers are willing to look past Minister Farrakhan's provocative rhetoric and name-calling because they believe in the core of his message: that Jews, other Whites, and, more recently, Palestinians, Arabs, Koreans, Vietnamese, and other Asians who own property and run businesses in the Black community do not reinvest their profits to improve the community and its people. Furthermore, many middle-class African-American men believe that the U.S. government has indeed not done enough to stop the flow of drugs into the Black community, and that there has been no all-out attack to prevent AIDS through education, needle exchange programs, and aggressive medical outreach to ensure that the latest medical treatment and support systems are available to Black inner-city AIDS victims.

Farrakhan is not as threatening as his rhetoric makes him seem. The real threat to American democracy is not Minister Farrakhan but White racism.

Farrakhan is a superb political performer who has mastered the style and rhythms of African-American speech. His caustic, biting, anti-White rhetoric is a form of playin' the dozens, signifyin', crackin', and snappin'—word games that can be heard daily in the Black community. Farrakhan's powerful allure can attract an audience like no other political performer can and keep them interested, entertained, and informed in speeches that last two hours or more. He regularly speaks to audiences of 10,000 to 20,000 people, not to mention the one million or more Black men who listened to him in Washington in 1995.[10] In Atlanta, a lecture by Farrakhan outdrew a 1992 World Series game that same night. In Chicago, when Black aldermen needed a speaker to raise funds for their legal defense in a censorship case, they turned to Minister Farrakhan, the one man who could fill any hall in town.[11]

Minister Farrakhan tells Black men who are angry and frustrated despite their successes in the mainstream that they are okay, that it is the White man who is evil. It is Whites who have divided the country by racism, not they. These are Black men who have tried the American way of education, hard work, and planning for the future, but remain skeptical of America's unwillingness to fulfill its part of the contract. In many ways they are like General Colin Powell, whom Whites admire, but these men come to different conclusions about the journey into the mainstream.

Successful Black males are using a variety of ways to cope with middle-class alienation and disillusionment. They are moving into upscale Black neighborhoods where they don't have to be around White folks after work. They are, to some extent, bypassing the dream of a fully integrated society, not because they are racial separatists but because it just isn't working. Some are moving out of their executive roles in White institutions to create careers that offer services to the Black community in areas such as education, job training, and business development. Black churches, fraternal orders, professional groups, and mentorship organizations are attracting large numbers of members. Interest in Black music, art, literature, and history is blooming. Many professional Blacks are becoming reborn into Black consciousness. Feeling betrayed, isolated, and disappointed, they are searching for answers by joining Black churches that preach African-American theology and have rites of passage programs for their children. They are establishing Black men's groups and Black literature clubs and are sending their children to predominantly Black colleges.

Explaining why he moved into a middle-class Black neighborhood and joined a Black men's consciousness-raising group, an airline executive says he needs to be away from Whites after work so he can let his guard down. Otherwise it would be like having another eight-hour job. Around other Blacks, he can be spontaneous, unedited, and genuine. Away from a homogenized White work environment, he can walk the walk, talk the talk, signify, jive, play the dozens, and get into the call-response dialogue. He doesn't have to seek White validation for his thoughts and reactions or constantly justify his behavior and feelings. With the men in his consciousness-raising group, there is a base of shared experience that creates intuitive understanding of cultural rhythms, male/female relationship styles, speech patterns, communication and expressive norms, and humor.

The Psychologically Healthy Black Male

Because achieving middle-class social and occupational status is not synonymous with mental health, it is legitimate to ask what constitutes mental health for a Black man in America. How can the psychologically healthy Black male be described? Based on his examination of several research studies, Howard Ramseur drew up a profile that consists of six primary psychological and social characteristics:

A positive self-concept and sense of self-worth

A positive Black identity and connection with the Black community and Black culture

An accurate perception of the social environment and of racism

Adaptation to Black and White cultural expectations and development of ways to cope with stresses resulting from conflicting cultural expectations

Emotional intimacy with others

An ability to work productively and to develop an overall level of competency and effectiveness[12]

Black males tend to rely on friends, family, and loved ones for affirmation of self-worth rather than on dominant culture stereotypes. Skip Gates's sense of personal worth as a child and adolescent evolved from close relationships with his family, extended family, peers, girlfriends, and mentors who valued him. Nathan McCall changed from a destructive, go-for-bad identity pattern to a positive Black identity under the guidance of Black mentors when he was in prison, and he continued the transition when he enrolled in college. Although Gates excelled in schools that were predominantly White, he accurately perceived the explicit and implicit racial boundaries at school and in the community. He knew that the Whites in control could arbitrarily change the rules to deny Blacks the prizes they had legitimately won. In high school, Brent Staples dated Black girls, danced Black dances, and joined the Black student activist group. At the same time, though, he was a member of an integrated community playhouse and participated in activities sponsored by the Quakers and the League of Women Voters. In terms of intimacy and sustaining close relationships, Vest Monroe maintained close relationships with his family and friends from the projects after he had moved away to attend school and later to work for *Newsweek* magazine.

Psychosocial competence, or what psychologists call "efficacy," refers to an individual's belief that he can take charge of his life and overcome barriers to achieve his goals. Highly competent, effective Black men like Gates and Staples are able to take charge of their lives by developing paradoxical beliefs to cope with racism. Like the successful Black men and women that Audrey Edwards and Craig Polite described,[13] they are aware of how racism can interfere with their goals. On the other hand, they believe that they are in control of their own destiny. They feel that ultimately what happens to them in life depends on their own efforts rather than on the obstacles created by racism. They acknowledge the reality of racism, but put their time and effort into discovering ways to accomplish their objectives. The research reviewed by Howard Ramseur suggests that high self-esteem, positive racial identity, good interpersonal relationships, adaptive coping strategies, work productivity, and belief in the control of one's destiny tend to combine to make for a competent, effective Black personality.[14]

Part

IV

MAJOR INFLUENCES ON

AFRICAN-AMERICAN

MASCULINE DEVELOPMENT

Chapter 10

The Influence of the Family

The family, the peer group, and the neighborhood influence the psychological perspectives of African-American males as they struggle to come to grips with the issues involved in self-definition, attitudes toward women, coping with racism, discovering adaptive possibilities within the African-American way of being, and integrating African-American and Euro-American lifestyles.

Controversial Issues Surrounding the Black Family

Discussions of Black family life have been shrouded in academic and political controversy for the past thirty years. Much of the controversy originated in Daniel Patrick Moynihan's 1965 report *The Negro Family: The Case for National Action.*[1] Moynihan, now the senior U.S.

senator from New York, was working with President Lyndon Johnson as an assistant secretary of labor. He concluded in his report that the Black family was a tangle of social pathology characterized by an unstable matriarchal structure. He based his conclusions on census data on the composition of Black families, divorce rates, the number of Black single mothers receiving financial assistance from the Aid to Families with Dependent Children (AFDC) program, and the increasing numbers of Black children born out of wedlock. His summary of these statistics indicated that 25 percent of Black families were permanently without a father figure in the home. Another 25 percent of Black children, according to his calculations, would spend extended periods of time in households without a father while growing up. Thus, on any given day, 40 to 50 percent of Black children were growing up in homes without a father present. In American society, where a two-parent, patriarchal family was the norm in 1965, the Moynihan Report, as it is called, hit Black and White communities like a bombshell.

Moynihan contended that Black males were at a disadvantage by being reared in female-dominated households in a larger society where public and private institutions were run by males and dominated by traditional masculine leadership styles. Coming from female-dominated households, Black males were at greater risk for unemployment, drug abuse, crime and delinquency, and failure to pass the mental and physical tests to enter the armed forces than were White males from two-parent, male-headed households. Because of their gender and lack of world experience, Black women were unable to teach the discipline and goal-directed behaviors that Black males needed to succeed in the world beyond the home or, for that matter, to assist young Black males in developing the stability and leadership skills they would need to guide their own families when they became husbands and fathers. The Black community was being flooded with males who had grown up in broken homes, never acquiring any relationship to male authority, and who were unable to succeed in mainstream society. The result was social chaos, crime, delinquency, school failure, and illegitimate births producing more female-headed families.

To rectify the situation, Moynihan called on President Johnson to develop a massive program to reconstruct the Black family so it would resemble the two-parent, patriarchal White family. According to Moynihan, if federal policy initiatives were not launched to prevent further deterioration of the Black family, Blacks would have trouble capitalizing on the economic, political, and legal gains achieved by the civil rights movement of the 1950s and 1960s.

Black and White progressive, liberal critics were quick to attack Moynihan. In retrospect, he states that he was surprised at the intensity of the criticism and how long it lasted. The attack on Moynihan and his report generally accused him of ethnocentrism, sexism, racism, and a failure to understand the extended structure of the Black family.

By using White family norms to assess the Black family, Moynihan repeated a familiar strategy used by White social scientists to judge Black institutions and behavior. Briefly, he seemed to assume that the only psychologically healthy family structure is a two-parent household headed by a male, which, supposedly, was the norm for Euro-American families in 1965. A family that did not meet this model was automatically suspect of being unstable, psychologically unhealthy, and unable to provide male children with the guidance they need to become effective, competent adults. Such a family would quickly deteriorate into poverty and social pathology.[2] In 1992, on Public Broadcasting's program *Frontline,* the writer Marco Williams presented a story about growing up in a household run by four generations of women that questioned Moynihan's contentions. In Williams's story, the fathers disappeared from the children's lives early, yet these women raised families without becoming dependent on welfare. They were hardworking, family-oriented, self-reliant women who coped without deteriorating into drugs, crime, or poverty.[3]

Feminists challenged the sexist themes in Moynihan's logic. They argued that a single mother who has internalized a balance of traditional male and female personality and behavioral traits can teach male children to be caring and nurturant, as well as tough, responsible, and rational. Personality characteristics are not inherent in gender. Both males and females can be adequate role models for male children by demonstrating a balance of expressive and instrumental traits.

Many critics felt that Moynihan misunderstood the debilitating effects of racism in the labor market. Rather than a lack of masculine responsibility, assertiveness, and motivation, it was racial discrimination in trade unions, relegation to low-paying jobs in industry and the corporate structure, and cyclical and long-term unemployment that made it difficult for Black males to carry out the provider role as heads or coheads of families. Furthermore, restrictive welfare policies often required the father not to be present in the home if the family was on

AFDC. A lack of good-paying jobs can easily start a cycle that contributes to poverty, welfare, crime, and other social ills.

Finally, Moynihan did not seem to understand the role of the extended family structure in Black life.

The Black Extended Family

By comparing the Black family to the Euro-American nuclear family, which exists as an independent unit in a separate household, Moynihan was unable to see the strengths of the extended family, which come into clearer focus when the Black family is viewed as part of an interdependent extended family network. The core structure of the Black family is an extended family that consists of mothers, fathers, uncles, aunts, grandparents, older brothers and sisters, nonrelated kin, and secondary family members—neighbors, quasi-relatives, and church members—who come together to meet the problems of living and raising children. The extended family spans three or four generations and operates across several households. Traditionally, neither a matriarchal nor a patriarchal leadership structure dominates. Both men and women work outside the home, do household chores, and participate in the day-to-day rearing of children. Sex roles are flexible, and an egalitarian decision-making structure prevails. The extended family has its roots in the legacy of African tribal culture, the slavery plantation system, and economic hardships that have always required both genders to work outside the home to ensure family survival. The structure was maintained because it was family and because it worked.[4]

Extended families exist in many different forms; they are not rigid and undergo change as their members go through life. For example, a young couple may start out living with the wife's parents to save money during the early years of their marriage. After the first child is born, they move out on their own and the wife's grandmother moves into the space they vacated. After several years of marriage, the couple breaks up. The grandmother moves in with the ex-wife to provide child care while she works. Thus, over a period of time, we have a nuclear family within an extended family, a nuclear family living in a separate household, and a single-parent family retaining its ties to the extended family. All three families coexist in the Black community within the extended family structure.

The guiding principles of an extended family are a combination of reciprocity, mutual aid, and interdependence. These can take many different forms, such as lending money, taking care of relatives' children or sick and shut-in adults, giving emotional support during times of crisis, and sharing information about jobs and educational opportunities. Additional strengths in the Black extended family have been documented by expert researchers in Black family life. The clinical psychologist Nancy Boyd-Franklin and the sociologist Andrew Billingsley include the ability to expand and contract to meet demands, dual socialization of children in Black and White lifestyles, teaching responsibility to children, flexibility of roles, egalitarian decision making, provision of multiple role models, and religion and spirituality.[5, 6]

Extended Black families have shown the ability to absorb others into the household. Brent Staples's mother, despite a constant shortage of money because of her husband's drinking, occasionally took in pregnant, single women who had nowhere else to go. She told Brent that it took only a cup of water to make enough stew to feed one more person. It was part of her Christian values to help others. Some Black families take in children of relatives when their mothers and fathers are unable to support them. "Taking in" children also extends to neighborhood children whose parents have suffered disabling misfortunes. Black families who live near colleges and universities take in college students who are related to them in order to reduce their fees for room and board. The extended family provides an extensive informal network of social services, foster homes, and nursing care.

Children growing up in African-American extended families receive dual socialization; they are socialized to get along in both the Euro-American and African-American cultures. Parents and grandparents who are proud of their African-American heritage teach it to their children. At the same time, they fully understand that in order for their children to succeed they must master the educational, occupational, and social competencies that are necessary for success in the mainstream.

Because both parents usually have to work to keep the family afloat, children in the extended family are taught home management skills, such as cooking and cleaning and responsibility for younger children, as well as how to survive on the streets. The oldest child, whether male or female, is usually designated as what family therapists call "the parental child." The responsibility for managing the family when the parents are away at work is delegated to the parental child. He or she makes sure that younger children do their chores, complete their homework, and come home after school if they are not involved in parentally approved, supervised activities. Parental children, like Brent Staples, may even shop, pay bills, and prepare meals. In a functional extended family, the younger children and the parental child understand that the parents are the final authority figures.

Gender flexibility and egalitarian decision making, as strengths of the Black extended family, arose out of economic necessity. Men and women both had to work and act interchangeably as both mother and father. Black women were not relegated to the kind of compliant, passive status in decision making that emerged in the Euro-American patriarchal family. Because children see both males and females working and operating in nurturing and decision-making roles, a rigid distinction between sex roles is not as likely to develop.

The Black extended family provides children with multiple role models. If the father is not present in the household or is not actively involved with the children, other extended family members—uncles, grandfathers, older brothers, church elders—may step in to fill the gap. In times of crisis, when adolescent males are depressed or spinning out of control, the family can call on male resources within the extended family for support, counseling, and companionship.

The Black Church as an Extended Family

A deep religious orientation has been one of the greatest strengths of Black extended families. Historically, Black family life was centered around the Black church. A continuing belief in the power of divine transcendence has been a source of resilience and vitality that has helped Black families survive the dark hours of slavery, segregation, and poverty. Extended Black families pass on the tradition of faith, transcendence, and survival through God's grace from one generation to another. Church elders tell folks how God watched over them in times of crisis, and they urge young people to keep the faith that troubles will pass. Spirituality as a coping mechanism is deeply ingrained in the Black psyche. People who grow up in the Black community are usually equipped with a core system of spiritual beliefs they can use to reframe potentially devastating experiences. As children, they learn that hardship is a test of faith, that God will not give you any more than you can bear, and that He will not desert you in an hour of need. Some Black psychologists like Nicholas Cooper-Lewter use a psycho-spiritual approach to counseling and psychotherapy based on the African-American religious experience.[7]

For many Black families, the church functions like a large extended family network. Members refer to each other as sisters and brothers. Older women in the church are reverently referred to as "Mother." For overburdened single mothers or new people in town, the church can be a surrogate family offering support and assistance. Older members of the church are there to assist young people and provide help and support. They recall troubled times in their own lives and encourage young people to draw upon faith in God and spiritual strength to overcome setbacks and challenges.

While not all Black people are officially church members, most Black people internalized religious beliefs as children and continue to respect the power of spirituality as adults. Although spirituality finds its deepest expression in the Black church, it spills over into the daily lives of most Black adults. The findings from a national survey of a representative sample of African-Americans indicate that an overwhelming percentage of African-Americans consider religion as a major part of their lives. Eighty-four percent of the survey participants designated themselves as religious, 76 percent said religion was important in their lives, 78 percent prayed daily, and 80 percent sent their children to church. The survey also revealed that men have stronger religious beliefs than women, but that women attend church more regularly.[8] Also, Black men who attended church regularly, prayed daily, and frequently listened to religious broadcasts tended to be highly involved in married life, child rearing, and extended family relationships.[9]

Black churches are active in the community and provide a range of programs for children, adolescents, adults, and elders. Black churches run parenting programs, after-school tutorials, day-care centers and nursery schools, prenatal clinics, food distribution centers, credit unions, scout troops, rites of passage programs, and centers for job training and family counseling.

Third Shiloh Missionary Baptist Church in New Orleans, located next to the Desire Housing Project, home for 8,000 people from mostly low-income and blue-collar families, bought abandoned houses in the neighborhood and tore them down to build new apartments. Construction of the apartments provided jobs for people in the project, where, as of 1992, the unemployment rate was 60 percent. From the low rents on the apartments, which are turning a profit, the church is supporting a tutorial program for children, a scholarship fund for students, and other community projects that include more low-income housing to rehabilitate the neighborhood. The church's priorities are decent housing for low-income families, educational support for youth, and a new church building.

In Washington, D.C., Shiloh Baptist Church, founded by a handful of ex-slaves in 1863, provides a range of activities for young people, adults, and the elderly. The church has a full basketball court, racquetball courts, exercise rooms, banquet halls, a complete restaurant, and meeting rooms, all of which are open to the community. It has an extensive Big Brothers program for low-income youth, Boy Scout and Girl Scout troops, after-school tutorials, parent education classes, a Boys' Club of America group, math and science learning centers, and sex and health education and drug prevention programs.[10]

America's Changing Family Structures

Back in 1965, Daniel Moynihan was unable to look into the future and see that new family structures were emerging in America. In 1995, *Ozzie and Harriet,* a popular TV family sitcom featuring a stay-at-home wife and a working husband, no longer exists as the dominant family structure in Black or White America. Children now grow up in a variety of family structures.[11] It is not uncommon for children to live with single mothers (with or without boyfriends), stepparents, grandparents, or other relatives or to be part of blended or reconstructed families that contain only one of their biological parents. Most mothers work, and increasing numbers of single moms are now a permanent fixture in family life. Working married women, inspired by the feminist revolution, are no longer content with patriarchal family leadership. Egalitarian leadership and shared decision-making authority are now the norm in most families.

Trends first noted in Black families are now becoming more visible in White families. Statistics indicate that, as of 1993 (and the numbers have remained relatively constant), White families were where Black families were in 1965. Twenty-five percent of White children now live in homes where there is no father figure. Another 25 percent will spend significant periods of time in homes without fathers. Approximately

50 percent of first marriages by women end in divorce; half of those divorced will remarry and about half of the second marriages will also end in divorce. The fastest growing group of White single mothers is composed of women who never married. Twenty-four percent of all unmarried women, ages 18 to 24, are now mothers, a 56 percent increase from ten years ago.[12] The number of out-of-wedlock births is augmented by many college-educated and professional women who are voluntarily choosing to be mothers outside marriage. For Black families, the statistics are even more dramatic. Fifty percent of Black children are permanently without fathers in the home; another 20 to 25 percent will spend significant periods of time in families where no fathers are present. In 1991, 57 percent of Black children were born to unmarried mothers.[13]

With the belated recognition that single-parent, female-headed families are now a fact of life in White America, family psychologists no longer see such families as inherently characterized by a tangle of social pathology. And they have devised a new language to discuss current family structures. Terms like "bastard" or "illegitimate," "broken homes," and "matriarchal" have been replaced by "out-of-wedlock births," "single parenthood," and "reconstructed families." Furthermore, questions about the roles of fathers in the family now extend beyond the African-American context. Despite the recognition of a variety of legitimate family structures, some family specialists like David Blankenhorn, director of the National Institute of Fatherhood, bemoan the loss of fathers as a permanent part of family life. Blankenhorn laments the fact that absence of the father has become an acceptable standard. He thinks that such absence is becoming so pervasive that America is on the verge of becoming a fatherless society. Through the National Institute of Fatherhood, Blankenhorn is on a crusade to move questions surrounding fatherhood to the center of the debate about families and bring the father back into a leadership role within the family.[14]

Blankenhorn contends that his statistics indicate that paternal absence is responsible for two major devastating social problems: teenage and young adult crime and teen pregnancies. Gangs feed on children from fatherless homes. Boys without fathers to guide them create their own rites of passage with gang initiations, getting girls pregnant, and macho violence. Seventy percent of the men in jail spent time in fatherless families. Teenage girls searching for father figures to boost low self-esteem are vulnerable to sexual exploitation and out-of-wedlock pregnancies. According to Blankenhorn, fatherless children are less successful in school, more prone to depression and behavioral problems, and are likely to be deficient in social skills and coping strategies. Fathers are needed to build safe neighborhoods. Mothers may set rules for behavior, but it is the fathers and older male figures who help keep boys in line on the streets. Blankenhorn claims that in 1992, then Vice President Dan Quayle was right when he condemned the TV sitcom character Murphy Brown for choosing to have a baby out of wedlock. By entering the debate on paternal absence in a political context, however, and not mentioning the role poverty and diminished social services play in increasing the pressures on single mothers, Mr. Quayle limited his effectiveness and incurred the wrath of many women.

Not only are fathers absent, but society no longer has a clear idea of what they are supposed to represent, Blankenhorn thinks. Are fathers expected to be firm disciplinarians in the family who set the standards and enforce the rules, or are fathers supposed to be nice guys who duplicate the traditional maternal role that involves affection, nurturance, and empathy?

Feminist scholars contend that Blankenhorn doesn't fully understand the cause/effect relationship of the stresses confronting families without fathers. Many single mothers provide safe, emotionally secure homes for their children, with clear behavioral expectations and consequences. The problem confronting these women, feminists argue, is poverty due to a combination of low wages and deadbeat dads who don't pay child support. Many times, when the father and mother divorce, the father divorces the family and children and exits from their lives. When he takes up with another woman, he devotes his time and financial resources to her children. The problems of single moms are further complicated by a lack of low-cost, safe, reliable child-care services. As single motherhood becomes more prevalent, millions of women are struggling with the problems of tight finances, child care, and medical services; averaging $20,000 a year or less in wages, their time and money are stretched. Single moms are constantly juggling bills and trying to find quality time for children between work, running errands, and household chores. Women who can barely keep food on the table, buy clothes for their children, pay the rent, and afford medical care, and who cannot provide quality child care for their children after school, are bound to experience stresses that eventually surface in their children's academic and social behavior.[15]

Family Organization and Psychological Development

From a psychological perspective, the most important aspect of family life is not its structure but how well the family meets the children's needs for safety, emotional security, affection, and guidance. The family is the first human unit children are a part of. It puts in place the psychological foundation that determines whether life will be tilted toward an optimistic or pessimistic view. Overtly and covertly, the family establishes standards and expectations for behavior. Family life provides opportunities for developing problem-solving and coping behaviors. The early learning of sex roles occurs within the family.

Single parenthood in African-American families does not automatically mean that the family is dysfunctional or pathological. A psychologically resilient, resourceful African-American woman with strong ties to an extended family network can create a stable, positive psychological environment for her children so that they learn the life management skills they will need in the world beyond the home.

Nancy Boyd-Franklin, who has worked extensively with African-American families as a family therapist, describes an effective single-parent family as one where there is a clear understanding of who is in charge. The family members know what their roles and responsibilities are. Rules and standards for behavior, along with consequences for violations, are clearly established. Whether the parent is employed or receiving public assistance, the children's basic needs for shelter and safety are met. The mother is flexible, willing to listen, and tries to develop two-way communication with her children.

Many African-American single-parent families have strong ties to the church. Rather than dwell on hardships, many spiritually oriented single mothers see difficult situations as God's test of their faith, and they hope for a better life for their children. An effective single mom teaches respect for authority, shows an active interest in her children's schooling, and respects values involving hard work, responsibility, obeying the law, and preparation for the future. Strong ties to members of the extended family provide support and additional role models for male children. It is important for single women to maintain a life of their own apart from their children in order to prevent stagnation and becoming overly enmeshed in their children's lives. Boyfriends, school, church, and community participation are adult activities that can fill up empty spaces. At the same time, single moms have to be careful of becoming overburdened with work, school, managing a family, and trying to have some adult social life. The key to survival for single mothers is balancing time, compromising on what can and cannot be accomplished, and making sure the family has a support system.

Case Example: Anita Taylor's Family

Anita Taylor and her three children—Dan, age twelve; Donna, age fourteen; and Jimmy, age sixteen—represent an example of an effective, functional single-parent African-American family. Anita had her first child, Jimmy, when she was a sixteen-year-old high school junior. She dropped out of school and lived at home with her mother and two younger sisters for a year after Jimmy was born. Finishing high school through an independent study program, Anita then worked part time as a dietitian's assistant in a hospital and started a nursing program in a local community college. She continued seeing Jimmy's biological father, Harold, age nineteen, who worked for a moving company as a driver. They decided to get married when she discovered she was pregnant with their second child. After Harold and Anita got married, they moved in with his mother until they could save enough money for furniture and for the first and last months' rent for an apartment.

Looking back, Anita feels the first five years of her marriage to Harold were the good years. She finished her nursing program, her youngest child, Danny, was born, and she and Harold were putting aside money for a down-payment on a home. Both grandmothers helped with child care while Anita worked and completed school. About five years after Danny was born, the marriage started to deteriorate. Anita discovered that her husband was using drugs and taking money out of the couple's savings account to pay off drug and gambling debts. She thought counseling might help, but he refused to attend the sessions. Anita went to the counseling sessions alone. Harold felt that he had married too young, was tired of the responsibilities of work and children, and wanted to see what life was all about. The couple split up when she discovered that Harold was staying with a girlfriend when he was supposed to be away on moving jobs.

The first few years of single life were rough financially; Harold had left Anita with a pile of debts and student loans. She continued with the counseling and relied on her church for support. The children participated in after-school activities and summer children's programs. Her parents helped with money for school clothes. For the first few years, Harold avoided paying child support by moving to another state. He had no contact with the children. With the help of family members and an attorney, Anita was able to track him down; after some legal pressure, he agreed to start paying child support. After the family breakup, Harold lost his job with the moving company and spent some time in a drug recovery program. He is now off drugs, attends a recovery support group, and works in an auto plant on the assembly line.

Five years after Anita and her husband separated, Anita's aunt, who had lost her husband during the Vietnam War, moved in with Anita and her children. The aunt, whose two adult children live in another state, receives widow's benefits and works part time as a grocery store clerk. The presence of her aunt in the family as a surrogate mother has freed up some time for Anita to attend school one night a week and on Saturdays to complete a bachelor's degree program in hospital administration. The children attend church two nights a week and on Sunday; they have household chores and are expected to study two or three hours a day. On afternoons when Anita and her aunt are at work, her daughter, Donna, starts dinner and supervises Danny with his homework and chores. Anita and her daughter attend the sex education class for mothers and daughters at the church. Driving back and forth from the class meetings also gives mother and daughter time to talk about dating, drugs, health issues, and other adolescent concerns.

When he was fifteen, Jimmy went through a period of rebellion. His grades deteriorated, he started experimenting with drugs and alcohol, repeatedly disobeyed curfew rules, and may have been having unprotected sex with his girlfriend. Jimmy's track coach threatened to drop him from the team unless he went to family counseling with his mother. After he began to feel comfortable in the counseling sessions, Jimmy told his mother and the therapist that he was tired of being controlled "by a house full of females." He felt his mother was overprotective, too worried about sex, drugs, and alcohol, and was "trying to make a sissy out of me." He also didn't like his mother's boyfriend, who sometimes spent the night on weekends. Anita, Jimmy, and the therapist worked out a contract according to which Jimmy could earn more freedom and get his driver's license contingent upon responsible behavior at home, outside the home, and in school. Jimmy, Anita, and her boyfriend worked on techniques to improve their communication. The boyfriend felt that Jimmy needed firm, male discipline because Anita let him get away with too much. Anita asked her brother to spend more time with Jimmy. She also asked Jimmy's father to attend some of the counseling sessions as a way of starting to rebuild his relationship with his son. The father reentered the picture, and Jimmy now plans to spend the summer with him working as a summer student employee in the auto plant. He would like to study auto design in college, and his father has agreed to help him.

Things have now settled down in the family. Jimmy is back on track in school and in the home. Anita is completing her bachelor's degree, and family members are trying to keep two-way lines of communication open.

The Underorganized Family

A chaotic, underorganized family environment, whether it occurs in a two-parent or a one-parent home, disrupts children's emotional balance and interferes with their learning problem-solving and life management skills. Children are likely to be confused about what is expected in terms of responsibility, rules, and standards for behavior. They learn that life is capricious, that the family can be overwhelmed by crises, confusion, or explosive outbursts at any time.

In *Parallel Time,* Brent Staples describes growing up in a chaotic, underorganized, two-parent family.[16] The family was continuously moving from house to house. His parents fought and argued constantly. His father had a good income, but his excessive drinking caused chronic shortages of money. The family was harassed by creditors and bill collectors. They sometimes had to move in the middle of the night to avoid paying bills or were evicted for not paying the rent. His mother was a good-hearted, hardworking, Christian woman, but she was overwhelmed by trying to cope with an abusive, alcoholic husband and the responsibility of managing a household with nine children born in quick succession. Visible cracks in the family structure started to appear as the children entered adolescence. There were runaways, unplanned pregnancies, drug abuse, arrests and jailings, and school dropouts. Brent's brother was murdered in a dispute that started over a drug deal.

Today, in the inner cities of urban America, many African-American parents are overwhelmed by the responsibilities of trying to raise a family in neighborhoods stricken by poverty, crime, crack cocaine, and lack of access to employment. Disconnected from the church and extended family ties, single mothers, who started having children as young teenagers, are ill-equipped to organize a good enough family environment. They love their children but are unable to meet the constant demands of parenthood. Young, poorly educated, and single, they often find it difficult to reconcile their own needs for independence and freedom with the needs of their children for support, companionship, and understanding. Children are sometimes left alone to fend for themselves while the mother stays with her boyfriend or goes out drinking or visits a crack house.

With only a limited understanding of planning and priorities, single mothers with few adaptive coping skills are easily frustrated by bills, shortages of food, and lack of money for rent and school clothes. Drugs and complicated relationships with males add to family frustrations. Arguments and fights ensue. Family discipline and rules are inconsistent. Children are allowed to run wild, but when mom's frustrations boil over, children may be severely beaten for minor infractions. Typically, no explanation follows verbal and physical punishment, so children develop a faulty understanding of the cause/effect sequence. Mom is not sadistic and doesn't hate her children, but harsh physical discipline is the only way she knows to control them. Children also see adults settling disputes by yelling and screaming and by physical violence. Children take on the characteristics they see modeled in the family environment. The family is the most important predictor of violence. It is where children first see how it works as a way of solving problems—that might makes right.[17] If adults don't know how to deal with their problems constructively, children won't learn to solve problems constructively. If children have no clear rules and see adults drinking excessively, abusing drugs, and having multiple sexual partners, they will do the same. The National Institute of Drug Abuse has estimated that children who spend ten hours a week after school without adult supervision are nearly two times as likely to smoke, drink alcohol, or use marijuana.[18]

Family Life and Sex-Role Learning

Young males initially learn about the characteristics associated with gender roles by observing adults in the family setting. The adults provide a looking glass through which children can see themselves reflected. Children tend to emulate what they see as they try on observed roles and imagine what it would be like to be an adult. The most common masculine roles African-American children are exposed to within the family circle are those of provider, egalitarian decision maker, defeated male, player of women, and street tough. Very little has been written about Black males in the father/provider role. Much of the literature on Black males in family life focuses on paternal absence and on Black males who have been unable to assume the role of provider or cohead of the household because of problems with drugs, incarceration, unemployment, poor health, and deficient educational preparation.

Noel Cazenave, a Black sociologist, has extensively studied the role of middle-class working fathers in African-American families. In one of his major research studies, Cazenave asked fifty-four Black letter carriers in New Orleans questions about what it means to be a man today. The letter carriers responded that it means responsibility, being a breadwinner, hard work, ambition, and standing up for firm guiding principles. They felt the major roles of a man centered around being a provider, father, husband, and worker. The most important responsibility for a father was to be a provider, followed by being a guide and teacher, authority figure, companion, and protector.

The men saw themselves as different from their own fathers. They were more active participants in child rearing than their fathers had been in terms of the amount of time they spent building relations with their children: playing with them, helping with homework, and talking to them about Black identity, racism, the future, and the responsibilities of parenthood. The letter carriers also saw themselves as less authoritarian and more egalitarian in decision making with their spouses. Cazenave concluded that when Black men have the opportunity to be providers and are present in the home, their role extends beyond the traditional patriarchal, autocratic one to combine expressive and instrumental traits. Their role is more utilitarian, expressive, and egalitarian than the traditional power-dominant male sex role.[19]

The egalitarian father role is a standard feature of the two-parent African-American family. Both parents work, and mother and father, along with grandfather, grandmother, uncles, and aunts, interchange roles in providing child care, monitoring play activities, supervising schoolwork, and nurturing and supporting children emotionally. In this type of family setting, young males are exposed to the instrumental and expressive traits of masculine role models. They learn that males can be supportive, caring, and empathic, and at the same time able to handle assertively the demands of work and employment outside the home.

The Trey-Nine Chicago housing projects described by Vest Monroe in his book *Brothers* were filled with Black males who had been defeated by life or who were barely hanging on.[20] Vest and his friends saw their fathers, uncles, and grandfathers suffering from unemployment, seasonal layoffs, low wages, and a general belief that the White man won't let you make it too high in this world. The message communicated to young African-American boys in such an environment is "Don't set your sights too high because, despite your best efforts, the White world will find a way to defeat you." Since White folks will let only a few Blacks through the door, chances of a high level of success in the mainstream are about the same as winning the lottery.

A more insidious message about African-American masculinity, power, and success was picked up by Nathan McCall growing up in a middle-class Black community.[21] The fathers of Nathan and his peers were employed in blue-collar jobs. In the neighborhood there were Black males working as postal clerks, mailmen, teachers, and businessmen, yet everywhere Nathan and his peers looked they saw White males in positions of power and control over Black males. In order to stay on the good side of the White man, their fathers and other older Black males had to assume a posture of compliance and passivity in the work setting. White power and control pose a dilemma for Black parents. What should they tell their male children about assertiveness and ambition? Black mothers are especially troubled by this dilemma. They sometimes try to shield their sons from disappointment by not pushing them too hard. They know that failure and heartbreak occur more often than success and masculine power in the world outside the home.

In families where there are no stable adult male figures and where the mothers, aunts, and grandmothers have short-term romantic liaisons or even compete with each other for the few available men, young males run the risk of internalizing the image of player of women. In some Black families, there are two and three generations of women who have had no long-term relationships with men. Boys learn that women are the ones who take the responsibility for supporting the household financially and protecting the children. Adult male activities are primarily sexual and fun oriented. With no images of responsible males around them, young males are vulnerable to repeating the role of player of women as adults.

Finally, if there are no males in responsible decision-making roles, with whom the boy can build a stable relationship as he goes through the formative years, he is at risk of being influenced by powerful forces outside the home. The masculine images in the streets, especially in urban areas, tend to emphasize macho toughness and sexual prowess. Boys are taught that in order to be respected and survive on the streets, they cannot show weakness. The message is to look tough and act bad, and even if you are afraid, don't show it; if a young Black man shows signs of weakness or fear, he will be ostracized by the peer group. As young men move into adolescence, they learn that scoring with females is a way of achieving status on the streets. With many areas of occupation and achievement sealed off by racism and poor educational training, sexual prowess is one of the few areas in which young Black men living in inner cities can demonstrate their power and dominance.

Chapter 11

The Role of the Peer Group

As Black males progress through late childhood, adolescence, and early adulthood, the peer group becomes a major influence on values, identity choices, masculine styles, attitudes toward women, strategies for coping with racism, and levels of Black consciousness. Peer groups usually consist of boys and young men of about the same age or level of maturity and who are at a similar stage of biological, psychological, and social development. Adolescent peers are confronting growth issues involving psychological and physical maturation, integrating sexuality into their lives, separating from parents, and defining themselves as men. During adolescence, the peer group replaces the family as the central source of support, understanding, and guidance. By adolescence, Black males—indeed, most other American males—spend larger and larger amounts of time in unsupervised activities with peer groups on the weekends and after school. They also see their peers at school, participate with them on athletic teams, and work with their cohorts on part-time jobs. Young people who are isolated from peer friendships and activities feel rejected and alone.[1]

Functions of the Peer Group

Harry Stack Sullivan, a pioneer in the field of adolescent psychology, believed that close friendships between agemates play a critical role in the transformation from late childhood to early adulthood.[2] Adolescent peer friendships fulfill basic needs for intimacy and closeness, help teenagers master social skills, offer adventure and excitement beyond the world controlled by parents, and provide emotional support during the ups and downs of the adolescent passage. The primary functions of the peer group consist of meeting psychological needs, setting standards for behavior, providing mentorship through rites of passage, and integrating the common pool of experiences that define Black males as "Brothers."

In psychological terms, the peer group meets the need for belonging, feedback, and new learning experiences. The peer group also provides a shield for adolescent rebellion. All human beings have deep-seated needs for close psychological attachment to others. During childhood, a boy's parents, extended family members, and other caretakers meet his needs for attachment and belonging. As adolescents move into the social environment beyond the home, peers take on the role of significant others in meeting these needs. Teenagers who are experiencing normal power struggles and authority conflicts with their parents about values, individuality, and rules cannot always get their support and understanding. It is easier to turn to peers who are experiencing similar problems.

The peer group acts as a stage on which the adolescent can present or project himself. As an audience, the peer group is like a mirror reflecting back to the teenager impressions of his persona. With feedback from the audience, the teenager can make adjustments and refinements to fit in more with the group's expectations. Adolescence is a time when new social skills, values, and coping strategies need to be learned to master the challenges brought about by the psychosexual changes and demands of the social environment. The old childhood behaviors are looked upon as immature and won't work in the adolescent context. The peer group provides an arena where young people can learn new behaviors and explore alternative values by observation, modeling, and experimentation. By watching and listening in peer group interactions, teenage males can learn dance steps, rap strategies, study skills, and dress fashions and how to talk to girls or initiate sex. More experienced peers act as role models and guides for the neophytes as they try out new roles.

Young people often use the peer group as a cover for rebellion. Away from the prying eyes of adults, they can experiment with behavior and values their elders disapprove of. Shielded by the peer group, teenagers experiment with drugs and alcohol, share their experiences with sex, sometimes engage in group sex, fight with rival groups, and break the law. A group of Black wannabe gangsters in Los Angeles invade department stores in shopping malls with a technique they call "racking." They enter a shopping mall and create a distraction to divert the attention of security guards by staging a fistfight or a loud argument. They then swarm into a store for a few minutes, grabbing clothing and escaping quickly. In the confusion, security guards have a difficult time putting up an effective defense and witnesses have trouble identifying the boys who participated in the raid.[3]

Peer groups set standards and expectations for masculine behavior, provide guidance and mentorship for younger members, and conduct informal rites of passage. Some peer groups revolve around partying, girls, and social activities; others stress academic performance or athletics. Gang-oriented peer groups emphasize fighting, physical aggression, and protecting homeboys. Skip Gates and his adolescent peers, called "the Fearsome Foursome," were interested in girls, fun, athletics, and school. In their senior year in high school, the Fearsome Foursome also participated in civil rights activities to protest segregation in their community and the failure of school authorities to properly acknowledge the meaning of Martin Luther King's assassination.[4] The norms of behavior and rites of passage for Nathan McCall's peer group involved gang rapes, fighting rival gangs, assaults, thefts, burglaries, armed robberies, and shootings.[5]

Sexual behavior and how women are treated are important dimensions of peer group norms. Skip Gates and his peers pursued sex as part of romantic love. Skip tended to idolize women and treated them with tenderness and respect. Nathan McCall and his associates, on the other hand, brutalized young women in gang rapes. His peers felt that only fools fell in love; women were perceived as objects of pleasure.

Pretending to be in love and manipulating women for sex were acceptable masculine behaviors. For boys from fatherless homes who do not have strong surrogate father figures in the extended family, masculine standards learned through the mentorship and bonding of the peer group can have a lasting effect.

The Positives of Peer Groups
Sharing Knowledge of the Black Heritage

A unique aspect of peer group activities for Black youth is the sharing of bits and pieces of information to form a common pool of experiences that define them as Black men.[6] In peer group interaction, they share information about the Black heritage, lifestyles, and survival strategies picked up in conversations with elders at home or in the neighborhood, discussions in barbershops and rap sessions, and from books, music, and church sermons. Internalization of these experiences allows them to refer to themselves and other Black men as "Brothers," "Cuzes," "Road Dogs," "Homeboys," and "Bloods." The bond established through common experiences permits Black men who meet as strangers at airports, conferences, and social gatherings to quickly establish rapport, with an easy flow of conversation.

Mastery of Black verbal styles is an essential component of Black masculinity. Within the peer group, young Brothers learn how to rap, signify, play the dozens, cap, mack, sweet-talk, and woof, using vivid figures of speech and singsong rhymes in a rapid-fire call-response dialogue. On street corners and playgrounds and at parties and other social events, Black youths continuously practice the intricacies of Black linguistic interactions. Kids who master the complexities, nuances, and timing of Black language patterns can hold the stage in social interactions, thereby enhancing their recognition and prestige.[7]

The Eager Beavers: Moving on Up

An example of positive peer group influence can be found in the life stories of a group of Black male teenagers who called themselves "the Eager Beavers." The Eager Beavers were adolescents in the predominantly Black Fillmore district of San Francisco in the mid-1940s. They were kids from working-class extended families. Their fathers and stepfathers were longshoremen, postal clerks, hotel doormen, shipyard workers, and janitors. Approximately half of the Eager Beavers had fathers or stepfathers in the home. As high school students, the Eager Beavers were fun-loving teenagers whose major interests were athletics, girls, and partying. They experimented with social drinking but discouraged excessive drinking, drug use, smoking, and delinquent behavior. As athletes, they wanted to keep their bodies in good condition. Delinquency was frowned upon because it could disqualify them from participating in high school athletics. The Eager Beavers established an unofficial coexistence with "the Lucky Twenties," the major Black gang in the Fillmore district. Everyone knew the Eager Beavers could fight. They would not attack others, but if their friends were abused they would respond quickly. Since many of the Eager Beavers had opportunities for part-time or full-time athletic scholarships at colleges and universities in the San Francisco Bay Area, they became more concerned about grades as high school juniors and seniors. All of the Eager Beavers attended college. Several were varsity athletes in football and track at San Francisco State, the University of San Francisco, San Francisco City College, and the University of California, Berkeley.

As undergraduates, the Eager Beavers joined Kappa Alpha Psi, a national Black fraternity. In college, they fanned out toward majors in education, premed, business administration, or history. Two of the Eager Beavers, Ollie Matson and Burl Toler, became All-American football players at the University of San Francisco. Matson won the Silver and Bronze medals at the 1952 Olympic Games in the 1600-meter relay and the 400-meter run, respectively. As a professional football player, he was an All-Star offensive back, kick return specialist, and defensive back for the Chicago Cardinals. Following a career-ending football injury in his first season with the Cleveland Browns, Burl Toler became a teacher, elementary school principal, and then assistant district superintendent of schools in San Francisco. He was also the first Black referee in the NFL.

Other members of the Eager Beavers went on to careers in law enforcement, medicine, education, government service, and the military. Rotea Gilford served as deputy mayor to Dianne Feinstein after completing a successful career as a police officer. He also served as a special assistant to Mayor Willie Brown of San Francisco. Hiwatha Harris entered medicine and was instrumental in starting Central City, the first community mental health center in South-Central Los Angeles. Staton Webster received a Ph.D. in education from the University of California, Berkeley, and spent his career in higher education as a professor and administrator. Verdice Carter and Donald Grant became teachers and district administrators in Oakland and Alameda, respectively. Marvin Crews served as a navigator in the U.S. Air Force and retired after thirty years with the rank of colonel. Ken Baker Stallings worked for the postal service as an administrator and finished his career as a postal superintendent in San Mateo County.

The Eager Beavers were role models and mentors for the next generation of Black males who were two to four years younger. As juniors and seniors in college, they provided visible evidence for the younger group that it was possible to succeed in college. Augmented by their affiliation with Kappa Alpha Psi, the Eager Beavers took the younger men under their wings like members of an extended family. They were helpful in assisting Black freshmen select responsive professors, schedule their classes, learn how to study, obtain part-time jobs, and get invited to social functions. By their demeanor, actions, and informal verbal and nonverbal communications, the Eager Beavers made it clear that they did not tolerate street behavior, go-for-bad attitudes, or drugs. They gravitated toward kids who had good social skills and who were willing to work hard to be good students. Athletics were respected, but athletic talent was not essential to be included in the Eager Beaver–Kappa Alpha Psi network.

The life accomplishments of the younger group mentored by the Eager Beavers are impressive. Willie Brown, who graduated from San Francisco State College in 1955, went on to become one of the most powerful Black politicians in the United States. After completing law school at the University of California, Hastings in San Francisco, Brown practiced law and served in the California State Assembly for thirty-two years. As Speaker of the State Assembly for fifteen years, he was second only to the governor as a political force. Nothing moved in California politics without Brown's consent. After retiring from the assembly, following the enactment of term-limit laws, Brown became the first Black mayor of San Francisco, in 1995.

Other men mentored by the Eager Beavers were K. C. Jones and Bill Russell, both of whom played basketball on two National Championship teams at the University of San Francisco, the alma mater of Ollie Matson and Burl Toler. Russell and Jones became internationally known for their outstanding play with the Boston Celtics, perennial professional basketball champions in the 1960s and 1970s. And both went on to coach in the NBA. Ed Barnes and Joe White became university professors of psychology and were active in the Black psychology movement that spawned major changes in psychology. Four others became lawyers, two pursued careers in medicine, and five were social workers, community activists, and program administrators. Others entered engineering, business, and public administration.

The group mentored by the Eager Beavers in turn mentored the next group, creating a chain that has yielded successive cohorts of productive citizens in a wide variety of occupations.

The Negatives of Peer Groups
Gangs: A Destructive Cycle

Gangs are generally regarded as an example of negative peer influence. For many Black urban youths, gangs are a win/lose situation. On the relatively positive side, for young Black males who feel locked out of access to high-paying jobs and status in the larger society, the gang offers companionship, physical and psychological protection, adventure, opportunities to earn a street reputation, and a chance to earn money in the drug trade. On the negative side, the longer a young man stays in a gang, the greater the likelihood that he will face felony charges, jail, and possibly death. It is not uncommon for gang youths to be involved in shoot-outs, assaults, armed robberies, and possession of illegal drugs. By the time they are fifteen or sixteen, they have usually done time in detention centers.[8] Monster Kody Scott, who joined the Eight-Tray set of the notorious L.A. Crips gang at the age of eleven, was arrested for car-jacking and assault at age fifteen. A year later, he was shot six times in an ambush by a rival gang. Subsequently, he was convicted of possession of a rifle, armed robbery, assaults, and mayhem. He served time as a young adult in several California prisons.[9]

The gang offers a career line for low-income Black males who see no other workable options. Under the mentorship of older gang members, known in street parlance as "shot-callers," new recruits start off as foot soldiers and work their way up to positions of authority and to financial remuneration from the gang's illicit activities. New gang members are expected to emulate the shot-callers, who set the standards for masculine demeanor, dress, and language. In many cases, the mentors who school the younger gang members are only a few years older. Monster Kody's mentor, Tray Ball, was fifteen years old when Kody joined the gang. In other cases, the shot-callers are adults with prison records who have been in the gang since early adolescence.

Foot soldiers, at the bottom of the gang's organizational chart, work their way up through violence. Bold, daring actions, like a violent raid on enemy territory or brutal assaults or the vicious beating of a rival gang member, are rewarded with upward mobility in the gang's hierarchy. Starting with the "jumping-in" ceremony, a rite of passage in which a new gang member fights two or three other gang members, violence is the glue that cements the gang together. Violence becomes a way of connecting, a way of belonging to the collective experience. Hurting someone in the rituals of fighting and shooting opens the door to inclusion.[10] Monster Kody says he felt an overwhelming sense of power and closeness to his homeboys when they were riding around on a mission with intent to commit deadly violence. For Kody and his peers, this was the ultimate power. Nathan McCall felt that his peers consolidated their identity as a gang after the first gang rape. After that, McCall and his associates escalated to more gang rapes, armed robberies, shootings, and assaults.

In the context of violence and hate directed toward their enemies and strangers who unwittingly get in the way, gang members express undying love for their homeboys. Nothing is more important than the psychological connection to the homeboys. Gang members are willing to die for one another. They feel the gang Brothers will take care of them and protect them in good times as well as bad. For youth from homes that are overwhelmed by poverty, joblessness, and loss of hope, the gang set becomes a family, a religion, and a career all in one. According to Monster Kody, joining a gang in South-Central Los Angeles is like going to college for those from upper-middle-class neighborhoods; everybody is expected to do it. Every day, the gang member is expected to put in some work for his set: writing graffiti on walls to display the gang's initials or symbols, going on reconnaissance missions into rival territories, selling drugs, patrolling and protecting the home turf, or acting as a lookout for the police. Some well-organized gangs have flowcharts of responsibilities, charge dues, hold weekly meetings, and even have gang prayers and songs. At any time, homeboys can be called upon to engage in dangerous missions including drive-bys, assaults, and executions. Many eagerly accept such assignments since they will enhance their status and move them closer to the higher ranks of shot-caller and O.G. O.G.s, or original gangsters, are held in the highest reverence because they have demonstrated extreme acts of aggressive violence and loyalty to the set.

Gang members know that death is always lurking in the shadows and that prison is inevitable. The ability to master the fear of death is a test of one's masculine courage. Prison is another test of masculine nerve and survival skills. In prison, youths can test themselves against the baddest of the bad. Gang Brothers who survive the prison test of manhood can return to the streets with an enhanced reputation as a ghetto star or O.G.

Caught up in the grip of the gang's philosophy and behavioral norms, bright, sensitive young men turn into aggressive macho types who engage in predatory sex and violence. Teenagers who were once promising, likable grade school students adopt an aggressive façade, talk tough, and take on the general physical appearance of the gang in dress and swaggering demeanor. Fifteen-year-olds, who in another time and place would be playing sports, working part-time jobs, and thinking about going to college, strut around the neighborhood with automatic pistols jammed into their waists. Privately, many have doubts about their roles in mayhem and violence, but it is against the gang code to express doubts. Doubts are perceived as weaknesses and deficits in masculine courage. Beneath his violent gang exterior, Nathan McCall heard the voices of morality, decency, and respect for others that he learned at home and at school. He did not stop to reflect on what he had become until he landed in prison. There he listened to the inner voices and gradually fashioned a new life for himself.

While gangs have always been violent, reliable statistics indicate that there has been an escalation in gang violence in the last fifteen years.[11] Disputes that once involved fists, knives, and chains are now settled with guns. What troubles most observers is the randomness of the violence. Kids are killed for being in the wrong neighborhood, wearing the wrong colors, dating the wrong girl, or looking at someone the wrong way. Dissing a gang member or his friends by an offhand remark or appearing to look at someone too long on a bus can trigger a lethal assault. In urban ghettos, where respect is a precious commodity because so little of it exists, young people are quick to perceive slights and feel they must protect their masculinity and the image of their gang.

The quick response of retaliatory violence has led to tragic mistakes. In 1984, gang members carrying out a contract retaliatory hit over a disputed drug deal mistakenly executed former UCLA and pro football star Kermit Alexander's fifty-eight-year-old mother, his sister, and two nephews. Four years later, a gang member spotted a member from a rival gang on the street in the Westwood neighborhood of Los Angeles, near the UCLA campus, and pulled out a gun. One of the shots he fired at his rival on the crowded street went astray and killed an innocent bystander, a young woman who was strolling with a friend. Community leaders who had grown used to gang members killing each other were shocked. It was a tragic reminder that gang violence can occur any time, anywhere.[12]

The proliferation of guns, especially semiautomatics, and the quick money to be made in the crack cocaine trade have contributed to the acceleration of gang violence. In Los Angeles, Chicago, New York, and other large cities, gang wars are no longer fought over neighborhood turf but over who will control the sale and distribution of drugs. To the Black gangs, the drug trade represents a fast money scheme, similar to the scams conducted by swindling TV evangelists, avaricious Wall Street insider traders, and greedy businessmen who ripped off the savings and loan industry for billions of dollars. Gang members admire people who stretch the limits of the law and get away with it. It reinforces their belief that upstanding White folks will lie, cheat, and steal if they think they can get away with it.

Before the advent of crack cocaine, gangs like Los Angeles's Rolling-Sixties, a set within the vast Crips organization, were like a family. They hosted family picnics in the park, played football, and threw parties for the set and their guests. They spoke the Black Panther party rhetoric of Black pride, community control, and loyalty to the neighborhood. The Rolling-Sixties took their name from the numbered streets between Slauson and Florence in South-Central Los Angeles. Their turf was a prized possession, a symbol of manhood to be defended at all costs. Beginning in the early 1960s, the Rolling-Sixties were one of the first L.A. gangs to cash in on the drug scene. As the Rolling-Sixties evolved from a group of neighborhood enforcers and protectors to a well-armed, for-profit group, fighting deadly battles for control of the drug enterprise, the neighborhood deteriorated into a war zone. Innocent bystanders are now killed along with rival gang members. Different sets within the Rolling-Sixties have turned against each other. Gang factions no longer battle about turf but about who will control the lucrative drug profits. High stakes make the game more deadly and control comes out of the barrels of easily accessible guns.[13]

A Rampage of Death and Funerals

In cities like Los Angeles, where gang violence has exploded into a rampage of death and destruction, elaborate funerals for fallen gang members are a regular occurrence. Hundreds of times each year, slain comrades are laid to rest in rituals mixed with love and hate. Eulogies profess love for the martyred hero and vow retribution to the assassins. Gang colors are waved, photos are taken of gang members bending over to kiss the deceased homeboy in his coffin, and gang salutes follow the coffin to the grave site.

The funeral of Cadillac Jim, a twenty-nine-year-old, high-level Rolling-Sixties Crip, was attended by 500 mourners. He was gunned down one night outside a cheap motel in Los Angeles. Befitting his status as an O.G., with a history of more than ten years of gangsterism, Jim's body rested in a casket fringed with a sparkling blue garland, the color of the Crips. Over his open casket hung an eight-foot banner that bore his name. Young men with blue scarves hanging from their pockets bent to kiss his forehead and have their pictures taken with the fallen hero. In addition to beautiful floral sprays, his deluxe funeral included a silver hearse and four stretch limousines. One hundred vehicles followed the seventeen-mile procession to the grave. He was buried in a section of the cemetery, called Brotherly Love, reserved for the gang while gang members flashed signs and held blue bandannas over their heads. Gang members told reporters that homeboys are what they fight and die for.[14]

Gang funerals have become so numerous in cities like Los Angeles that a cottage industry has developed to meet the demand for specialized services. Some store merchants produce custom-made T-shirts with gang symbols and special messages. Photographs of the deceased appear on sweatshirts. Florists create special arrangements with gang colors. Embalmers have started using special putty to rebuild the faces and bodies of young men ripped apart by gunfire. Caterers serve barbecue for the homeboys on cemetery lawns.[15]

For some young gang members, a funeral can be a turning point. The reality of death jolts them into questioning what's happening with their lives. Fear of an early death motivates them to start searching for a way out. For others, a hero's death strengthens their resolve to stay with the set, to vow their loyalty to retaliate, even if it means their own death.

Tragedy and Death for a Young Recruit

Gang recruits are getting younger and younger. In metropolitan areas, boys as young as ten and eleven are affiliating with powerful street gangs. In the late summer of 1994, Robert Sandifer, a pint-sized, eleven-year-old member of Chicago's notorious Black Disciples gang, was apparently executed by fellow gang members for botching a killing assignment. Police claim that Robert, acting on orders from the gang's shot-callers, sprayed semiautomatic pistol fire into a group of rival gang members playing football. He wounded one boy in the hand. A stray bullet killed Shavon Dean, a fourteen-year-old girl who was standing a few yards from the front steps of her home. Shavon, who was hit in the head, had no gang affiliations. She was about to start high school in a few days. She was denied her rightful opportunity to meet the challenges of life and dispatched to an early grave because of a deadly weapon in the hands of a boy who had not yet entered his teens.[16]

According to the police, the gang hid Robert out for three days, then executed him. Police found him under a graffiti-scarred Chicago railroad viaduct with two .25-caliber bullets in the back of his skull. They believe he was killed because he knew too much about the gang's operations and wanted to turn himself in. He had brought heat on the gang by mistakenly killing Shavon Dean. His alleged executioners were two brothers, ages fourteen and sixteen, who had joined the Black Disciples gang when they were ten and eleven. The brothers, who admitted killing Robert, wore the same gang tattoos as Robert.

Robert was an abused, neglected child who sought refuge in the gang. He was taken from his mother's home at the age of three, when social workers found cigarette burns on his neck, shoulder blades, and buttocks, cord marks on his abdomen, and scars on his face. From 1986 on, he was shuffled between his grandmother's home, group homes, detention facilities, and treatment facilities. His mother was addicted to crack cocaine and, supposedly, prostitutes were working out of his grandmother's home. In his short life, Robert amassed a lengthy criminal record. He was first arrested at the age of eight for shoplifting. Subsequently, his rap sheet shows twenty-seven arrests for a range of offenses including armed robbery, property damage, stealing, and attempted assault. The gang that killed Robert was able to offer him more of a home and family than the overburdened child welfare system or his abusive mother. The real tragedy of Robert

Sandifer's case is that there are thousands of neglected and abused boys on city streets who are easy prey for gang recruiters.[17]

Protection versus Discussion

Young Black males like Robert Sandifer, who fall through the safety net of extended families and youth services and who feel locked out of mainstream society, will look for alternatives to meet their needs for safety, protection, status, support, and recognition. What the public sees as antisocial gang activities is the creation of another world. Homeboys in gangs like the Crips, Bloods, and Black Disciples know that their chances of being accepted and succeeding in mainstream society are close to nil. Members of straight society shy away from angry young Black males who are growing up in neighborhoods that are being overwhelmed by poverty, crime, and drugs. So the homeboys create their own world. It is a world in which violence is not only acceptable but mandatory to prove one's masculine worth and courage. Young people need to feel protected, heard, and acknowledged by important people in their lives. Despite the tendency of teenagers to rebel and distance themselves from adults as they struggle with issues of independence and individuality, they still need the help and support of adults to find their place in the world and keep hope alive for the future. Children and adolescents need adults to mirror a reality where they can see themselves accomplishing something worthwhile in life. No one held up that mirror for Robert Sandifer, and the alternatives he found in the hostile streets destroyed him and Shavon Dean.

Chapter 12

Neighborhood Influences on Black Masculine Development

In addition to the family and the peer group, the neighborhood where young men live exercises a strong influence on their self-identity, attitudes toward women, strategies for coping with racism, and motivation to fulfill dreams for the future.

Distressed Neighborhoods

The findings of a 1996 report prepared by the Annie E. Casey Foundation indicate that one-fourth of young Black people are growing up in distressed neighborhoods. Another quarter live in transitional neighborhoods that are starting to deteriorate because of loss of blue-collar jobs, declining housing values, and the movement of middle-class Blacks to the suburbs where there are better schools and safer streets. The loss of middle-class Blacks, who have the skills to provide political and cultural leadership, accelerates neighborhood decline.[1]

The Casey Foundation study used five indicators to define a distressed neighborhood: drugs, crime, violence, welfare, and teen pregnancies. In these neighborhoods, these negative indicators are much more prevalent than safe schools, high school graduation, and good-paying jobs. Distressed neighborhoods offer young African-American men very little in the way of constructive opportunities for mentorship, positive recognition, or part-time jobs. The possibilities to actualize dreams for economic, occupational, and social empowerment are restricted. The traditional social infrastructure—the Black church, men's clubs and fraternal orders, strong extended family networks, effective schools, and the community's old heads—that once nurtured boys into men is overwhelmed, fragmented, or nonexistent. Crime, gangs, street hustling, and the underground economy, fueled by the drug trade, have replaced established institutions as the major influences on masculine development. The breakdown of the neighborhood and its traditional institutions leaves children growing up in a social vacuum.

The Code of the Streets

In cities where large sections of urban turf are controlled by street hustlers, drugs, crime, gangs, and violence, a code of the streets defines norms of masculine behavior and governs interpersonal interactions between males. The code prescribes guidelines for conduct and how one should respond if challenged. In order to survive on the streets, all males are expected to know the rules once they venture outside. A misstep can result in a savage beating or, in the worst-case scenario, homicidal violence. According to the code, masculinity is defined in terms of toughness and a capacity for physical aggression. Humility and passivity are not respected. Young men are told by their elders and their friends to watch their backs, to fight back if anyone messes with them, and not to back down or punk out if challenged. At the heart of the code is a near pathological obsession with acquiring and maintaining respect.[2] Respect is defined as being treated right or granted the esteem one deserves. In the street culture, respect is difficult to win and easy to lose. The proper amount of respect generates status, recognition, and a sense of personal power.

Getting Respect

The street code has guidelines for both defensive and offensive conduct. The goal of defensive comportment is to carry oneself in such a
way that others are deterred from aggressive action. The basic requirement of defensive self-presentation is to send subtle but unmistakable
signals to others that you can take care of yourself and that you are
capable of violence if the situation demands it.

In order to gain enough respect to deter violence, the young man
must have the right look. Stylish clothes and jewelry are important
components of the right look. Wearing fashionable sneakers, jackets,
and sweat suits signals that the person is hip and not afraid to display
things that might require defending. Conversely, if the young man
avoids wearing expensive clothes and sneakers, he may be sending a
message that he is afraid of being attacked or robbed. Messages of fear
suggest that one is weak and can be moved on or dissed without fear
of retaliation. A young man who by his physical presence looks capable of taking care of himself may not have to campaign actively for status and self-respect; others will defer to him because they know he is
capable of violence. If someone attempts to take his possessions or
money, or abuses a member of his family, he will have to retaliate to
maintain his status in the streets. There are no guarantees against challenges. There is always someone around looking to build up his respect by taking on someone with a reputation.

The offensive quest for respect on the streets is guided by an
aggressive, go-for-bad style; those actively campaigning for respect either
forcibly take the possessions of others or violate their honor. Taking
someone's jacket or gold chain symbolizes arrogant strength. Getting
in someone's face, or dissing him with derogatory remarks about his
mother or girlfriend, shows that the young man is not afraid to take
bold, provocative actions. In the streets, manhood means being able to
take aggressive action against another man, like throwing the first
punch in a fight or pulling out a gun.

Targets of provocative aggressive action tend to react in one of two
ways: They either back down or they retaliate. In the first instance,
aggressive action can create an image that the Brother is not to be
messed with; he is a bad dude, no doubt about it. Others quickly back
down and show proper deference. Aggressive behavior fits the old saying that the best defense is a good offense. Few people are willing to
challenge a young Black man who is known as one of the baddest

Brothers in the hood. A second possible consequence of aggressive action is that it leaves one open to retaliation, sometimes when least expected. Members of a rival gang lay in wait for Monster Kody Scott and pumped six bullets into him. Fortunately for Monster Kody, he survived. Other ghetto bad men like Cadillac Jim, who was gunned down in front of an L.A. motel, and hundreds of other victims of Black-on-Black pay-back violence have not been as lucky.

What inner-city Brothers refer to as "nerve" is a central component of ghetto manhood and respect. True nerve means a willingness to risk death to maintain one's respect. Middle-class White people outside the ghetto feel they can ignore slights, but hard-core, street-oriented Black youths are required by the code to defend their honor. Many young Black men believe that death is preferable to being dissed by others. The most fearsome Brothers in the hood are those who are not afraid to die. When others know that a young man is not afraid to die, it gives him a real sense of power on the street. His manner conveys a message that nothing scares or intimidates him.

An Oppositional Culture

According to Elijah Anderson, an African-American professor of sociology at the University of Pennsylvania, the code of the streets and its obsession with respect and tough masculinity is part of an oppositional culture that has developed in America's inner cities. Anderson is a street sociologist of the old school. Rather than analyzing behavior with elaborate statistical tools, he relies on the ethnographic methods of listening and observing. His classic book on the Black ghetto, *A Place on the Corner* (1978), was based on three years of observations and listening at Jelly's Bar and Liquor Store in Chicago. In 1992, he published *Streetwise,* a book about the emergence of go-for-bad Brothers as heroes and role models in two Philadelphia neighborhoods.

Anderson contends that ghetto men, frustrated by poverty, racism, lack of decent-paying jobs, and the fallout from drug traffic, have organized their identity around an oppositional culture. Pervasive despair, hopelessness, and alienation from mainstream society have spawned the code of the streets with its own norms for masculinity and respect. Since most young inner-city Black men feel they have little opportunity to gain respect, recognition, and power in the larger society, they have created their own rules to convey respect and status. People outside the inner city find it difficult to understand why ghetto youths can't just walk away from the wrong kind of stare or minor insults. For the ghetto Brothers, manhood is a precious commodity that cannot be achieved through high-paying jobs, civic accomplishments, or academic pursuits. They have no investment in the goals of conventional society, and conventional society has no investment in them.

For many inner-city males, respect and masculinity are part of a zero-sum game. Since conventional channels of respect are sealed off, there is only a limited amount of respect available; therefore, respect can only be achieved by taking it from someone else and then being prepared to defend it with one's life if necessary. Profound lack of faith in the police has contributed to the oppositional culture and its obsession with respect. Since people in the ghetto feel the police either cannot or will not protect them and their loved ones, they must be prepared to defend themselves and, by their demeanor, discourage others from trying to move on them.

Everybody is expected to know the rules in order to negotiate the inner-city's mean streets. If a victim of a mugging or a robbery responds in the wrong way, by staring too long, for instance, the perpetrator may feel justified in killing him. When this happens, people in the community shrug their shoulders and say the victim should have known better, since everybody has an opportunity to learn the rules.

Young men who don't subscribe to the code of the streets—and, according to Anderson, many don't—are referred to in the streets as decent people. Decent people still have an investment in conventional society. They are usually preparing for a better future by working and going to school. Yet, if challenged, decent youths must be prepared to respond by defending themselves or talking their way out of a potentially violent situation. In the midst of the anger, despair, and frustration that is part of ghetto life, violence can erupt at any time and claim decent youths as its victims.

Case Example

Sixteen-year-old Rashad King would certainly qualify as a decent young man by the code of the streets. He was one of the best and the brightest. An honors student who liked basketball, girls, and fun, he was not into drugs, gangs, or crime. His room was filled with athletic trophies and school awards. Rashad's high school principal described him as a young man of decency and promise who was definitely on his way to college. Rashad wanted to become an attorney. On Easter Sunday night in April 1994, Rashad was killed on a subway platform in Brooklyn, New York. He was on his way home from an outing to Coney Island and trying to make his midnight curfew. Police said there had been a stare-down and some verbal sparring with two other young Black men in a subway car. The argument spilled over onto the platform when the youths left the train. Rashad had started to run when three shots were fired. One bullet struck him in the lower back and killed him. He was pronounced dead at 12:30 A.M., thirty minutes past his mother's curfew.

Because deaths of young men are so common in the projects where Rashad lived, mothers have developed an informal death ritual. When mothers who have not lost a child meet the eyes of mothers who have, they make a silent promise to pray. Rashad's best friend says it's hard to figure out how to handle interactions on the street. He doesn't want to get violent, but on the other hand, limits have to be placed on people who behave in a threatening manner.[3]

An Epidemic of Death, Violence, and Fear

In neighborhood streets ruled by gangs, drugs, crime, and the masculine code, violence has reached epidemic proportions. FBI crime statistics indicated that the number of young people under the age of eighteen arrested for violent crime rose 42 percent between 1988 and 1992; young Blacks were arrested for violent crime at five times the rate of Whites.[4] A study conducted by the National Crime Analysis Project at Northeastern University found that the number of seventeen-year-olds arrested for murder climbed 121 percent between 1985 and 1991, and the number of sixteen-year-olds arrested for murder rose 158 percent. The biggest increase in murder arrests was for fifteen-year-olds: 217 percent.[5] The victims of teen murders are, disproportionately, Black youth. According to the 1996 edition of *The State of Black America*, published annually by the National Urban League, the leading cause of death of young Black men between the ages of fifteen and thirty-four is homicide, and Black youths are victims of homicide at a rate six times that of White youths.[6]

A national telephone poll of teenagers conducted by CBS News and the *New York Times* in 1994 reinforces the repeated finding that

Black teenagers are more likely than Whites to be victims of crime and violence. Seventy percent of Black teenagers responding to the poll knew someone who had been shot in the past five years, compared to 31 percent of White respondents; 37 percent of Black teenagers compared to 19 percent of Whites said violence was a big problem where they attended school.[7] Although the numbers involving Blacks and violent crimes leveled off in 1993 and 1994 and dropped slightly in 1995, the numbers remain astronomically high, particularly for Black males.[8]

The Personal Face of Violence

In conversations with social workers, teachers, child psychologists, and reporters, young people put a personal face on the violence surrounding them. Death and mortality from gunfire and violent assaults are frighteningly real and have invaded the psyche of today's youth. In interviews with Ron Harris, a reporter for the *Los Angeles Times,* students at predominantly Black Washington High School in South-Central Los Angeles expressed concerns about being assaulted at parties, after school, while visiting friends, or just walking down the street in their own neighborhoods. Every one of a hundred students expressed a fear of being shot. Almost all of the students knew of someone under eighteen who had been shot, stabbed, or assaulted. In three randomly selected classrooms, one-third of the students told Harris that they had been shot, shot at, or caught in gang gunfire. A seventeen-year-old boy was standing outside a school when a car drove by and started shooting. Another was shot in the hip while walking in the park. A car drove by and started shooting; he tried to run, but the gang members chased him down. Another was caught in a gang cross fire while visiting a friend.[9]

Youngsters tell stories, draw pictures, and write essays about violence and death. In an elementary school in Laurel, Maryland, a suburb outside Washington, D.C., a young girl telling the class about her most memorable experience talked about a man coming into her home when she and her older sister were having breakfast. The man pointed a gun at her sister's head and said he would blow her brains out. The child had to be comforted by her teacher when telling the story.[10] Young people write essays about what their funerals will be like, who will cry, what the preacher will say, and who will read the eulogies explaining why they had to die and leave so young. Kids draw pictures of drop-down drills they practice at home when the sounds of bullets rip through the night. Boys who are barely out of puberty serve as pallbearers for friends killed by gunfire. In many communities, when a young man is killed, his name is added to the graffiti murals in vacant lots.[11]

What has surprised many observers is the extent to which worries about death and violence have intruded into the suburbs and smaller cities. In St. Paul, Minnesota, a teacher was shocked when a number of her students raised their hands in response to a question inquiring whether they knew a neighbor, relative, classmate, or friend who had been shot. At the high school in Laurel, of twenty-six tenth-grade students in one class, sixteen knew a person under the age of nineteen who had been killed and thirteen knew of someone who had been knifed. The victims were friends, cousins, neighbors, or friends of their sisters and brothers.[12]

Childhood vanishes quickly for inner-city kids who have little time to savor its joys before they start worrying about violent death and physical injury. It is difficult for young men to concentrate on learning when they are terrorized by such fears. Schools surrounded by high fences with metal detectors at entrances and policemen patrolling the hallways look more like prisons than sanctuaries of learning. Many kids consider the day a victory if they make it safely from home to school in the morning and back home again after school.

The paradox surrounding young people's preoccupation with fears of violence is that the source of violence, namely, other young people, is also the source of their greatest support. Most young people turn to other teenagers for companionship, empathy, and solace. Teenagers as a group are closer to their peers than they are to adults, yet most teens feel other teenagers are far more likely than adults to commit crimes against them.[13]

Coping with Violence and Death

Young men encircled by violence that can erupt at any time struggle just to survive; death is a monster that can become real at any time. To cope with the constant anxiety caused by the unpredictability and randomness of violence, kids have adopted a variety of coping strategies. Avoidance, danger seeking, aggressive behavior, joining gangs, staying focused on goals, and pursuing the easy money in the drug trade are some of the different ways of coping that teachers, parents, child psychologists, youth workers, and probation officers have observed.

Some youths use strategies based on a combination of caution, vigilance, observation, and avoidance. At L.A.'s Washington High School, students avoid wearing certain colors or expensive items of dress that might draw the attention of gang members and provoke an attack. They avoid catching the bus at a certain corner near the school where there have been drive-by shootings; instead, they walk to another bus stop three blocks away where they think it is safer. Before going to a party, many kids find out who is going to be there, whether the parents going to chaperone, and who might crash the party. There are no exact rules for handling approach/avoidance dilemmas. For example, a boy walking down the street sees some teenage boys standing together or walking his way. His fear level rises because he doesn't know them. What should he do? Should he cross the street to avoid them? Does he keep walking toward them? Should he speak to them? Any action he takes could be interpreted as a sign of disrespect. Kids say that no matter how careful they are, sometimes fights cannot be avoided. They run into people who want to fight because they are trying to establish a go-for-bad reputation.[14]

Anxiety about safety and avoiding danger makes some kids withdraw and isolate themselves. Fear takes over their lives and restricts their movements and activities. Ironically, some kids would rather be in juvenile detention facilities than out on the danger-filled streets. They feel safer in a protected, highly structured environment. After a drive-by shooting that occurred in his neighborhood while he was in a juvenile detention facility, a Black teenager told his counselor he was glad he was locked up because he could have been killed in the shooting.

Some young Black men engage in the opposite of avoidance behavior. They employ what psychologists call "counterphobic behavior." Rather than avoid danger, they throw caution to the wind and seek out danger, living a life characterized by high-risk behavior. In some communities young African-American males play a death-defying game called "chicken": They drive fifty miles an hour going the wrong way down a one-way street. In economically distressed Black neighborhoods of Newark, New Jersey, part of the rites of passage for Black male teenagers is stunt-driving stolen cars. Kids return to the neighborhood in stolen cars late on summer nights and perform high-speed turns, circles called "doughnuts," and sharp twists that leave a trail of skid marks on the streets. High-risk behavior like stunt driving can lead to fatal results. A teenager riding in a stolen car with his friends pointed an unloaded gun at two off-duty police officers. They identified themselves as policemen but the teenager continued to point the gun; the officers fired and killed one young man. As the car sped away, the officer fired again and killed another. All the participants were Black.[15]

When adolescents live with a constant fear of death, they may feel that they can conquer the fear by challenging death. High-risk sexual behavior and drug abuse may also be related to the constant preoccupation with death. Why put off sex and drugs if one is going to lead a short life? Unplanned pregnancies are a way of leaving something behind in the world. Why fear sexually transmitted diseases, AIDS, or drug addiction if life can be snuffed out at any time? In an atmosphere of daring and defiance of danger, sex gets disconnected from love. Sex is part of reckless fun seeking rather than a meaningful commitment between two people. Unconsciously, death-defying behavior may be part of what psychologists call "the adolescent fable."[16] Adolescents can objectively understand the consequences of danger-seeking behavior, but because they feel they are special and unique, disastrous outcomes will not befall them. A boy consciously knows that high-speed twists and turns in a car are dangerous, but he believes he is blessed with a special immortality that gives him personal immunity from death and injury. Another boy repeatedly plays Russian roulette. Logically, he knows the odds will eventually catch up with him, but he feels his uniqueness will protect him.

Some youths try to protect themselves from fears and intimidation by becoming aggressive bullies. They harass weaker kids, take their clothes, jewelry, and expensive sneakers, shake them down for lunch money, steal their pets, and won't let them enter certain apartment buildings. In his autobiography, *Black Boy,* Richard Wright described the abuse he suffered both from his father and from southern racists while he was growing up in Mississippi in the early part of the century.[17] Full of anger and hatred, he burned a cat. Burning the cat symbolized how abused creatures often identify with the aggressor and find weaker creatures to vent their hostility on. In today's inner cities, abuse is passed down. Stronger boys pick on the weaker ones, who, in turn, look for more fragile kids to take advantage of.

Youths who have been threatened, shot at, beaten up, shaken down, or robbed frequently get weapons to protect themselves. Guns are easy to purchase on the streets in urban neighborhoods. However, possessing a gun for self-protection in the urban killing fields can lead to tragic results. Will Wright, an African-American college-bound student in Los

Angeles, bought a gun to protect himself. He had been harassed by gang members in his Dorsey High School neighborhood. Somehow, he ended up in a game of Russian roulette and shot himself with his own gun. Will had everything going for him. He was smart, likable, a good student, and a varsity athlete in baseball, and he had strong emotional support from two loving parents. Yet he ended up becoming a statistic of teenage gunfire; a gun he had bought for protection destroyed him.[18]

Case Example I: Shaul Linyear

After he had been robbed twice at gunpoint, fifteen-year-old Shaul Linyear bought a .22-caliber gun on the streets for protection in his Crown Heights, Brooklyn, neighborhood. Violence was all around him there. As a teenager, he started hanging out with friends in the streets, cutting school, and defying his mother's authority. His lawbreaking behavior progressed from taking neck chains from other kids to robbing deliverymen and people walking home from work. As time went on, he fell for a girl who liked expensive things. He used some of the money from his robberies to buy gifts for her and fashionable clothes for himself. Shaul and his friends say that girls in their neighborhood won't look at a boy unless he has money and wears stylish clothes. Shaul shot a man during a robbery and got away with the man's gun. Later, he used the stolen gun in a holdup of two deliverymen, one of whom Shaul shot and killed. The fatal robbery occurred outside a police precinct station, and Shaul was quickly apprehended. Asked why he pulled a robbery so close to a police station, Shaul said he didn't think he would get caught.

Shaul pleaded guilty to murder and robbery and was sentenced to seven years to life. The man he killed left behind a widow and four children. Shaul's mother, who is a single parent of four children herself, is relieved that Shaul is in a prison for young offenders: He is off the streets and he will have adult supervision and the kind of day-to-day structure that she could not provide as a single mother working full time and going to school.[19]

In neighborhoods where gangs and violence are facts of life, many teenagers cope with their fears by joining a gang for protection and kinship. They hope that by joining a gang they won't become victims of a gang. In impoverished Black neighborhoods on Chicago's South and West Sides, young people tell reporters that because gangs control the turf, people can't go where they want or walk down the streets without permission from the gangs. Safety in the hood is about being part of a group. Since the gang offers protection and backup, it is easy to acquiesce and become affiliated. The kids don't like the possibility of being wounded or killed in the inevitable gang violence or going to jail, but it's a trade-off. Children have needs for protection and safety. The police and their families can't protect them, so they join existing gangs or create their own crews and posses.[20]

Some teenagers try to stay focused on future goals despite their doubts and fears. They write essays showing that hope and motivation are still alive regardless of the dreariness and dangers of their surroundings. One boy writes that although crime and drugs are everywhere we must strengthen our hearts and face the problems. Another writes that he and other Black people need more racial pride to overcome hate, racism, violence, and other problems.[21]

Case Example II: Cedric Jennings

Sixteen-year-old Cedric Jennings, a junior at Ballou High School in Washington, D.C.'s, inner city, had his heart set on attending Massachusetts Institute of Technology. He struggled to learn in a high school where failure occurs much more often than success. In September 1993, 836 sophomores were enrolled; by Thanksgiving, 172 were gone. The expectation was that by the time they were seniors, the graduating class would probably be down to less than 250 students. Kids dropped out or disappeared because of deadly shootings, drugs, jail, or unplanned pregnancies, or they simply stopped coming. Gangs and bullies ruled the school, which is surrounded by housing projects and deteriorating buildings. Only a few students have hope for the future.

Cedric gets an early start every morning and doesn't leave school until after dark. He's in the computer lab by 7:15 A.M., long before classes start. He spends his spare time in the chemistry lab where he meets regularly with his mentor. At Ballou, where failure is the rule, Cedric is ridiculed by his classmates, especially male students, for working hard to succeed academically. He has been pushed around, beaten up, and called a nerd. One boy threatened to shoot him. To be accepted in the school culture, most bright males deliberately make C's and D's. It is not cool to make A's or B's or to take advanced courses. Being a good student is perceived as trying to be like the White man, and trying to get ahead in the

White man's world as showing disrespect for Black folks. Teachers call it the crab bucket syndrome: When one student tries to get out, the others pull him down.

Cedric soldiers on, despite being the object of derision. He has strong support from his mother (his father is in prison) and the Black church he attends.

The reason more young African-American males like Cedric fail to move ahead is not because they lack the ability. Without support from overstressed parents and teachers, they succumb to a peer culture of failure, gangs, and acting cool. They become disillusioned before they can establish a solid academic foundation.[22]

In violent, crime-ridden, inner-city neighborhoods, few opportunities exist for constructive mentorship, for achieving recognition and status, or for legitimate jobs. The largest economy is the drug trade, which is usually controlled by gangs, hustlers, and operatives of major drug traffickers. It is difficult to resist the lure of easy money. Youths who a generation ago would have been working as bag boys, store clerks, and stock boys are now hustling drugs. There are no supermarkets, auto parts shops, or department stores to hire young men. In some urban areas, the unemployment rate of African-American youths runs as high as 75 percent.

The heroes on the streets for young boys are often older youths and young adults with money, fashionable clothes, attractive women, and fancy cars acquired with money made in the drug trade. In communities like Harlem and Chicago's South Side, it is easy to get hooked up to the drug trade. Everyone knows who the main dealers are. Street dealers, called "scramblers," use teenagers and kids fresh out of grade school to do a variety of jobs. They can make $600 a week and more by serving as lookouts, carrying drugs from one place to another in bookbags, and hiding drugs, and gradually work their way up to street sales. The money, status, and girls make kids feel like somebody, that they have some power and control over their lives. Money and guns are shields they can use to insulate themselves from attack. With money, they can buy protection; with a gun, they can defend themselves.

Some community elders have mixed feelings about drugs. On the one hand, they can see how crack cocaine has devastated the community and increased the deadly violence between rival groups battling for control. On the other hand, the drug traffickers are their sons, nephews, boyfriends, cousins, and friends, who bring home money to pay the electric bill, buy groceries, catch up on the rent, and purchase school clothes for younger children.[23]

The Power of Positive Neighborhood Influences

In contrast to today's distressed inner-city Black neighborhoods, the West Adams district of Los Angeles, where Johnnie Cochran, O. J. Simpson's lead attorney, grew up in the 1940s and 1950s, was a thriving middle-class Black community with a strong social infrastructure. At the center of the community was a network of Black churches that conducted outreach programs ranging from preschool centers to programs for senior citizens. Alumni chapters of the Kappa Alpha Psi and Alpha Phi Alpha fraternities supported athletic teams, raised scholarship funds, and encouraged young Black men to set high goals. Women's organizations like Jack and Jill and the Links sponsored coming-out balls, cotillions, and oratory contests; they also raised money for scholarships and encouraged young people to participate in community service activities. The nucleus of Black civic organizations—composed of fraternal organizations, sorority alumnae chapters, churches, social clubs, and the Men of Tomorrow, a Black professional group made up predominantly of World War II veterans—became a powerful voice in Los Angeles politics. Indeed, this civic/political group was instrumental in helping to elect Tom Bradley as the first Black mayor of Los Angeles. In the West Adams neighborhood of the 1940s and '50s, the streets were controlled by the residents and the police, not gangs, drugs, and criminals.

Under the tutelage of the churches, fraternal orders, and civic organizations and backed up by strong extended families, many young men were ushered into the responsibilities of manhood with a rich awareness of the African-American heritage. A steady stream of young Black men attended Southern California colleges, including UCLA, the University of Southern California, Loyola, Pepperdine, Los Angeles State College, and Los Angeles City College. Some others went to Black colleges in the South where their parents had matriculated.

A number of young African-American males who were nurtured by the West Adams social infrastructure became attorneys, medical doctors, ministers, social workers, educators, civil service workers, government administrators, and police officers. Johnnie Cochran and the late Sam Williams are two of the outstanding products of the guidance provided by West Adams institutions.

Johnnie Cochran, whose father was a star salesman for Golden State Mutual, a Black-owned life insurance company, has lived in the West Adams district most of his life. After graduating from UCLA, he attended law school at Loyola University in Los Angeles. Even before he became nationally and internationally famous for his leadership of "the Dream Team" in the controversial Simpson murder trial, Cochran was regarded as one of California's outstanding trial lawyers.

While a police officer, Tom Bradley became a mentor and father figure for Sam Williams. Bradley started working with Sam Williams as a coach when Sam played in the playground football leagues sponsored by the Los Angeles Police Department. After a stellar high school football career in Los Angeles, Sam played football for the University of California, Berkeley, on an athletic scholarship and then attended law school at the University of Southern California. As an attorney, Sam was an integral part of the political nucleus that elected Tom Bradley four times as mayor of Los Angeles. During his career, Sam was a corporate attorney and an official with the California State Bar Association.

Violence and Gangs Spill Over into Middle-Class Neighborhoods

What worries many parents in today's middle-class Black neighborhoods is the creeping spread of the code of the streets and gangster styles among their children. In cities like Los Angeles, where gangs are omnipresent, young Black men from affluent families are coming under their sway. The excitement, adventure, and macho image of gang life and go-for-bad street behavior exude a seductive aura. In many metropolitan areas, the street Brothers have a following of beautiful girls and a reputation for live parties and throw-down dances. Gangsters and go-for-bad Brothers are glorified in movies and rap videos as the real thing—the truly authentic, down Brothers who are tougher than life. The media say to Black kids that this is the way to be. It is difficult for many young Brothers from stable middle-class families to resist the lure of the steady bombardment of exciting video images and singsong rhymes of gangsta rap music. As aspiring gang wannabes, these kids reject their middle-class status, discount their parents' advice, and identify with the grittier aspects of underclass life on the streets. For middle-class Black youths, emulating gang fashions and behaviors is a way of proving their masculinity, achieving notoriety, and gaining respect as a bad dude.[24]

The conversion from the middle-class values instilled by one's parents to a gangster lifestyle doesn't happen all at once. The transition begins in small, barely discernible steps and progresses as the young man edges closer to the danger zone of thefts, robberies, assaults, and excessive drug use. If the progression continues, kids can end up deeply entrenched in a full-blown gangster and macho identity. Guns replace fists and knives in fights, armed robberies turn deadly, and disputes are settled with shootings.

The first stage consists of harmless attempts to imitate the gangster look, language, and demeanor. Kids affect the pose of street life, dress like gang members, and try to emulate the walk and the talk. They sprinkle their conversation with terms from gangster rap music. Baseball caps turned inside out, saggy pants, baggy flannel shirts, and sweatshirts become part of their dress style. Teenagers call it "dangerous dressing"; they adopt the gangster look, but not the gangster life. Kids hold hip-hop dance contests and stage competitive rap contests to see who can come up with the hippest raps. For most teenagers, adopting the gangster, hip-hop look is part of normal adolescent rebellion. Teenagers have always used clothing, music, and in-group terminology to rebel against adult control and express individuality. Since adolescents don't have real power, one way they can express power is by clothes, talk, and cool poses.[25]

In the second stage of the transition kids begin to spend more time hanging out and cruising. Peer group culture now exists in a space somewhere between youthful pranks and drive-by shootings. They engage in vandalism, spraying graffiti, and fistfights. Preppy gangs and wannabes call themselves "crews" or "posses." The danger of preppy gangs is that hanging out can become addictive, and fistfights and minor lawbreaking can escalate into shootings, drug sales, and robberies. Experts say that preppy gangs and posses are stepping over the line and are becoming increasingly violent.[26]

Case Example: Salmon Daniels

In Los Angeles, eighteen-year-old Salmon Paul Daniels, Jr., son of a prominent Black physician, was a member of a preppy wannabe gang called "the Sex Pistols." He told his father it was a dance group of guys who enjoyed parties, looking for girls, acting crazy, and hanging out. Unbeknownst to his father, the Sex Pistols were stealing, vandalizing, fighting, and dealing a few drugs. Salmon was busted in a high school drug sting. Although he was not allowed to graduate on the stage with his class, he received his diploma. The Sex Pistols vandalized a Los Angeles Transit bus, with damages totaling $10,000. They invaded shopping malls and engaged in group thefts from department stores using the mass attack technique called "racking." A week before he was to leave for college, in August 1992, Salmon was killed by a rival preppy gang called "the Mobsters." Apparently, he had argued with some boys from this gang earlier on the day he was killed. Later that fateful Sunday, when he was with a date at Venice Beach in Los Angeles, he was attacked by fifteen to twenty-five members of the Mobsters. Salmon tried to run, but the group pursued him. Witnesses told police that he was caught, dragged down, and beaten. One of his attackers pulled out a gun and shot him.[27]

The final step in the progression from middle-class values to gang life involves teenagers who start running with established gangs. Hanging out becomes addictive to the point that youths pursue ever more intense highs of excitement, danger, and thrills.

Case Example: Che Avery

Che Avery, a Los Angeles Black teenager, led a double life. In the daytime, he attended school and worked. At night and on weekends, he hung out with one of Los Angeles's most violent gangs, the Rolling-Sixties Crips. Before he was arrested and sentenced to jail, pleading guilty to nine counts of felonious armed robbery, Che's life showed every sign of promise. He was an ideal son. He had a B+ grade average, was well liked by his friends and teachers, and never gave his parents any trouble. He was accepted at two high-ranking universities, UCLA and Berkeley. But behind the backs of his hardworking parents, Che was changing from a model youth into one completely identified with hardened gangsters.

Che started his descent into gang life by associating with a preppy group called the Scandals. They mainly hung out, went to parties, and loitered around movie theaters and hamburger stands looking for girls. Their worst indiscretions, according to Che, were a few excessive drinking episodes. At Beverly Hills High School, a predominantly White upper-middle-class school that

Che attended on a special integration transfer, he adopted the gangster look, wearing baggy clothes and a bandanna. The upper-middle-class White kids at the school looked up to him because they thought he was the real thing, one of the authentic gangsters they idealized in gangster rap videos and movies. Che wasn't really into gangbanging, but it gave him something to prove, an image to look up to.

Next, he started hanging out with a group called the DGFs, short for Don't Give a Fuck. The DGFs were more of a posse than a gang; they didn't sell drugs or engage in gangbanging. They stole a few things, partied, and chased girls. Hanging out with the DGFs only whetted Che's appetite for more excitement and thrills. He found himself admiring members of the Rolling-Sixties. They were tough, macho, had a following of pretty girls, and were not afraid of illegal activities, danger, or death. Soon, Che was running with the Sixties, robbing and fighting. He enjoyed the intense highs from the danger and adventure. The death of gang peers from gunfire and shootings cemented Che's identity with the Sixties. On weekend nights, he was out stealing jewelry and jackets with a .22-caliber revolver. He enjoyed the satisfaction of seeing people scared. Busted for robbery in March 1991, he spent seven months in jail before pleading guilty to armed robbery.[28]

The descent of Che Avery is a chilling example of what can go wrong when young men of talent and promise get caught up in the fast life of the streets. The struggle of middle-class teenagers to demonstrate their Blackness and their manhood can thwart the most diligent efforts of families to keep their children out of harm's way. For parents, the dilemma is how closely they should supervise their children. Do they raise their kids in a hothouse and shield them from experiences they will need to survive? Or do they give teenagers some leeway to discover the adventures and excitement of the streets, hoping that they will not engage in destructive behavior? In searching for the true definition of Black masculinity, many privileged Black teenagers reject the upwardly mobile advice provided by their parents. They feel the only valid version of Blackness and masculinity comes from the oppositional culture with its code of the streets and tough arrogance. Rebellious teenagers, under pressure from peers and the temptations of adventure, often feel they have something to prove to everyone except the right people.[29]

Part

Part

V

INTERVENTIONS,

RECOMMENDATIONS,

AND CONCLUSIONS

Chapter 13

Fatherhood, Manhood Training, and Education

Discussions, debates, initiatives, and interventions are now going on in the Black community that show promise of changing the conditions of Black males from being controlled by external forces to empowering them with the personal and institutional resources to understand, act on, and control their own environments. Men's clubs, fraternal orders, educators, ministers, psychologists, ex-gang members, and former prison inmates have been reassessing and redefining the meaning of masculinity, exploring ways to facilitate positive masculine development in young people, disseminating information designed to assist Black males, and recommending public policy.

A number of commissions, organizations, conferences, and research centers have sponsored events to provide leadership for what is becoming a Black men's movement aimed at understanding and solving the complexities and pitfalls Black men living in America must cope with.

Black Men Mobilize for Action

In 1990, the psychologist Richard Majors, author of the widely read book about the psychological styles of Black men, *Cool Pose,* and a colleague, Jacob Gordon, founded the National Council of African-American Men (NCAAM), an umbrella organization to coordinate the search for long-term solutions and monitor the activities of the many groups that work on behalf of Black males. NCAAM is a nonprofit organization whose primary goal is to expedite policy changes at the national, state, and local levels that will enable Black males to take advantage of a wide range of educational, occupational, and economic opportunities. In addition to coalition building, advocacy, and self-help initiatives, NCAAM sponsors workshops on manhood training, family responsibility, and how to take charge of one's life. NCAAM developed the *Journal of African-American Male Studies,* the first academic journal devoted exclusively to the affairs of African-American men; and the Council plans to publish an *Annual State of the Black Male* booklet that will review information on poverty, education, law enforcement, employment, medical treatment, and social policy and prevention from a Black male perspective. NCAAM also has a youth affairs division committed to mentorship and guidance for young men.[1]

Another national organization that is working to change the adverse conditions confronting Black males is a group called 100 Black Men of America. Founded in New York City in 1967, following the urban race riots, this group of concerned businessmen, educators, religious leaders, government administrators, and other professionals provides leadership and programs in mentoring, housing, education, economic development, employment, and health care in sixty-eight chapters across the country. 100 Black Men has gained national recognition for its programs to help young African-American men focus on long-term goals and stay clear of drugs and violence. Also, Black educators and social scientists have developed research centers at Morgan State University in Baltimore and at Morehouse College in Atlanta, both predominantly Black institutions. Spurred on by Black elected officials, state legislatures in California, Illinois, Maryland, and Ohio have created commissions to study the conditions of Black males and make recommendations for changes in policy and for programmatic interventions in education, housing, health care, law enforcement, criminal justice, and employment.

The Congressional Black Caucus initiated the 21st Century Commission on African-American males in an effort to bring together corporate leaders, educators, elected officials, and community leaders to recommend solutions to the critical problems that Black males encounter. Finally, the Urban Institute in Washington, D.C., is studying policy regulations with reference to five areas of concern to Black males: teenage parenting, high school dropouts, female-headed/welfare-dependent families, unemployment, and crime and drugs.

At the core of the fledgling Black men's movement are several key programmatic interventions: returning fathers to a place in the family, manhood training and mentoring, educational interventions, special programs for high-risk young people, prison and drug rehabilitation, and an appeal to include aging gang members and ordinary blue-collar men in outreach programs. Black churches are, once again, being called upon to step into the arena and provide leadership, resources, and program implementation. In this chapter we discuss the first three concerns in some depth.

Reestablishing Fatherhood

In many inner-city Black communities, more than half of the babies are born to unwed mothers and 70 percent of children grow up without a biological father in the household. In Cleveland, Charles Ballard, a fifty-seven-year-old Black social worker, is trying to teach teenage fathers to be responsible parents and adults. At the National Institute for Responsible Fatherhood, which Ballard founded, he recruits blue-collar workers, businessmen, and professional men from the community to work with young fathers as counselors and mentors. The National Institute for Responsible Fatherhood grew out of A Teen Father Program, which Ballard created in 1982. Graduates of the fatherhood program are trained to become role models and peer counselors in turn for young men entering the fatherhood program.[2]

Ballard's program has turned around more than 2,000 young fathers. His goals for young men entering the program are clearly stated. They are expected to legitimize their child or children, be in school or in a prep class to complete the high school equivalency exam, find a job, no matter how menial, and learn to handle work and financial responsibility. Young men work closely with other young men who have become successful fathers and family members. They learn how to feed and diaper babies, how to schedule their time, communicate with their mates, and make family decisions. The program is run in a family atmosphere. Counseling is available twenty-four hours a day and often takes place on street corners and basketball courts. Ballard has found that many young men are highly motivated to become good fathers. They are fed up with the violence around them and want their children to have a better chance in life than they did.

Ballard himself not only talks the talk but has walked the walk. He grew up in Alabama without any adult male role models. He became a father at age seventeen, ran away to join the Army, and ended up spending time in prison. In prison, he went through a rebirth of Black consciousness and responsibility. After being released, he gained custody of his five-year-old child, went back to school, and earned a master's degree in social work and family development. As a social worker at Cleveland General Hospital, he saw all around him Black mothers and babies with no fathers and decided to do something about it. Under Ballard's leadership, the National Institute for Responsible Fatherhood is expanding into a nationwide effort. A national office has opened in Washington, D.C., and additional programs are now underway in Baltimore, Nashville, Kansas City, and Detroit. In 1990, Ballard and the Institute were awarded the Presidential Achievement Against All Odds Medallion. The White House ceremony was convened by Lewis Sullivan, director of the U.S. Office of Health and Human Services. Another successful fatherhood program calling men to higher standards of fatherhood and marriage is being conducted by the Apostolic Church of God, based in Chicago's South Side.

Many young Black men would like to become an integral part of family life but lack the means to support their families because of the high unemployment rate in the Black community. Noel Cazenave's research with employed Black letter carriers demonstrated that Black men were more likely to participate in family life as husbands and fathers if they had the financial means provided by secure employment. Providing for one's family and parenting were viewed as major male roles.[3] Inspired by the Million Man March, the Reverend John Wardlow, director of the Public Housing Authority in Hartford, Connecticut, has started a program to reunite fathers with families by providing them with jobs that pay a living wage. In what is called the Family Reunification Program, fathers who have children living in the projects, where 83 percent of the families are headed by single mothers, are offered $22 an hour to work on demolition and asbestos abatement jobs at the projects. Other incentives, such as fixed rent for six months and medical care, are included. In return, the fathers agree to take their children off welfare and move in with their children's mothers. To be eligible for the program, fathers must meet three criteria: They must have children living in the projects; they are expected to sign a pledge to strive to become good role models and participate in the children's activities; and, once employed, they must move their children off welfare. The men are required not to use drugs and to submit to regular drug testing.[4]

One of the novel features of the Hartford Family Reunification Program is that it appeals to both sides of the liberal/conservative welfare debate. It supports the liberal view that families are falling into poverty because of economic forces beyond their control. The government has a role in helping family providers obtain training and experience that will qualify them for jobs that pay enough to support their children. The program also accepts the conservative notion that people should not be given a handout while sitting around idle. Welfare without work perpetuates dependency.

Henry Cisneros, former national director of the U.S. Office of Housing and Urban Development, saw encouraging signs in the Hartford program and thought it should be expanded to other housing projects across the country. Cisneros and other experts in family life have noticed that once inner-city young men establish a bond with their families and assume an active role in providing for and raising their children, a spiritual transformation occurs. Young men see the destruction caused by gangs and want to leave street life behind them.[5]

Returning fathers to an active role in family life is an effort that extends beyond ideological and racial lines. Governor Pete Wilson of California has declared the absence of fathers the most urgent problem in America. Governor Wilson's observations were seconded by Eleanor Holmes Norton, a Black Congresswoman representing Washington, D.C. Thirty percent of babies born to women of all races are not products of legal marriages. According to statistics compiled by David Blankenhorn, president of the National Institute of Fatherhood, 40 percent of America's children do not live in a home where their biological fathers are present. Children in homes without fathers are more prone to delinquency, teen pregnancy, dropping out of school, gang membership, and drug abuse. Even in two-parent homes, fathers' lack of involvement in their children's lives is a problem.[6]

Efforts to help men become actively involved with their children are being sponsored by an expanding group of civic and religious organizations, grassroots organizations, and corporations. Across the country, thousands of men are attending mass rallies sponsored by the evangelical Promise Keepers crusade, which urges men to recommit themselves to fatherhood and family life. Churches are offering fatherhood fellowship meetings where men can share their common concerns about fatherhood and family life. The U.S. Army, Navy, Air Force, and Marine Corps and several corporations and government agencies provide workshops on fatherhood taught by facilitators from Family University in San Diego. Family University is devoted exclusively to parenting issues, especially fatherhood. In addition to seminars, it provides an extensive list of parenting books, pamphlets, tapes, and videos.[7]

Fatherhood experts are encouraging fathers to look beyond parenting as a duty and to see it as an opportunity for growth and fulfillment. Kyle Pruett's research on fathering at Yale University indicates that men who are actively involved in rearing young children tend to be happier and more stable at home and at work. Pruett was amazed by how hands-on nurturing relationships with their children profoundly changed the lives of fathers. Many of the fathers told Pruett they had no idea how the power of their child's love and spontaneity could revitalize their lives.[8]

Manhood Training and Mentoring

Training programs for adult male roles for Black boys and young men are growing in popularity across the country. These programs are built around mentorship, symbolic and actual rites of passage, and African-American values. The belief that mentorship is an essential part of the passage from boyhood to manhood is based on the rationale that Black youths need active hands-on guidance from African-American adult males as they strive to master the challenges involved in defining their identity as men, building mutually satisfying relationships with women, constructively coping with racism, discovering adaptive possibilities in the African-American way of being, and integrating African-American and Euro-American values into a workable framework. Growing up in a complex society where they are likely to encounter economic and racial barriers that hamper their psychological and social development, Black males need to be nurtured from an early age with a core of positive developmental experiences in order to successfully carry out male responsibilities in the areas of work, education, marriage, and family.

The philosophy of contemporary manhood training programs is based on traditional African initiation rituals and rites of passage. In his classic saga *Roots*, Alex Haley describes African rites of passage training. Around the time of puberty, boys were isolated from their families for an extended period and given rigorous physical and mental training as part of a process leading to becoming recognized by the tribe as men. The training was supervised by mentors called tribal elders. Boys were taught the skills and attitudes necessary to assume the responsibilities associated with the male role in family life, fatherhood, and tribal affairs. Completion of the training was followed by a ceremony formally recognizing the boys as men, with several days of celebrating, feasting, and dancing.[9]

Remnants of rituals, rites, and ceremonies symbolizing the passage of life from one stage to another can be found in religious and cultural customs that cut across ethnic lines. Bar Mitzvahs and confirmation ceremonies symbolize the readiness of early adolescents to assume adult responsibility for their conduct and actions. Graduations symbolize the completion of a phase of academic training and readiness to enter the next stage. Marriage ceremonies symbolize the leaving of single life and consolidate the commitment to spouse and family life. Anthropologists and social psychologists believe that people in the modern urban world still need rituals and ceremonies to help them define roles and move from one stage to another of the life span.[10]

There are many Black manhood training formats, but most involve a common core of African-American history, values, and principles of living.[11] Guided by both individual and group mentors, most programs emphasize responsibility for self and others, wellness and bodily care, educational skills, respect for others, teamwork, problem-solving and conflict resolution skills, household management, economic and life management skills, responsibility for family and community betterment, discipline, respect for women, responsible sexual behavior, and drug prevention. Boys learn how to incorporate the African principles of spirituality, connectedness to others, harmony with nature, and collective work and responsibility into their daily lives as key factors of masculinity. They are taught that Africans were the original men of the Earth and have a long history of respect for learning and education. Boys are encouraged to identify with African pioneers in science, economics and trade, and mathematics. They are taught that men of African descent built engineering marvels like the pyramids. They could not have accomplished these significant human achievements without discipline or while high on drugs.

Through stories, fables, plays, music, and oral and written literature, young men in manhood training programs learn about the heroic African-American men who led the struggle to overcome slavery and oppression. They are exposed to the sources of power in the African-American ethos. The seven principles of *Nguzo Saba* are taught as a minimum foundation for lifelong values.

Black boys in America are surrounded by historical and contemporary images of White superiority. Exposure to African-American history, values, and principles in manhood training programs counterbalances the one-sided emphasis on White superiority and protects Black youths from feelings of inferiority that can arise from negative comparisons to a pantheon of White male competence. African-American boys need to know that people like themselves accomplished heroic deeds and made a contribution to the world.

Inner-city Black youths who are growing up in distressed neighborhoods without fathers or stable father-figure surrogates are vulnerable to adopting the tough guy, player of women images of masculinity that are projected in the streets. Manhood training, which teaches responsibility, discipline, resilience, respect for women, and positive relationships with others, gives youths an alternative to the destructive features of inner-city masculinity.

Middle-class Black youths face a double dilemma. As adolescents, they can be tempted to pursue the glitter and glamor of street life as an expression of the authentic Black masculine persona. But as they climb the mainstream success ladder as adults, they run the risk of becoming alienated from the Black community. They often end up in a no-man's-land, stuck under a racial glass ceiling occupationally and excluded from the White good-old-boys' club while, at the same time, estranged from day-to-day relationships with the Brothers. An identity firmly grounded in Black consciousness, internalized through manhood training, can provide the emotional fortitude, psychological centeredness, resilience, and resourcefulness needed to transcend the dilemma of street versus boardroom.

The goal of manhood training, according to the psychologist Nathan Hare, is to imprint on the psyche the requirements of African-

American manhood during the critical stages of preadolescence and adolescence, in order to help the boy understand that there is a difference between the biological and the social man. Biological manhood is based on physical attributes, sexuality, and the ability to reproduce the species that comes with puberty. Social manhood, in an African-American context, requires learning to be disciplined, competent, responsible, and aware of the history and ethics of Black people; it also means setting long-range goals that require persistent effort and making the commitment to uplifting oneself, family, and community.[12]

Manhood training in preadolescence is important because it is a time when boys are pulling away from the world dominated by women schoolteachers, babysitters, and mothers. Often, without the guidance of fathers or responsible adult male figures, Black boys struggle to establish an acceptable level of competence in peer relationships, sports, and other competitive activities. Many preadolescent African-American boys come under the sway of street-oriented peer pressure, which causes them to deemphasize school-oriented learning. Boys who fail to develop basic academic competencies in reading and math in the preadolescent years will find it impossible to move ahead in education or training for high-paying jobs that require technical competencies.

Adolescence is a critical time for establishing one's gender identity, internalizing values, and setting the direction for adult living. According to Erik Erikson's theory of development over the life span, each psychological stage of development builds on the previous stage. Successful resolution of the adolescent identity crisis is essential for developing reciprocal male/female intimacy, becoming a productive father, and acquiring wisdom in subsequent stages.[13]

Usually, manhood training programs consist of two hours of group meetings and two hours of individual mentorship meetings a week, extended over a period of several months. At the end of the program, a graduation ceremony certifies that the initiate has completed the training course and is ready to enter the next stage of masculine development. The graduation at Browne Junior High School in Washington, D.C., is heavily laden with African rites of passage symbolism. Boys in African dress and hats (called *kufis*) walk toward the front of the auditorium as drums sound out African rhythms. On the stage, the boys step across a symbolic threshold, which indicates their passage from boyhood to the first stages of manhood. An African Kinte cloth as an emblem of the passage is placed around each boy's shoulders by the elders—teachers and administrators dressed in African clothing. Following the ceremony, elders, parents, community people, siblings, and friends join the boys in the celebration of the passage.[14]

Courtland Lee, a professor of educational psychology at the University of Virginia and consulting psychologist for several school districts in Virginia and other states, has designed manhood training programs for African-American preadolescent and adolescent youth. The training module for both age groups uses a format of weekly individual mentorship meetings and semimonthly group sessions. The manhood training takes place over a period of thirty-six to forty weeks, approximately the length of an academic school year. Individual and group meetings are worked into the student's normal day. The manhood training is culminated by a graduation ceremony that affirms the boy's passage into the next stage of masculine challenges and demands.[15]

Group sessions in the preadolescent module stress the development of motivation and skills necessary for educational success and positive and responsible behavior. The curriculum promotes Black consciousness by emphasizing African-American culture and history. The training module for elementary school boys in grades 3 to 6 is called the Young Lions—A Gathering of Pride. The lion is respected in African culture for his strength and survival skills. In some manhood training programs, the boys are referred to as *simbas,* an African word meaning young lions.

In Lee's program, the boys examine the lives of African kings and think about what life was like for the future kings when they were boys. They review the lives of African-American men like Malcolm X, Martin Luther King, Jr., Langston Hughes, and George Washington Carver. They write essays on the meaning of the contributions of these historical figures to African-American liberation, and what can be learned by emulating famous Black men as role models. The boys think about the future and what they will be like in the twenty-first century as fathers, husbands, and wage earners. They role-play home and school problems that require nonviolent conflict resolution skills. Toward the end of the training program, the boys write out an action plan that includes goals for academic achievement and responsible behavior.

In the weekly two-hour individual mentorship sessions, the focus is on improving reading and math skills, learning to organize time to complete homework and household chores, improving social behavior, and developing self-confidence. Mentors are introduced to the boys with the title of elder. The boys are informed that in Africa and in America, men with this title are to be treated with respect. Elders are people who have accumulated much wisdom in the process of living. They can teach the boys a great deal about how to become men because they represent the same gender and ethnic group as the boys. The elders are selected from the African-American community on the basis of their commitment to young people and because of the position and respect they hold in the community.

Lee's manhood training module for adolescent boys in grades 7 to 12 is designed to strengthen the mind, body, and spirit by modeling positive Black male images, fostering responsible behavior and personal mastery, developing achievement motivation and educational success, and promoting an understanding of African-American culture and history. In these training sessions, young men discuss the challenges facing Black men in America, reflect on the meaning of masculinity from a Black male perspective, and define what constitutes a strong Black male. Music, poetry, biographies, and current events are used as catalysts for discussions. Sessions on the body focus on wellness and grooming. To strengthen the mind, participants study the lives of Black men like Arthur Ashe, James Meredith, and George Washington Carver who placed a high premium on education. Soul is defined as the unshakable spirit of Black men who fought for Black pride and glory like Jesse Owens, Jackie Robinson, Joe Louis, Jesse Jackson, and the buffalo soldiers. Responsible sexual behavior and fatherhood are primary topics. The teenagers keep a journal and end their training with an action plan that outlines educational, occupational, and personal goals and strategies to achieve their goals.

The manhood training modules for preadolescents and adolescents outlined by Lee and others can be modified to fit a variety of settings. Adults who work with young people in churches, community centers, and social service agencies, in fatherhood education and delinquency and drug prevention programs, and in Boys' Clubs, Boy Scouts, and Big Brothers programs have recognized the value of manhood training based on an African-American perspective, and they include it in their work. The programs can be augmented with field trips, films, art, holiday feasts and rituals, plays, drumming, martial arts, dance, and sports.

Groups sponsoring manhood training programs for young people have found an abundance of volunteers who want to serve as mentors and elders. Roland Gilbert, a successful real estate broker who runs a mentoring program for Black boys in an inner-city neighborhood of Oakland, California, has over 600 Black men on waiting lists to become volunteer mentors/elders. In return for a long-term commitment to work with his program, Gilbert offers the volunteers training in real estate management and sales.[16] One Hundred Black Men has enough volunteers to staff mentoring programs in over twenty-eight cities. Volunteers can usually be found in African-American churches, community agencies, fraternities and lodges, youth service centers, Black businesses, labor unions, and colleges and universities. Courtland Lee suggests six criteria for selecting volunteers: expressed commitment to helping Black youth; insight into the struggles facing Black males; understanding of the educational and social challenges confronting Black men; demonstrated success in reaching personal goals; a strong sense of personal responsibility; and a willingness to grow as an African-American male.[17]

Preliminary research by psychologists at the Urban Institute in Washington, D.C., suggests that manhood training programs conducted over a period of several months show strong signs of success. Boys who participate in these programs for an extended time display a positive self-concept, improved grades, and less involvement in drugs and delinquent behavior; they also stay in school longer.[18]

The idea of manhood training for African-American men is not limited to preadolescents and adolescents. Louis Farrakhan's Nation of Islam (NOI) offers weekly manhood training meetings at Muhammad's Mosque No. 7, in Harlem, to Black men who are not NOI members. Every Saturday morning about 200 men ranging in age from twenty to fifty gather for several hours of training at the mosque, which was once the headquarters of Malcolm X. They are a mixture of working-class men, businessmen, students, and unemployed men looking for work. The sessions are part lecture, part group therapy, part paramilitary training, and part catharsis to relieve the urban blues and burdens that all men carry. The NOI instructor teaches that Black men must be responsible and disciplined. Men are warned of the perils of gambling, adultery, drug use, lying, improper diet, and idleness. Self-respect, self-love, and self-reliance are stressed. A well-rounded man, according to NOI teachings, should respect his wife, spend time with his children, and know how to manage a household, budget his money, and balance a checkbook. NOI teachers emphasize self-improvement, community betterment, pooling economic resources, and building business enterprises. Brotherhood and proper direction and planning of life are stressed.[19]

The Nation of Islam has built a strong Black urban male membership by retrofitting men with old-fashioned values. NOI has a solid history of recruiting and helping Black men whose lives were overwhelmed by drugs and crime. Many nonmembers, while they may not accept its mysticism and harangues, especially NOI's tendency in the past to refer to all White people as devils, admire NOI's commitment to race pride, Black consciousness, empowerment, and doing for self.

The module Courtland Lee uses to instruct mentors/elders can also be used for manhood training and retraining for adults. The program begins with reflections and consciousness raising. Participants discuss excerpts from film versions of Richard Wright's *Native Son,* Lorraine Hansberry's *A Raisin in the Sun,* and Spike Lee's *Malcolm X* and scenes from the motion picture *Glory.* They analyze stereotypes of Black men and reflect on how they see themselves as fathers and husbands. The men recall their own identity struggles as adolescents and how they resolved conflicting values and choices. They look back on their own childhood and discuss the role of their fathers and other men who influenced them. Relationships with women are important components of men's lives. They explore their feelings about women as companions, mothers, and lovers, and how they manage conflict in heterosexual relationships. Finally, they examine the role of spirituality, purpose, meaning, and feelings in their lives.[20]

Educational Interventions

The Black community recognizes education as a powerful tool that can equip people to meet the challenges of life effectively. However, educational institutions in America have uniformly failed them, and frustration, failure, and underachievement are realities for legions of young Black males. In school systems across the country, Black youths start to fall noticeably behind by the third grade. From the middle of elementary school and continuing into high school, Black males lead all other groups of students in suspensions, expulsions, behavioral problems, and referrals to special classes for slow learners. In most inner-city high schools, the dropout rate for Black males is over 50 percent, and those who remain in school are four to five grades behind in reading and math.[21] Many young Black males view school as a "White thing." They resist involvement in school because they fear it will make them more like White people, whom they regard as their enemies, and will alienate them from their friends. At a time when rapidly changing industrial technology requires a highly educated work force, Black males are being left behind. For youths on the streets with no jobs and no skills, it is only a matter of time before they will be swept into the vortex of drugs, crime, and teenage fatherhood.

The major innovative educational interventions advanced by Black educators center around an Afrocentric curriculum, culturally based teaching and learning strategies, and establishing a greater male presence in schools by recruiting Black men as teachers, mentors, and tutors who can serve as role models. An Afrocentric curriculum highlights African and African-American history and culture. Contributions of ancestors in Africa and America are emphasized. Children are taught to be proud of the heroic liberation struggle Black people in America have waged against overwhelming odds. They learn how the African-American ethos permeates American culture and how American society has been influenced by African-American culture in music, dance, language, dress styles, athletics, science, medicine, agriculture, and religion.

Teaching and learning strategies in public schools, especially at the elementary school level, reflect White middle-class feminine norms. Students are expected to be quiet, passive, and emotionally controlled. Boys reared in African-American neighborhoods are likely to be highly expressive; they display style and flare, use colorful rhythmic speech, play the dozens and rap, and exhibit a considerable amount of emotional energy in their interpersonal and peer interactions. Their spontaneity and energy set the stage for conflict in the classroom between student behavior and teacher expectations, which interferes with the learning process and results in negative evaluations for Black male students.

Culturally based learning/teaching strategies, on the other hand, capitalize on the active, emotionally expressive style of the students. Using music, dance, powerful visual imagery, spontaneous recitations, story animations, and constructive raps, teachers can incorporate the natural learning style of the students and use it as a bridge to develop academic competencies. Courtland Lee has designed a teacher training module to help teachers develop learning strategies that are consonant with the cultural styles of Black boys.

Special outreach programs in Waterloo, Iowa, and in Milwaukee and New Orleans are recruiting Black men to serve as tutors and mentors in elementary schools where there is a preponderance of Black male students. Black youths in homes without fathers who attend elementary schools where there are few Black male teachers often have no direct day-to-day contact with strong African-American males they can emulate. Because Black male teachers are so uncommon in inner-city schools, school systems are starting innovative programs to rush more male minority teachers into the classrooms. Philadelphia, Milwaukee, and Seattle are hiring Black men with B.A. degrees as teaching interns and are paying their tuition while they take night classes to finish work for standard teaching credentials. Interns are required to serve three to four years in return for the tuition payments and their teaching positions.[22]

Black Male Academies

The most controversial educational innovation designed to enhance the academic competence and facilitate the masculine development of Black boys is the all-Black male educational academy. Three predominantly Black elementary schools, supervised by the Detroit Public School Board, are pioneers in the creation of these academies. Located in the midst of Detroit's urban landscape, littered with crumbling buildings, crime, drugs, and unemployment, the three schools—named after the powerful African-American heroes Marcus Garvey, Malcolm X, and Paul Robeson—appear to be flourishing. The educational cornerstone of the all-Black male academies is an Afrocentric curriculum reinforced by building self-esteem and by high expectations, strict discipline, respect and love, and parental involvement.[23]

A typical day at Detroit's Paul Robeson Academy begins with an affirming call-response chant. All 350 students, teachers, administrators, and volunteers gather for a *harambee,* an African term for coming together. A boy dressed in the school's uniform of dark trousers, a white shirt and tie with a Kinte cloth around his shoulders stands in front of the assembly and starts through a recitation of "I Am Somebody." His fellow students answer back as the boy progresses through the recitation, which includes themes of love, respect, helping others, and self-esteem. The recitation is followed by chants, poetry readings, expressions of praise by the staff for the students, and a brief meditation to help the students settle into the day and focus on concentrating during their classroom work. The *harambee* ends when the students shake hands with every teacher and guest in the receiving line.

Inside classrooms named after African countries, the students start out by reciting the meaning of the African colors: green, red, and black. Green stands for the fertility of the motherland of Africa, red stands for the blood that people of African descent have shed fighting for their freedom, and black stands for the race of African peoples around the world. After the morning rituals, the children in one second-grade class concentrate on math, science, reading, and writing speeches that they will deliver in front of the class. In their work with students, teachers express a mixture of caring, discipline, and high expectations. Students' uniforms are regularly inspected. Assignments are due on time, neatly done, with no excuses for lateness. Students are expected to speak in complete sentences and to address adults and fellow students with respect. Teachers make frequent home visits to talk with parents and students, help with homework, and play games with the children. Parental involvement is required. Parents sign a contract to supervise homework and commit several hours a month to volunteer in their child's school. Parents are graded on the level of their participation.

The combination of an Afrocentric curriculum, love, discipline, and high expectations has resulted in increased student performance, reduced disciplinary measures, and fewer behavioral problems. The three academies have outscored most other Detroit schools on statewide tests in math, reading, and science. One thousand youngsters are on the waiting list to gain admission to the schools. Boys who were on the verge of failure are now making A's and B's. Kindergarten children are reading out of first- and second-grade workbooks; first and second graders are doing algebra. One parent said that her son, who was starting to act up at home and at school, now showed a desire to learn, did his homework, and was respectful toward adults at home and at school.

The three Black male academies in Detroit encourage community participation and involvement. In accordance with the African principle that "it takes a village to raise a child," the academies have reached out to the community. The schools are overflowing with an abundance of community people, parents, university students, professional men, and blue-collar workers volunteering to mentor students, serve as teachers' aides in classrooms, tutor and supervise homework, accompany classes on field trips, and teach students about the importance of Africans and African-Americans. Young men from Michigan State University, who are affiliated with a program called Brothers Keepers, work with the kids as Big Brothers, classroom helpers, playground monitors, and lunchroom aides. At the Paul Robeson Academy, 200 men who volunteer as part of a Man-to-Man Program take students on camping trips and accompany them on cultural enrichment tours, repair broken-down neighborhood homes, and raise money. Students in the fifth and sixth grades at Malcolm X Academy frequently visit Detroit's Benjamin O. Davis Aerospace Center where they learn the fundamentals of how to fly airplanes.

The academies remain open in the evenings and on weekends for educational activities and community programs. On Saturdays, special enrichment programs, plays, musical events, speech contests, and other events are conducted. Tutoring and mentoring programs are available in the evenings and on the weekends. During the holidays, the teachers, students, parents, volunteers, and community people have a *Umoja Karamu,* an African-American unity feast celebrating Kwaanza and the seven principles of *Nguzo Saba.*

The academies have been involved in several controversies since their inception. On August 22, 1991, only four days before their opening, the American Civil Liberties Union and the National Organization for Women filed a lawsuit on behalf of three African-American women who contended that the creation of all-male academies discriminated against their daughters. Federal Judge George Woods granted an injunction on August 31, 1991, and ordered the Detroit Public School Board to find a compromise that would not discriminate against females. Following the judge's order, the school board agreed to open the schools to all students; however, the Afrocentric curriculum—firm discipline, high expectations, parental involvement, and male-centered educational focus—remained intact. The schools were officially designated as "African-Centered Academies." As of 1994, nearly 90 percent of the students enrolled in the academies were Black males. Many of the parents who enrolled their daughters in the schools say they did so because the male academies are the best Detroit has to offer.[24]

In the summer of 1992, when the Malcolm X Academy moved into a mostly White neighborhood, a swastika was painted on the door. Some White residents in the neighborhood complained to the school board and urged the board to relocate the academy. During the winter of 1993, a lawsuit was filed against the school claiming it was teaching religion in violation of church and state separation rules. In the spring of that year, shots were fired at teachers and students practicing baseball on a field adjacent to the school. One neighborhood parent accused the school of teaching racism and extreme discipline. Many observers feel that the neighborhood's White residents were upset for two reasons. They felt uneasy about having Black children in their predominantly White neighborhood, and they mistakenly thought that the school was teaching hatred of Whites because its curriculum was centered in African-American history and culture.

Despite the controversies, the academies have continued to flourish. Since the opening of the first three, thirteen schools have added the Afrocentric curriculum, and plans are underway to introduce the Afrocentric curriculum into all of Detroit's public schools.

Other cities, such as Baltimore, Chicago, Portland, and Milwaukee, are experimenting with Afrocentric curricula in all–Black male schools. Examples are the African American Immersion Academy and the Malcolm X African Immersion School in Milwaukee and the UJAMAA Institute at Medgar Evers College in Brooklyn. Single-gender classrooms in regular schools, with special emphasis on African-American male students, taught by African-American males, have been introduced in Miami, Baltimore, and Washington, D.C.[25]

Some school districts have set up outreach programs designed to augment the education of Black males at existing schools. The East End Neighborhood House in Cleveland, Ohio, conducts African-American rites of passage programs at two Cleveland public schools. The School/Community/Helping Hands Project operated by the Wake County Public Schools in Raleigh, North Carolina, matches African-American role models from the community with Black boys in grades 3 to 8 to work on improving school achievement, self-esteem, interpersonal relationships, and leadership.[26]

Other innovative educational interventions that show considerable promise for helping Black male students achieve academic success are community schools, smaller high schools, and conflict resolution and emotional skills training conducted by the schools.

Full-Service Community Schools

Also following the African proverb that "it takes a village to raise a child," the community school goes far beyond the traditional focus on academics and assumes responsibility for the child's emotional, physical, and social well-being. Anything that affects the child is the school's business, from nutrition to drug abuse prevention, health care, and psychological counseling. Community schools, also known as full-service schools, operate under the philosophy that if children are to be rescued from the dangers of urban ghettos and housing projects, families must be rescued along with them and neighborhood schools must be transformed into full-service communities. What is better equipped to rescue impoverished families than the schools, institutions that are already in the business of serving children?

Full-service elementary schools start early and take responsibility for children's needs from the prenatal period until they are twelve-year-old sixth graders. Using a holistic approach, community school educators tackle any problem at home or on the streets that is preventing a child from learning. Educators conduct developmental screenings for families with preschool children and offer training in parenting skills. They assist parents in helping young children with the foundations of learning so the children won't fall behind before they reach school.[27]

An example of a full-service community school is Bowling Green Park Elementary School, located in the midst of a crime-ridden public housing project in Norfolk, Virginia. A sign over the school's front door says "A Caring Community." The principal, Herman Clark, a Black Ph.D. in educational psychology, moves the rhetoric of standing for children beyond talk. Bowling Green Park's program starts with preschool kids and continues as children progress through elementary school. Parent educators work with toddlers. They make home visits to teach preschoolers to recognize letters and colors and read them stories. They hand out flyers in food stamp lines, encouraging new mothers to sign up early for programs.

Bowling Green Park staff members and teachers informally adopt children who are being neglected by overwhelmed single moms or whose parents are on drugs, dead, or in prison. They take the kids home on the weekends, get their hair cut, purchase new clothes, and take them on trips. They also have heart-to-heart talks about discipline, schoolwork, the future, and even sex when the topic seems appropriate. Parent involvement is one of the keys to success. Bowling Green Park has two parenting technicians who conduct meetings to find out what parents need and who follow through on requests for job training, parent education, exercise classes, or budget planning. The school's approach is paying off. Student attendance is up 97 percent daily, and test scores have shown considerable improvement.[28]

The community school's holistic approach is moving beyond schools that serve poor inner-city children. Thirteen schools in middle-class neighborhoods in Independence, Missouri, have adopted a full-service school approach, called "the 21st Century Model." These schools are now offering family services, preschool programs, day care, after-school activities, tutoring, and mentoring.

Smaller Schools

Many Black male students get lost in the shuffle in large urban high schools. They end up dropping out or drifting through school without members of the educational staff being aware of their presence. In his book *Brothers*, Vest Monroe noted that most of his male peers either went through high school without any purpose or direction or dropped out because no one encouraged or nurtured them.[29]

A generation ago, educators favored large urban high schools because they could offer a wide range of subjects and extracurricular activities at relatively low cost. Now educational experts and researchers see big urban high schools with 2,000 to 5,000 students as pathology-ridden institutions that breed violence, academic failure, alienation, and dropouts. What was once a place of opportunity has become a place of fear that stifles the interest and curiosity of many Black male students and of students in general.

By contrast, schools limited to about 400 students have fewer behavioral problems, better graduation and attendance rates, and in most cases, higher test scores and a larger percentage of students going on to college. They offer students experiences hard to find in big high schools, such as something to belong to, something to believe in, and someone in authority to believe in each student. At a time when many students have less support from fractured families and neighborhood institutions in deteriorating communities, students in smaller high schools can build close bonds with teachers to help them through the troubled times of adolescence. In small schools, it is easier to create a close-knit community that emphasizes achievement, work, and discipline, and keeps the lines of communication open between parents, students, and teachers.[30]

Educators across the country are moving to replace large urban high schools with smaller ones. The University of Chicago and Temple University in Philadelphia are helping Chicago and Philadelphia high schools create smaller schools within their walls. The Philadelphia Board of Education has implemented a plan to convert all twenty-two remaining large neighborhood high schools into smaller ones. Efforts are under way in Denver, San Francisco, Boulder, Colorado, and

Providence, Rhode Island, to do the same. In New York City, thirty new small high schools opened in the fall of 1993.[31] Central Park East Secondary School, a small high school in New York's predominantly Black Harlem, is outstripping many high schools in the city in achievement rates, test scores, and percentage of students going on to college. At Central Park East, every full-time teacher is responsible for building a close relationship with fifteen students and their families. In 1993, Central Park East graduated 71 percent of its ninth-grade class in four years, and 90 percent of the graduates went on to attend college, an astonishing success rate for a ghetto high school.

The crown jewel of the smaller schools movement is Harlem's Frederick Douglass Academy, a highly successful combined junior–senior high school. Frederick Douglass was once Intermediate School 10. It counts among its distinguished alumni the writer James Baldwin, the psychologist Kenneth Clark, and Congressman Charles Rangel.[32] Lorraine Monroe, the principal of Frederick Douglass Academy, set out to create a public school for Black students that would contain all the advantages of a private academy. She wanted to build a center of educational excellence in a poverty-stricken, drug-ridden, low-income neighborhood. Monroe and her teaching staff demand high academic standards and strict discipline. Students adhere to a dress code: navy blue slacks with white shirts and ties for the boys, and navy blue skirts and white blouses for the girls.

The rigorous academic curriculum includes math, French, global studies, literature, science, computer technology, and African-American history and culture. Students are surrounded by a school environment bustling with activity and creativity. They have the opportunity to engage in tennis, dance, music, basketball, soccer, cheerleading, and science clubs. The school has an extensive art program and offers creative writing and journalism courses. Students can publish essays and stories in the school's newspaper. They go on field trips to the Metropolitan Museum of Art, Broadway plays, the South Street Seaport, and Chinatown.

Students are not permitted to leave the school at lunchtime. Youngsters participating in after-school activities can have dinner at school. Everyone is assigned homework, and there is a quiet center where kids can study. Tolerance and diversity are learned through group meetings and activities with young people from Jewish organizations and other ethnic groups. Every year Frederick Douglass students attend summer programs at prestigious colleges, including Dartmouth,

Barnard, Bard, Hunter, and the various campuses of the State University of New York. Academically, the academy is on a roll. As of 1994, it had the highest math and reading scores in the district, and all of its students planned to attend college.

Emotional Skills Training and Conflict Resolution

Finally, in terms of school-based interventions, educators and psychologists are working with students in programs to help them control intense emotions, resolve disputes peacefully, and mediate disagreements that have the potential to escalate into violence. Statistics on student violence indicate that every hour in the United States 2,000 students are attacked on school campuses, 900 teachers are threatened by students, and 40 teachers are actually attacked physically. Every day 100,000 kids bring guns to school, and every day 40 children are killed or injured by guns. Forty-four percent of public school students report personal experiences with angry confrontations and encounters. Police and metal detectors may reduce the presence of weapons in schools, but they do not address the underlying issues triggering violent conflict. Conflict resolution and interpersonal skills training programs provide students with ways to resolve conflict nonviolently.[33]

Several school districts have instituted anger management training programs. The Los Angeles city schools use such a program aimed at middle school students. The program, entitled Think First, teaches students to recognize anger and what triggers it, and constructive ways to handle anger. Students meet with a facilitator an hour a day and parents attend one session a week. Think First encourages students to be responsible for their own behavior.

They learn to describe the intensity of their angry feelings on a ten-point scale. Kids are taught to understand what causes anger, such as mad-dog stares, being yelled at, gossip, or being dissed. They become aware of anger's physical cues in themselves and others, like facial tension, tightness in the stomach, and clenched fists. Students discuss how they act out anger by fighting, screaming, throwing things, yelling, and other hostile behaviors. Gradually, they learn anger reducers and alternative ways of expressing anger. Anger reducers include deep breathing, slowing down, meditation, visualizing calm scenes, and mellowing-out mantras. Once the intensity of the anger is reduced, students can think about alternative ways of responding. Used to thinking until they find a nonviolent solution, they will be less dependent on automatic hostile reactions like hitting, kicking, fighting, and verbal tirades, which can easily escalate into extreme violence. Students attending the program show improved grades, fewer referrals for behavioral problems, and less arguing and fighting with parents and siblings at home.[34]

School districts in Chicago, Seattle, Nashville, and Durham, North Carolina, as well as in many other cities, have instituted programs in violence prevention and conflict resolution. The program in Chicago, which reaches 5,000 students in dozens of inner-city schools, uses a three-tier approach that includes students, teachers, and parents. Junior high school students role-play violent confrontations, then stop and discuss what happened and why. Next the students play out the psychodrama again, this time focusing on nonviolent alternatives.[35]

The psychologist Rodney Hammond has developed a video-based training program for violence prevention and dealing with anger for African-American teenagers. Hammond's program, called Dealing with Anger, uses culturally relevant language patterns, verbal and nonverbal expressions, and dress styles. The program is built around three instructional videotapes that reflect the social environment of African-American male adolescents. Each tape begins with a conflict situation that has the potential to escalate into a dangerous confrontation. At critical points in the interaction, the narrator freezes the action and describes a skill that could have been used to diffuse the violence. The same situation is played out again, but this time an effective conflict resolution skill is used and the problem is solved without resorting to violence. In the three tapes, students are taught how to express angry feelings in a calm, nonthreatening manner, how to accept criticism without blowing up or acting irrationally, and how to negotiate a solution or work out a compromise to a conflict without resorting to aggressive or violent behavior.[36]

DuVal High School in Lanham, Maryland, is one of 5,000 public and private high schools across the United States that now use peer mediation programs to settle disputes between students and sometimes between students and teachers. Peer mediators work in pairs to help other students resolve disputes that arise from insults, rumors, stare-downs, gossip, offhand comments, and the like. The peer mediators rely heavily on effective listening techniques. They teach potential adversaries to listen carefully to what the other person is saying and not interrupt, to restate the problem in one's own words, and to agree to solve the problem. The peer mediators listen, clarify and reflect feelings, and paraphrase while remaining calm and respectful of both parties. By the time the session is over, the adversaries are usually talked out.[37]

Since the peer mediation program started at DuVal High School, in 1990, suspensions and fighting have dropped dramatically, and the school's climate has become more relaxed. Tensions that used to escalate into fights and verbal threats are now resolved nonviolently. Staff and students have learned to trust the mediators, and now watch for signs of troubled situations so they can be routed to the mediators before things get out of hand. Halfway through the 1994–95 school year, DuVal's peer mediators had resolved 150 disputes; one involved thirteen students and took a whole day to resolve. School mediation specialists feel that most students want to avoid violence and angry disputes. Conflict resolution through mediation gives them the tools to work through potentially violent disagreements and helps build a school atmosphere that allows students to learn in peace.

The peer mediators at DuVal High School do a lot of teaching. They hold classes in conflict resolution and travel to middle and elementary schools to help them set up peer mediation and conflict resolution programs. According to the peer mediation coordinator, the things that make DuVal High School's program successful are carefully trained mediators, outreach to students, staff, and parents, confidentiality and trust, the solid support of staff and administrators, and an emergency system capable of quick action.

Anger management groups, conflict resolution skills training, and mediation are part of what educators call student assistance programs. In these, counselors and facilitators work with students on issues of mental health and psychological growth: drug and alcohol abuse, self-esteem, breakdowns in communication with parents, and recovering from breakups with boyfriends and girlfriends. Through student assistance programs, educators are trying to provide support, stability, and shared values for young people in neighborhoods where traditional institutions like the extended family, churches, and fraternal orders have either collapsed or are overwhelmed. Student assistance programs are now operative in over half the nation's rural, suburban, and urban high schools. Modeled after human resources training and employee assistance programs in large companies, they have their own journal, called *Student Assistance*. These programs have adopted some of the New Age vocabulary, and their discussions are filled with terms like self-help, empowerment, recovery, taking responsibility for one's life, making choices, and dealing with consequences.[38]

The Limits of Intervention Programs

While the efforts of student assistance programs to help students attain personal growth are laudable, and they have achieved results inside schools, it is doubtful that programs like anger management, conflict resolution training, and mediation can significantly alter the tide of violence and fear surrounding the lives of many inner-city young men when the causes of violence stem from the mean streets outside the school. The problem confronting violence prevention strategies is that violence has complex roots. It is endemic to poor, urban neighborhoods where drugs, gangs, and crime are rampant. School-based programs can change violence in school hallways and cafeterias, but can they really change violence on the street corner? Growing up in crime-ridden neighborhoods heightens the risk that young Black men will be confronted with violence they cannot avoid or resolve peacefully. We are asking Black kids to do the impossible unless we as a society deal with the larger picture. If the ethos of the peer group and the neighborhood street culture glorifies violent, go-for-bad behavior, kids are being taught ways of preventing violence and solving conflicts that are not highly valued or reinforced outside the school.

Chapter 14

High-Risk Youth, Rehabilitation, and Extending Outreach

Black psychologists and social workers frequently refer to young Black males as an "endangered species." Indeed, those living in distressed urban neighborhoods are in danger of being consumed by the social pathology that surrounds them. They face a high risk for sliding down a slippery slope that will ultimately destroy them.

Intensive Youth Programs

The greatest potential for helping high-risk Black youths lies in programs that involve an intensive casework approach, where a supervising youth advocate serves as a surrogate parent to coordinate an integrated package of social services, mentoring, educational support, and delinquency prevention. As of 1994, intensive, all-out intervention programs designed to prevent destructive behavior were operating in Baltimore, Austin, Texas, and six other cities.[1]

Children in Baltimore, in a program called Choice, get daily supervision from caseworkers, sometimes referred to as shepherds, who
meet with teenagers referred by agencies that work with high-risk and
delinquent kids. The caseworkers have contact with the kids as much
as three to five times a day. They make sure they are in school, do their
homework, get tutored, and come home on time for curfew. They see
to it that the children and their parents follow up on medical appointments and school conferences. Shepherds do whatever it takes to keep
youths out of trouble and their families stable, including helping parents learn home management skills, find jobs, enter drug treatment
programs, pay electric bills, and renegotiate evictions. The idea is to
provide the child with a secure environment by helping take care of
family problems.

The key to intensive casework programs is providing high-risk
kids with time, attention, structure, and a firm but caring hand. Many
young men in the ghettos are part of crumbling extended families
where fathers have not been present for two or three generations. No
one pays attention to them; the adults are overwhelmed by their own
problems. The children have no structure or routine around which
they can organize their lives. Shepherds try to provide the structure,
time, attention, and organization. These caseworkers concentrate on
behavioral socialization using a carrot-and-stick approach. High-risk
teenagers have to be taught how to behave and are encouraged when
they do well and punished when they break the rules. They are taken
on field trips to museums and historical sites, encouraged to join athletic teams, and promised summer jobs.

Early results from Austin indicate that school attendance and
grades have improved and arrests are down for participants in the program. The barrier that all-out interventions like Choice face, however,
is that they are very labor-intensive. Caseworkers at Choice spend seventy hours a week dealing with a caseload of twenty kids or less at a
cost of approximately $4,000 a year for each child. Regular social
workers and school counselors have caseloads of over 100 young people. The cost of intensive casework, however, is much less than what it
takes to keep a teenager in a juvenile detention facility. Right now the
programs are small and scattered, but more will be needed as more
parents are put to work in welfare reform programs.[2]

The city of Boston has launched Winner's Circle, an ambitious
program to reach high-risk youths. The goal of Winner's Circle is to
provide a well-coordinated package of services to every identified

high-risk youth in the city. It seeks to eliminate bureaucratic agency boundaries and draw together a solid coalition of all appropriate groups to monitor the lives of the city's troubled youths. No high-risk kid will be left unknown, lost, or untouched by an extensive array of services provided by school programs and health, law enforcement, and social agencies. Youths are sent for help when they need it, and youth service workers are able to intervene quickly when youths are faced with a major life crisis.[3]

Winner's Circle involves a cooperative effort between the mayor's office, business communities, school officials, universities, social services, and law enforcement. The key to its success is a youth services coordinator who works out of each school that participates in the program and who brings together all these community representatives to discuss the progress and problems of the kids, monitor their academic performance, review their physical and mental health, make sure appointments are kept, assess the family situation, and be aware of any law enforcement problems. The coordinator also works with churches, recreation programs, and job placement agencies. The city's core of eighty street workers keeps track of youths who are no longer in school.

Programs like Winner's Circle and Choice are trying to provide the guidance and support that generations ago were given by extended families, neighbors, shopkeepers, churches, and other community groups. Now, many young African-American males are left without critical adult guidance to make the passage from early adolescence into young adulthood. By contrast, most families living outside Black urban ghettos have a number of support systems beyond the family that they can draw on during their transition from adolescence to early adulthood. There are extracurricular activities and field trips at school, organizations like the Boy Scouts, athletics, summer vacations or jobs, and community-based programs. Most middle-class White families take all this for granted. Yet we seem to expect ten- to sixteen-year-olds from poor, single-parent families, living in high-risk neighborhoods with few community support services, to make it into adulthood safely on their own. On their own, ghetto youngsters turn to their peers for nurturance, guidance, and solace. These peers in crime-ridden neighborhoods are likely to be gang members, drug dealers, gunrunners, and street hustlers.

Efforts are under way in many urban areas to reduce the street violence that prevents many high-risk African-American young men from following through on plans to pursue productive goals. It is difficult for young people to concentrate on educational or job training goals when they have to spend much of their time on the alert for signs of danger: avoiding potential violent encounters or posturing with a go-for-bad attitude to ward off attack. U.S. Justice Department statistics indicate that youths between the ages of twelve and fifteen are victims of crime more than any other group. Teenagers of all ages are crime victims at twice the national average and ten times the rate of the elderly.[4]

In Detroit, a group of Black men called Brothers on Patrol go into the housing projects in the morning to make sure children have a safe corridor to school. After school, they set up a safe pathway for children to walk home. Some of the Brothers on Patrol are fathers, others are young men from the community who volunteer to help out. In Boston, youth street workers for the Mayor's Safe Neighborhoods Program are constantly on the alert for signs of impending violence and have been credited with warding off gang rumbles and violence between groups. Jawanza Kunjufu, an African-American consulting psychologist, has created a nonviolence laboratory to help young men on the streets learn to resolve conflicts peacefully. Under the auspices of the National Crime Prevention Council and the National Institute for Citizen Education in the Law, the Teens Crime and Community Program runs violence prevention and social service programs in forty states.[5]

Guns in the hands of teenagers are the most frequent cause of death in street crime. In July 1994, President Clinton announced the creation of a federal computer system to track the illegal sale of guns to young people, as part of an initiative to help local police reduce the supply of firearms and halt the sharp rise in armed violence among young people. When a police officer catches a juvenile with a gun, the gun is confiscated and the serial number reported to the Bureau of Alcohol, Tobacco, and Firearms. The bureau will trace the gun to the original seller and purchaser to find out who is selling guns to teenagers. If the original purchaser says the gun was stolen, the police check to verify if such a theft was reported. If the story checks out, the juvenile is charged with felonious possession of a gun. During a six-month test of the program in Boston, no juveniles were killed by gunfire.[6] The gun-tracking program has received strong support from NOBLE, the National Organization of Black Law Enforcement Executives, which has always advocated gun control.

A 1995 nationwide poll of 2,000 teenagers conducted by Louis Harris and Associates documented a widespread willingness on the part of Black and White teenagers to take an active role in reducing crimes of violence inside and outside of school. Approximately nine in ten of the young people interviewed said they would be willing to participate in mentoring, education, and community awareness programs. These figures suggest that young people, who are often the victims of violence, are likely to be receptive to adult guidance in solving the problems that lead to violence.[7]

Prison Rehabilitation:
Informal Ministries and Prison Penology

Mentorship and manhood training sponsored by informal prison ministries have achieved spectacular results in turning Black convicts toward productive paths. Such ministries, which usually are an informal mix of Black Nationalism, Afrocentric values, Black consciousness, and Nation of Islam (NOI) and Orthodox Islamic beliefs, have provided countless numbers of Black prisoners with an opportunity to reassess what it means to be a man.

Black Nationalist and NOI doctrines clearly spell out who the enemy is, blaming the White devils for the nearly 400 years of oppression that have created the dismal conditions found in urban Black ghettos. Black Nationalists and NOI ministers clearly separate blame from responsibility, however. While the White man is to blame for oppression, Black men cannot wait on White men to free them; oppressors never give up power without a struggle. Black men must take the responsibility for developing a set of values that will psychologically liberate them—values that include discipline, self-determination, racial pride, being directed from within, and spiritual centeredness. Acting out anger and frustration at the White man by go-for-bad behavior or escaping through drugs is understandable, but ultimately destructive of self and others. By acting out and engaging in criminal behaviors or drug abuse, one becomes an unwitting accomplice in the oppressors' ongoing effort to destroy Black males. Empowered with the tools provided by an Afrocentric way of being, a Black man can reclaim his life and avoid such traps as imprisonment, which allow the White man total control. Two of the most outstanding successes of the Black prison ministries' manhood and mentorship training are Malcolm X and the journalist Nathan McCall. (See Chapters 6 and 8, respectively.)

More and more Black men in prison are turning to the Nation of Islam and Orthodox Islam to find spiritual solace and masculine direction. It is estimated that at least one-third of the one million or more Black men in prison are claiming affiliation with these sects; most of them converted after being locked up.[8] Despite the fact that groups like NOI have shown again and again that they can turn angry, crime-prone Black men into responsible citizens, husbands, and fathers, prison officials are reluctant to give the formal stamp of approval to Black Nationalist–oriented prison ministries. Prison officials are caught between opposing forces; on the one hand, they espouse prison rehabilitation, on the other hand, if they support Black Nationalist groups, they might seem to be acknowledging that the militant Brothers are right when they say that America is a racist society controlled by White devils.

Another innovative intervention, being developed by Black men serving long prison terms, shows considerable promise in transforming the lives of Black convicts and preventing young men from slipping into lives of repeated crime and imprisonment. Long-term inmates like Eddie Ellis, who spent twenty-three years in New York State prisons for murder, have created study groups and informal think tanks inside the prisons to try to understand the relationship between depressed social environments, personal choices, and involvement in criminal behavior. During his years in prison, Ellis earned bachelor's and master's degrees in sociology and theology. As part of the Black Resurrection Study Group, he and his fellow inmates at Green Haven Prison in Stormville, New York, analyzed the symbiotic relationship between New York's sixty-two state prisons and seven neighborhoods in New York City. They found that 88 percent of the inmates in the state prisons were Black or Latino and that 75 percent of these prisoners came from just seven neighborhoods: the Lower East Side, the South Bronx, Harlem, Brownsville, Bedford-Stuyvesant, East New York, and South Jamaica. Citing research findings from his prison think tank, Ellis pointed out that the social environment in underclass neighborhoods, with eroded schools, few jobs, fatherless families, and a drug economy, presents young Black men with a powerful tide of negative influences that predispose them to crime.

Ellis and his colleagues recommend that older men, like himself, who have served long prison sentences, shepherd and mentor young men along a path that leads away from crime and prison. In prison, these inmate penologists are conducting classes to help convicts become creatively involved in the community when they are discharged. They have petitioned the New York State Legislature to require ex-convicts to train for community service and crime prevention as a condition of parole. Ellis currently works as a community educator in Harlem, using his firsthand experience to mentor high-risk young Black men. He believes that change begins with the individual but must be nurtured along the way by old heads and given state and local financial support.[9]

Drug Treatment

To increase the rate of success in drug rehabilitation achieved by informal prison ministries, mentorship programs, and grassroots penology approaches, more treatment programs are needed inside and outside prisons. Drug possession, drug use and abuse, and drug dealing on the streets are part of inner-city Black male lifestyles. Seventy to eighty percent of Black males arrested in urban America test positive for drugs. In Baltimore, where 56 percent of young Black men are on probation or parole, in jail, or awaiting trial, drugs are involved in all but a few of the cases. Get-tough law enforcement policies and mandatory sentencing for drug possession have disproportionately affected Black males. Although they make up 12 percent of the population and constitute 13 percent of all monthly drug users, they represent 30 percent of all arrests for drug possession, 55 percent of all convictions for drug possession, and 74 percent of all those who receive prison sentences for drug possession.[10] Cheap, addictive crack cocaine has been a menace to the Black community for the past fifteen years, destroying thousands of African-American men and rendering them useless as family breadwinners.

Despite the overwhelming numbers of Black men involved in drug-related arrests, very few prisons offer drug treatment; nor is cheap, low-cost drug treatment easily accessible in Black urban communities where it is needed most. Even the police have said that turning the tide of drug use cannot be done by law enforcement alone. The police are often overwhelmed, outgunned, and outmanned on the streets. Unless the public is willing to put police on every corner in urban America twenty-four hours a day and spend billions more dollars building and staffing prisons for young Black men, treatment is the best approach to working with the social and medical problems arising from drug use.[11]

Effective treatment and follow-up in public nonprofit drug centers cost about $14,000 per patient. This is far less than the cost of keeping a man in prison for several years. People who want help should be able to get it quickly, while they are highly motivated to stop using drugs. Long-term follow-up studies of drug treatment conducted by the Research Triangle Institute in North Carolina indicate that in most cases the financial benefits of drug treatment are substantially higher than the cost. Virtually all income measures show that following drug treatment, costs of crime and law enforcement were reduced, prison costs declined, and more men were working and contributing to the support of their families.[12]

Effective drug treatment programs for African-American males need to incorporate the African-American ethos and the manhood training and mentoring principles that have proved successful in prison ministries and rites of passage programs. Internalizing a mix of African-American and Black Nationalist values definitely facilitates recovery.

Reaching Out: Gangs and Ordinary Brothers

To maximize the effectiveness of manhood training and mentorship programs for students, shepherding for high-risk youth, prison ministries and inmate penology, drug rehabilitation, and programs aimed at reducing street violence, the Black community needs to extend its outreach to include both ordinary, working-class males and gang members, two groups that are often left out of program planning and implementation.

Gangs: Mobilizing for Social Activism

All over America, aging gang members and ex-gang members in their late twenties and thirties are becoming exhausted by turf battles, violent death, and long prison terms. As weary and battle-scarred members of gangs enter adulthood, there is a rising consciousness of the waste and destruction their behavior has caused in their own lives and in the community. Many gang veterans have come to realize that violence, once justified by vague ideas about community control, has careened out of control. They are tired of going to prison and funerals, tired of seeing parents weeping for innocent children gravely wounded or killed by stray bullets in gang cross fires. They want a better life and a chance to turn their notoriety into something that can rebuild the communities they helped destroy.

At a gang summit conference held in Kansas City, Missouri, in May 1992 and attended by over 200 gang leaders, civil rights activists, and church leaders, the message was that it's time to stop the violence and rebuild urban communities. They talked about building self-esteem, empowerment, and taking responsibility for improving the lot of Black people. Gang leaders expressed a strong interest in building a coalition with government, corporations, and churches to raise money to start businesses, refurbish deteriorating houses, and fund job training centers. Annual follow-up meetings have since been held in other cities. The gang Brothers hold few illusions that it will be easy to turn gangs around or raise money for businesses and community programs, but they are willing to start. The fact that 200 of the baddest homeboys in America are willing to sit down and talk is a sure sign of progress.[13]

Some of the efforts by ex-gang leaders and older gang members are starting to show signs of progress. In Los Angeles, the truce between the Crips and Bloods, two of the city's largest, heavily armed, notorious gangs, is holding. At the Million Man March, one of the speakers, an ex-L.A. gang member, apologized to the audience for gang killing and mayhem. Former professional football star Jim Brown's Los Angeles–based organization, Amer-I-Can, is working with the corporate structure and government agencies to help aging gang members redirect their lives, start businesses, and train for high-paying jobs.

In Chicago, Black gangs are becoming involved in politics and community activism, just as White street gangs did generations before them. "Street organizations," as gang members in politics prefer to be called, have registered thousands of new voters, conducted voter education classes, backed candidates for school board and city council elections, and courted politicians. Gang members organized several thousand people in a march to protest dismal conditions in the school system and the lack of community-based health care facilities. Candidates for city elective offices have talked at meetings organized by the gang street organizations. Two ex-convicts, including a former leader of the 10,000-member Gangster Disciples gang, made it to the runoffs in Chicago's city council races in 1995 before losing to their opponents.

Twenty-first Century Vote, an organization at the forefront of channeling the power of street gangs into politics, has ties with the Gangster Disciples. Twenty-first Century Vote's chairman claims he has helped register thousands of new voters, many of whom were probably gang members. The organization has also entered into negotiations with Arab and Korean merchants to work on economic development ventures in Chicago's Black neighborhoods. Carl Upchurch, chief organizer of the annual Gang Peace Summit, known as the National Urban Peace and Justice Movement, says political power is the key to gaining access to economic power.[14] The movement to trade bullets for ballots is spreading to other cities, including Cleveland, Kansas City, and Los Angeles.

Moving gangs into politics and community activism has been talked about since the 1960s. Martin Luther King, Jr., recognized that Chicago street gangs represented one of the strongest grassroots organizations in the Black community. Although he was unsuccessful in his efforts to stop gang warfare and get the gangs moving in the direction of social activism and politics, it now appears that his dream is showing signs of becoming a reality.

However, the go-for-bad gang Brothers will not be able to turn away completely from the death, destruction, and terror they have wrought on urban streets until they find an economic replacement for the drug trade. In most poor inner-city neighborhoods, gang members control the drug trade at the street level. The gang Brothers are not going to give up the rich profits for long-term unemployment or minimum-wage, "chump-change" jobs. They are asking politicians, government agencies, churches, and the corporate structure to work with them to start businesses and finance job training. Gangbanging started off as a quest for respect. Society can show respect for the gang Brothers by working with them on mutual terms. If respect by mainstream society is not forthcoming, the mayhem and destruction will continue.

The Ordinary Brothers: A Forgotten Resource

Blue-collar, working Brothers represent a vast resource of untapped potential that is often left out of manhood training, mentorship, and rehabilitation programs. In *Slim's Table,* his ethnographic study of a group of working-class Black men in Chicago who eat their meals at Valois Restaurant, Mitchell Duneier suggests that these men have a lot they could teach both Black and White males about what it means to be a man in contemporary society. At a time when macho, patriarchal images of masculinity are being challenged, the men described in *Slim's Table* appear to be holding fast to a definition of genuine masculinity that emphasizes psychological strength, responsibility, and respect for others.

The Black men who gather regularly for meals at the restaurant on Chicago's South Side are characterized as inner directed; their feelings of self-worth are not derived from material worth or power over others. They are low-keyed, sincere men who respect wisdom and experience. The men gain respect from honesty and telling it like it is, even if this means revealing shortcomings, not by boasting about false accomplishments. They know how to be tender without being perceived as soft or fragile. They know when to stand their ground and when to back down graciously. These Black men treat Whites with respect and civility. They expect the same treatment in return.[15]

As Black community organizations search for dependable role models and mentors to work as volunteers with youths, ex-convicts, and patients in drug programs, they would do well to extend invitations to men of this sort. Black psychologists need to study how the character of these men was formed and what can be done to imprint their positive characteristics on the identities of today's Black youths and young adults.

In Omaha, Nebraska, a group of ordinary Black men formed a community-based group called MAD DADS, an acronym for Men Against Destruction—Defending Against Drugs and Social Disorder. MAD DADS was started in May 1989, when John Foster's son, home from college on spring break, was severely beaten by gang members who wanted to take his Suzuki Jeep because it had red and blue colors. When his son came home beaten and bloody and told his father what had happened, Foster went to the streets with two loaded guns—a .357 and a .44 Magnum—to seek revenge. After spending hours looking in vain for his son's attackers, Foster returned home and turned his rage into something positive.

MAD DADS attempts to restore order to gang-infested neighborhoods by means of weekly street patrols, mentoring, manhood training, rites of passage programs, teen centers, gun buybacks, prison visitations, and supervised youth activities with male chaperones.

The group seeks opportunities to support youth involvement in community, educational, and occupational activities. Their mission is to bring about positive change in troubled communities by seeking out and encouraging other men who are committed to the struggle to save people from the ills that plague urban neighborhoods. MAD DADS now has forty-seven chapters in thirteen states. Since 1989, more than 100,000 children have been involved with MAD DADS; over 30,000 of them were runaways, drug abusers or drug sellers, gang members, or otherwise troubled.[16]

The Black Church and Masculinity Concerns

Once again, the Black church is being called upon to take a central role in the Black man's quest for liberation, psychological wholeness, and spiritual fulfillment. From its inception in the eighteenth century, the Black church has been a source of solace in times of trouble and need, and has provided a spiritual and secular base with an array of educational, economic, medical, financial, and burial services that Blacks could not obtain elsewhere in a segregated society. Historically, the church was the beacon in the long struggle for civil rights, social justice, and equal opportunity.

To assist Black men in meeting the sociological and psychological challenges they face in present-day America, the Black church will have to retool its theology and secular activities. Many Black men, especially young adults, are reluctant to become involved in the church for two reasons. First, the images of Jesus, God, and the angels generally projected are White. Such images once led an eight-year-old boy to ask if Black people could get into Heaven. Based on the fact that the deities he saw were all White, he thought that only White folks could get into Heaven. Angry young urban Black men have trouble looking to a White, blue-eyed Jesus for spiritual and psychological guidance in a society dominated by images of White male superiority. Some Black men feel that White Christians aided and abetted slavery and White oppression by telling slaves that God meant for them to suffer in this life so they could be rewarded in the next life. A second reason for reluctance to join the Black church is that in most congregations, women dominate church activities; the social and spiritual programs are consequently geared to the needs of women and children. Younger Black men find little in the fiery sermons delivered by aging ministers to help them with pressing secular issues such as coping with racism, job training, drug abuse, gangs, Black-on-Black violence, unemployment, rehabilitation following prison terms, and development of Black consciousness.

A growing number of Black men who are dissatisfied with Black Christianity are turning to the Nation of Islam and other Islamic sects. The National Survey of Religious Identification estimates that about 600,000 Blacks in the United States are members of Islamic groups—roughly 20 percent of the adult religion-affiliated population. In 1989, there were 2,000 declared Muslims in the U.S. armed services; in 1996, there were 10,000. In Philadelphia, the number of Muslims rose from 40,000 to 60,000 in five years. A third of all Blacks in federal prisons are members of Islam; most converted after being locked up. Islamic rhetoric was very prominent at the Million Man March in Washington, D.C., in 1995.[17]

Most Black Americans who are members of Islamic groups adhere to the Orthodox teachings of mainstream Islam, which believes that the prophet Muhammad, born around A.D. 570, was the last messenger of Allah. A smaller number of Muslims, which researchers estimate to be about 20,000, belong to the Nation of Islam. NOI achieved prominence in the 1960s under the leadership of Elijah Muhammad and Malcolm X and is currently led by Minister Louis Farrakhan. Black Orthodox Muslims and NOI members believe that racism has not been fully addressed in America. All Islamic groups stress self-help and personal improvement. Orthodox Muslims open the door to men of all races.

The group known as the Nation of Islam is respected in the Black community for its success in keeping its members away from the destructive effects of drugs, alcohol, street crime, and extramarital sex, and for its stress on the work ethic, discipline, prudent money management, responsibility, and marital and family stability. Critics, however, are uncomfortable with its patriarchal style and history of racial separation. NOI teaches that the male is the head of the family and has the final voice in family decisions, that he is expected to be responsible for the well-being of his family and to treat all family members with respect and courtesy. Women, though respected as mothers, wives, and adult partners, are not appointed as ministers or heads of mosques, nor are they encouraged to seek positions of authority in religious affairs. At a time when women, Black and White, are still struggling for recognition, status, and equal access to decision-making roles in family life, work, and community affairs, NOI seems to be out of step with the times.

The three most visible NOI leaders, Elijah Muhammad, Malcolm X, and Louis Farrakhan, have preached racial separation, feeling that the racial animosity of Whites towards Blacks in America is too deeply ingrained ever to permit equal integration. Recently, however, Farrakhan seems to have modified his separatist teachings slightly. While he has not completely renounced racial separation, he has hinted that there may be areas of mutual interest in politics, economics, and urban affairs where Blacks and Whites can work together productively. He says his door is open to any one, Black or White, who is willing to sit down with him to discuss America's racial problem seriously.[18]

Proponents of Islam feel it is more compatible with Black consciousness than Christianity. Since Islam rejects visual depictions of God, Blacks can pray to a formless, raceless Allah. The emphasis on discipline, self-help, and responsibility symbolizes strength to many Black men. Muslim men are expected to take care of their families, work hard, abstain from drugs and alcohol, and follow a ritual of five calls to prayer a day. Teenage boys and young men who join NOI dress neatly in suits and ties and drop their swaying, hip-hop walks. Because Islam is a complete way of life, Muslim clergy pay a great deal of attention to the secular needs of men. Urban mosques run manhood training, mentoring, and job training programs, sponsor economic collectives and business development seminars, staff computer labs and homework centers, and teach living skills, such as budgeting, health maintenance, household management, and parenting. In a rundown section of Philadelphia's Black community, Suetwedien A. Muhammed, a former gang member, runs a small mosque that has a homework association, computer lab, crime watch, and a Big Brothers' program for young men. Suetwedien says he is trying to rebuild a neighborhood he helped destroy when he was a gang member.[19]

Islam's growing popularity is forcing the Black church to find new ways to become relevant to Black men. Some Black churches are Blackanizing Christianity. Ministers wear African Kinte cloths over their vestments during services, which are often accompanied by African drums beating in the background. First African Methodist Episcopal church in Los Angeles has a stained glass image of a Black Jesus on three windows; some churches in Philadelphia have images of Christ, Solomon, and Moses portrayed as Black. The Reverend Ivan Hicks of Bright Hope Baptist Church in Philadelphia runs a rites of passage program in which male church elders guide young men spiritually and psychologically into manhood. Reverend Hicks teaches that Jesus Christ was a revolutionary who stood up for the rights of oppressed people. The Reverend Jesse Jackson has encouraged all Black churches to adopt high-risk young men and shepherd them through the passage into productive manhood.[20]

Although there appears to be a widening gender gap in the Black religious community, with men joining Islamic groups and women adhering to Christianity, what is important, however, is not whether Black men are Christians or Muslims, but whether they can find and develop a strong enough spiritual foundation to protect them from the destruction of the streets.

Chapter 15

What Next?
Confronting Racism

The mobilization of African-American men to address concerns of identity, intimacy, and racism, and to find adaptive possibilities in the African-American way of being and specific interventions in the Black community (as discussed in Chapters 13 and 14) needs to be augmented by efforts in the larger society to face the issue of race.

Race: America's Unfinished Business

Several major studies (cited in Chapter 1)—from *The Philadelphia Negro* in 1909 to *The Black Middle Class Experience* in 1994—have documented that race, racism, and racial discrimination are continuing problems that negatively affect the quality of life for Black men in America. Because of the persistence of racism, which is now more covert, institutional, and structural than it was in the past, Black males face an undue burden in their struggle for identity, education, and access to political and economic power.

At the beginning of this century, W. E. B. Du Bois, the first African-American man to receive a doctorate from Harvard, predicted that the problem of the twentieth century would be the problem of the color line. As we move toward the twenty-first century, the color line is still part of society's unfinished business, one that both Black and White Americans will ultimately have to confront.[1] The problem must be resolved before Black men as a group can realize their full potential occupationally, educationally, politically, economically, and in family life.

Confronting the problem will not be an easy task, however. A vast perceptual gap separates Blacks and Whites on questions surrounding race. Evidence from racially tinged recent events and public opinion polls shows that Blacks and Whites view the meaning of race-related events differently. The not-guilty verdict in the 1995 trial of O. J. Simpson for the murder of his wife, Nicole Brown Simpson, and her friend, Ron Goldman, is a vivid example of the Black/White perceptual chasm. Polls taken after the trial show that two-thirds of Blacks accepted the not-guilty verdict by a predominately Black jury; two-thirds of Whites, on the other hand, felt that Simpson was guilty.[2]

Other examples of the perceptual divide come from polls by social scientists assessing differences in Black/White perceptions of racial progress, stereotypes, and leadership. Blacks generally feel that the civil rights movement has not gone far enough in ensuring equal opportunity and equal justice. Conversely, many Whites feel that the movement has gone too far, and this may explain the growing resistance to programs like affirmative action and special admissions to universities, which were initiated as attempts to reverse centuries of racial discrimination. Polls conducted at the University of Chicago indicate that many Whites cling to stereotypes of Blacks as being less intelligent, and that Whites are more likely than Blacks to associate Blacks with welfare, crime, homelessness, drugs, and AIDS. Other polls consistently show that Louis Farrakhan is viewed more favorably by Blacks than Whites. Whites tend to see Farrakhan as a negative force and as a poor role model for youth, whereas Blacks tend to see him as a positive force for social change and a strong role model for young people.[3] The most straightforward explanation of the Black/White perceptual gulf is that the two groups live in different experiential worlds, which leads to different perceptions and interpretations of race-related events.

Renewing the Call for an Interracial Dialogue

What's needed in America today is an ongoing, candid Black/White dialogue about the role of race in society—a dialogue about how race covertly and overtly influences attitudes, perceptions, opinions, and behaviors, how race confers advantages and disadvantages, how race opens up or closes down opportunities, and why Black and White Americans have such different views of racially connected events. Americans tend to shy away from discussing race; it seems to make us uncomfortable. After events like the Million Man March, the O. J. Simpson trial, the Rodney King beating and the 1992 Los Angeles riots, after White police officers accused of beating him were acquitted by a mostly White jury, race takes center stage as a discussion topic for a few days then fades away from the public's attention. The perceptual gap, compounded by generations of suspicion and hostility on both sides, interferes with the mutual understanding and communication that are essential for effective biracial problem solving. The problems associated with race in America will not go away by ignoring them or waiting until the next crisis develops to spend one or two days in intense discussion before going back to business as usual. Long-festering racial problems, which interfere with the quest for a better life for Black males and their families, will only be resolved by active, prolonged efforts by Blacks and Whites to engage one another across the table in an honest dialogue as equals. Society needs a continuing dialogue that moves beyond the dominance–submissiveness paradigm that has historically characterized race relations in America. It is also essential to transcend the recent tendency to polarize racial debate with loaded, subtly race-baiting words like merit-based hiring, welfare, crime, and drugs.

Blacks and Whites, living in the same geographical space, do not have to love each other to get along, but they must be able to communicate to solve problems of mutual concern. There are pressing problems in housing, education, health care, employment, job training, and family stability that can only be addressed in an open, frank, biracial dialogue. To reach across the perceptual divide and achieve the level of mutual understanding and empathic awareness that is essential for productive dialogue, each side will have to confront and express intense, and sometimes painful, emotions. Blacks will most surely express anger and resentment about America's racial history and their personal experiences of what it is like to live in a society where Whites possess political, economic, and legal power and control the mass media. Blacks are likely to be a bit more reluctant to express hurt and fear; it is not easy for them to reveal their deepest feelings in front of Whites. In a frank dialogue, Whites would probably at some point express anger and resentment toward Blacks for wanting what Whites perceive as special preferences in university admissions, employment, career advancement, business loans, and government contracts. Whites will also, no doubt, accuse Blacks of not taking responsibility for the violence, crime, drugs, teen pregnancies, welfare, and gangs that plague inner-city neighborhoods.

Along the way, Whites will have to work through such defense mechanisms as denial, rationalization, minimization, and projection of blame, postures that have prevented them from facing the horrible destruction created by centuries of racial oppression. The two most difficult problems for Whites will be developing empathy for the Black experience in America and acknowledging that White skin carries with it certain advantages from birth.

Whites need to go beyond the words and learn to feel what it's like to be Black in America. They need to walk in Black people's shoes and stretch to experience the world from an African-American frame of reference. Academic discussions will not do the job; it is easy to sit through a lecture, hear the words, and still remain untouched at an emotional level. Whites need to hear Black voices, imagine what it's like to be Black, reach across the chasm that divides us, and learn to see the world through a different lens. Evasions, denial, and fantasies about a race-blind society will not get the job done. The majority of Whites do not really know Black people; they are divorced from the day-to-day lives of people of color. The only way they will be able to move past their insulation is through a deep interpersonal encounter with Blacks. Major changes in perception come about through involvement and struggle.

It will be troubling for most Whites to admit that their skin carries privileges in our society. When they accuse Blacks of seeking advantages through affirmative action and other programs designed to address legitimate social grievances, they fail to recognize their inherent privileges. Because they are used to being in the driver's seat and do not carry with them a legacy of oppression, they can dismiss race as irrelevant and deny the set of advantages they possess simply because they are born with the physical features that Western society so highly values.[4] Peggy McIntosh, a professor at Wellesley College, is a leader in a new field of study called "Whiteness." She equates the privilege of being White with being right-handed. Society is designed for right-handers. Pick up a pair of scissors, sit at a lecture hall desk, or grasp a door handle—they are all designed for right-handed people. Whiteness works in a similar way. Children born into White society on average have more money, more education, and more power than Blacks. They have unearned advantages simply by virtue of being White, according to McIntosh. Furthermore, their privileges include not having to be worried about being stopped by the police while driving through a White neighborhood at night simply because of their skin color, or being viewed suspiciously when walking through a White neighborhood.

In the fall of 1996, a nonprofit organization called the Center for the Study of White American Culture sponsored a two-day workshop advertised on the Internet as a "dialogue on Whiteness." The intent was to allow Whites the opportunity to examine their ethnicity and understand that their color provides unearned privileges. While Whites have special entitlements, most of them don't consciously perceive themselves as privileged. Whites seem to think that what Whites feel, see, experience, and think is the norm. As the old Black folk saying goes, "If you're White, you're right." Other colors are considered aberrant: "If you're Black, get back." Non-Whites are expected to adapt to White norms.[5]

Other issues Whites will have to face involve acknowledging the contributions that Blacks have made to American life and thought, recognizing the heroic struggle Blacks have made to survive in America, and redefining integration from a one-way to a two-way process. Whites should extend their vision beyond the social pathology of urban inner-city ghettos and move beyond the stereotypes of Black men as street corner Brothers, athletes, or entertainers, and recognize the pervasive influence of African-American culture in American life and thought. Black rhythms, themes, and concepts permeate much of American folk humor, music, speech, dance, dress, drama, and nonverbal expressive styles. Blacks have made significant contributions to American literature and science. It is difficult to imagine what America would be like without the creative contributions of African-Americans.

Also, the Black struggle for equal justice has enriched America. It has opened up the doors of opportunity for other minorities and for women of all races. It has forced America to reexamine the true meaning of equality and fair play. More important, African-Americans have translated pathos and tragedy into the exultation and sorrow of gospel music, the sensuality and hardship of the blues, and the tragicomic ethos expressed in Black folk poetry.

Finally, the meaning of integration needs to be redefined to fit the realities of the twenty-first century. In the past, Whites defined racial integration as Blacks becoming assimilated into White America on terms controlled by White people; Whites would set the pace, determine the standards, and decide who and what was appropriate. The 1967 movie *Guess Who's Coming to Dinner* is a prototype of the old order of one-way integration on terms acceptable to Whites. In the movie, Sidney Poitier plays an outstanding Black physician, a candidate for a Nobel Prize in medicine, who plans to marry a wealthy young White woman (played by Katherine Ross) who has been raised in a racially liberal tradition by her parents (Spencer Tracy and Katharine Hepburn). The Poitier character is the perfect Negro. He is well educated, bright, articulate, soft-spoken, desexualized, urbane, and cultured (in a Euro-American sense). The liberal White parents face a dilemma: Should they accept this Black man who has met all the criteria for success as defined by Euro-American standards, or should they reject him because his skin is still Black? Embedded in this old concept of integration is the arrogant presumption that Whites have the final power to accept or reject and that what Blacks as a group are seeking is affirmation or the stamp of approval from Whites.[6]

In the new order of racial integration, Blacks are demanding a two-way process in which both sides contribute to the definition of what is acceptable in terms of behavioral standards, dress, dance steps, language, how political power is distributed, and how interracial relationships should be conducted. Whites seem surprised when they are reminded that the rules and norms of behavior set up to make them feel comfortable represent only one perspective. In a healthy adult relationship, both parties need to participate in defining rules and standards for conducting the relationship. The reason many middle-class Blacks avoid Whites after work and increasingly prefer to live in Black neighborhoods is that they are tired of the implicit rule that Whites have the final voice of approval. Blacks who resist White control are not Black racists; they simply want to be recognized for what they are without always having to seek White affirmation or validation.

In a frank Black/White dialogue, Blacks will, no doubt, be confronted with their responsibility for the tough guy, go-for-bad images and behaviors that many inner-city Black males project. In the past, Black leaders like Jesse Jackson focused exclusively on White discrimination that restricted Black access to jobs, housing, economic empowerment, political power, and career advancement. Now Jackson and others in the vanguard of Black leadership are reluctantly speaking against the Black-on-Black crime, violence, drugs, teen pregnancies, school failures, and family deterioration that plague poor Black communities. Jackson, who started out trying to change the system, is increasingly forced to look within and ask his people to take responsibility for destructive behaviors that they have the power to change. He is encouraging churches, fraternal orders, and men's groups to get involved and join hands with a new street leadership to work for progressive change from within the Black community. To his credit, Minister Farrakhan has always been an advocate of Black men taking responsibility for their behavior. He has consistently preached moral values involving hard work, abstinence from drugs, taking care of family, avoiding violence, and limiting sexual activity to the confines of marriage. Understandably, those who agree with Jesse Jackson and Louis Farrakhan worry that focusing on what Blacks can do to reduce destructive behavior will reinforce stereotypes of their irresponsibility and provide White conservatives with a rationale for eliminating government programs. Self-help, individual responsibility, and personal transformation will only go so far; society must do its fair share in removing the barriers that keep Black men from thriving optimally.[7]

Blacks also need to face the fact that there is a diversity of opinion within their own community. When someone speaks out or breaks the code of silence, it does not mean they are "Uncle Tomming," or selling out. Growth occurs through constructive criticism and confronting the dissonance of conflicting ideas. A monologue within the Black community that suppresses dissonance and the creative tension it produces retards both intraracial and biracial progress.

Dr. Martin Luther King's dream of a beloved community where all men can sit down together at the table of brotherhood in a spirit of love and reconciliation is not realistically achievable in the short run during these troubled times. It is possible, however, for Blacks and Whites in a biracial dialogue to move beyond loaded words, polarities, elliptical talk, and divisive issues to a point where we can seriously examine promising solutions to many economic, social, and educational problems. Small-scale model programs that show signs of working already exist in the areas of health care, housing, imprisonment, drug rehabilitation, and job training. According to Lisbeth and Daniel Schorr, in their book *Within Our Reach,* most successful, innovative social programs are small, with clearly defined objectives. Staff members are free to use their best judgment and collaborate with their clients and families to figure out what will work best in a given situation. They are not bogged down by paperwork and bureaucratic rules; like the "shepherds"—the caseworkers in Baltimore's Choice program—they can respond to problems as they arise and reach out to other community groups for support, guidance, and services.[8]

The U.S. armed forces have been in the forefront in the development of training programs for improving race relations that could be adapted to civilian life. Within a patriarchal culture, the military has established itself as one of the most successful multiracial institutions in America. Blacks are represented at every rank from privates to generals and admirals. Retired General Colin Powell, White America's most admired Black man, was the country's highest-ranking military officer as chairman of the Joint Chiefs of Staff. General Powell freely admits that without the Army's affirmative action program, led by an African-American, Secretary of the Army Clifford Alexander, he would not have received the opportunities and training to rise to his rank and position. Until well into the 1970s, despite President Truman's 1948 desegregation order, the officer's corps of the military remained a bastion of White, mostly southern, males.

What's interfering with racial progress in America is not a lack of ideas or know-how. What's missing is a commitment to get to the heart of what separates us and to persevere until we find areas of agreement on goals, strategies, priorities, timetables, and allocation of resources.

Religious Groups Step Forward

The still unanswered question is what groups in our society are able to facilitate the beginnings of an interracial dialogue. Churches and other religious organizations are in an excellent position to start the first phase of a nationwide Black/White dialogue. Preliminary discussions are already under way between some church-affiliated groups.

In June 1996, Ralph Reed, head of the predominantly conservative Christian Coalition, called a meeting with Black church leaders to protest the burnings of Black churches. He pledged to raise over a million dollars from his mailing list of 100,000 churches to rebuild more than forty Black churches in the South that had been destroyed. Reed designated Sunday, July 14, 1996, as Racial Reconciliation Sunday and issued a call for an ongoing reconciliation dialogue. He made it clear at the meeting that his commitment to this cause went beyond assistance to restore the burned-out churches. He asked the gathering for suggestions and said he was willing to do whatever it took to move forward in the direction of racial progress.

Reed acknowledged that in the past, Evangelical Christian groups had not only been on the sidelines in the struggle for racial justice but on the wrong side. In the 1960s, when the Reverend Martin Luther King, Jr., and his followers were being gassed, jailed, shot, beaten, and attacked with high-power fire hoses, conservative Evangelicals were claiming a biblical base for segregation and derisively referring to Dr. King as the Communist-inspired "Martin Luther Coon." Reed now preaches a spirit of repentance, asks for forgiveness, and calls on his followers to repudiate bigotry and racism in all its forms. He fully understands that the Christian Coalition and other church groups that make up the Christian Right cannot lead a moral movement to uplift America without addressing the question of racism.

Understandably, Black religious groups are skeptical of Reed's commitment. His conservative positions on affirmative action, welfare, and voting rights have not won him many friends in the Black community. The Reverend Joseph Lowery, head of the Southern Christian Leadership Conference, is one of the skeptics, but he feels Reed's commitment should be tested by action and is willing to work with him.[9]

Other Christian groups are stepping forward to lead the movement toward racial reconciliation. At a 1994 meeting in Memphis, a coalition of twenty-one White Pentecostal groups voted to disband and join forces with Black Pentecostals. The two groups held an emotionally releasing foot-washing ceremony to demonstrate their sincerity; members of each race bathed the other's feet. In 1995, the Southern Baptist Convention, America's largest Protestant group, voted to repent for past racism and seek forgiveness from their African-American brotherhood and sisterhood.

Racial reconciliation and interracial brotherhood are a major focus of Promise Keepers, a rapidly growing Christian men's group. At their revival rallies in football stadiums, which annually draw over one million men, each gathering of around 50,000 or more participants features a sermon on racial healing. One of the Promise Keepers' seven promises is to reach beyond the racial barriers and demonstrate the power of biblical healing and unity. At each rally, White participants publicly bear witness and confess to past acts of racism on their part and on the part of their ancestors. Spurred on by the leadership of the Promise Keepers, White suburban churches and Black inner-city churches are joining hands to form biracial men's ministries to work toward reconciliation. The Promise Keepers believe that racial barriers can only be broken down by direct contact, repentance, catharsis, renewal, and building coalitions.

The former University of Colorado football coach Bill McCartney, founder of Promise Keepers' Revival Ministry, has achieved a level of interracial understanding that most White men don't possess. Recruiting young Black male athletes in the inner cities, he learned firsthand the hardships they experienced growing up in deteriorating neighborhoods. He has successfully mentored many young Black men through the difficult passage from late adolescence to adulthood. Along the way, incidentally, he has acquired two biracial grandchildren.[10]

At a giant rally in Washington, D.C., on October 4, 1997, attended by several hundred thousand participants, the Promise Keepers' leadership clearly indicated that improving race relationships is at the top of their agenda. A survey conducted by the *Washington Post* found that one out of seven participants at the Washington rally was Black. Bill McCartney, who still likes to be called Coach, told the crowd gathered at the rally that his goal is to hold a multiracial rally in every state capital in the Union at noon on January 1, 2000, to announce that every Christian congregation has rooted out racism within its own ranks.

While he supports Coach McCartney's goal of ending racism in Christian churches, the Reverend Robert Franklin, president of the Interdenominational Theological Center in Atlanta, the largest predominantly African-American seminary in America, thinks the Promise Keepers' effort to eradicate racism will be successful only if it is linked with serious attempts to work with the Black church to reduce poverty and crime in low-income Black communities. Franklin, who attended the 1997 Promise Keepers' rally, told reporters that he was impressed by the way Black men and White men mingled during the gathering.[11]

Christian radio and TV stations could extend the reach of a biracial dialogue by broadcasting a series of small group sessions and town hall meetings. Eventually, public broadcasting stations and network TV could do the same, using formats similar to CNN's *Talk Back Live* and other discussion shows. The goal of a Black/White dialogue is for racially mixed groups of citizens to talk directly to each other as much as possible, rather than for experts with prepackaged lines to debate one another. The facilitators and discussion leaders will have to make sure that a diversity of views is expressed in the dialogue. We cannot make racial progress when the converted talk only to each other. Intellectual Blacks talking to White moderates and liberals or Black conservatives talking to White conservatives does not make for real biracial dialogue. White southerners need to talk to northern Blacks. White conservative suburbanites need to talk to angry inner-city Black males. Controversial figures like Nation of Islam leader Louis Farrakhan need to be brought into the dialogue. As a nation, we cannot continue to suppress controversial ideas and expect to make racial progress.

What We Can Do

In *Color Blind: Seeing Beyond Race in a Race-Obsessed World*, Ellis Cose lays out a model to guide America toward an interracial dialogue.[12] Based on his extensive study of racial reconciliation efforts under way in South Africa and ongoing racial problems in America, Cose thinks that we should acknowledge that we live in a color-conscious society and seek to become color neutral rather than color blind. Color neutrality seeks to remove disadvantages based on skin color but recognizes that skin color is a reality of life in American society. According to Cose, as he noted in an earlier book, *The Rage of a Privileged Class: Why Blacks Are So Angry* (1993), one reason for the Black-White chasm in America is that not only are we afraid to talk to each other, we seem unwilling to listen.[13] His plan for initiating a cross-racial dialogue that includes both talking and listening, geared to move us in the direction of empathic racial understanding, is based on the following recommendations:[14]

1. *We must stop expecting time to solve the problem for us.* Time doesn't heal all wounds; it certainly doesn't solve all problems. It is often merely

an excuse for allowing problems to fester. Our problems, including our racial problems, belong to us, not to our descendants.

2. *We must recognize that race relations is not a zero-sum game.* As a society, we need to move beyond the assumption that America is a zero-sum society in which if one race advances another must regress. In large measure, zero-sum thinking often accounts for the illogical reaction to programs that aim to help minorities.

3. *We must realize that ending hate is the beginning, not the end, of our mission.* If we tell ourselves that the only problem is hate, we avoid facing the reality that it is mostly decent, nonhating people who perpetuate racial inequality.

4. *We must accept the fact that equality is not a halfway proposition.* We made a mistake when we assumed that social, economic, and political equality are not interrelated, that it was possible to go on living in largely segregated neighborhoods, socialize in largely segregated circles, and even attend segregated places of worship, and yet have workplaces and a polity in which race ceased to be a factor. As long as we cling to the notion that equality is fine in some spheres and not in others, we will be clinging to a lie.

5. *We must end American apartheid.* There is something fundamentally incongruous in the idea of judging people by their character and yet consigning so many Americans at birth to communities in which they are written off even before their character is shaped.

6. *We must replace a presumption that minorities will fail with an expectation of their success.* Creating an atmosphere in which people learn that they cannot achieve is tantamount to creating failure. The various academic programs that do wonders with so-called at-risk youth share a steadfast belief in the ability of young people in their care. These programs manage to create an atmosphere in which the "success syndrome" can thrive. Instead of focusing so much attention on whether people with less merit are getting various educational or occupational slots, we should focus on how to widen and reward the pool of meritorious people.

7. *We must stop playing the blame game.* Too often in America's racial debate, we get sidetracked by searching for racial scapegoats. It hardly matters who is responsible for things being screwed up; the only relevant question is "How can we make things better?"

8. *We must do a better job at leveling the playing field.* As long as roughly one-third of Black Americans sit at the bottom of the nation's economic pyramid and have little chance of moving up, the United States will have a serious racial problem on its hands. There is simply no way around that cold reality. It is pointless to say that the problem is class, not race, if race and class are tightly linked.

9. *We must become serious about fighting discrimination.* Making discrimination a felony is probably not a solution, but more aggressive monitoring and prosecution—especially in housing and employment situations—would not be a bad start. Just as one cannot get beyond race by treating different races differently, one cannot get beyond discrimination by refusing to acknowledge it. We can only get beyond discrimination by fighting it vigorously wherever it is found.

10. *We must keep the conversation going.* Dialogue is clearly no cure-all for racial estrangement. Yet, as limited as the dialogue's audience may be, ongoing discourse is crucial. It gives those who are sincerely interested in examining their attitudes and beliefs an opportunity to do so, and, in some instances, can even lead to change.

11. *We must increase opportunities for interracial collaboration.* Even those who have no interest in talking about the racial situation can, through the process of working with people of other races, begin to see beyond skin color.

12. *We must stop looking for one solution to all our racial problems.* The reality is that there is no single or simple solution. If there is one answer, it lies in recognizing how complex the racial issue has become and in not using that complexity as an excuse for inaction. In short, if we are to achieve a solution to a complex of problems, we must attack the enemy on all fronts.

There are powerful forces in American life that have a vested interest in inhibiting a constructive racial dialogue and preventing a new biracial vision for the future from emerging. Some White southern politicians, neoconservative intellectuals, and governors of northern states use loaded words, with covertly racist implications, as wedge issues to maintain their power base. It's time for President Clinton to step up and bring the topic of racial reconciliation to the center of society's public and private dialogue. In February 1997, the Citizen's

Commission on Civil Rights, a bipartisan group that monitors federal civil rights policies, urged President Clinton to develop a more aggressive plan to combat racial discrimination.[15]

The president has been moving slowly but steadily in the direction of taking on race as the major unresolved conflict in American life. Starting in Memphis in 1993 at a Black church, where he feels comfortable with the religious rhythms and speech cadences, Mr. Clinton appealed to the congregation to concentrate on self-help and responsibility. Invoking the nonviolent, brotherly love theology of Martin Luther King, he urged the church members to take responsibility for the violence, crime, drugs, and other social pathologies that engulf poor Black communities. In 1995, his "mend it but don't end it" speech on affirmative action helped refocus a debate that at times seemed beyond civility. In April 1997, he appeared alongside Jackie Robinson's widow at the celebration of the fiftieth anniversary of the courageous baseball star's breaking of baseball's color bar. Later that spring, Clinton apologized to the victims of the infamous Tuskegee experiment, in the course of which Black men were secretly denied treatment in a government-sponsored syphilis research project.

Speaking at the commencement ceremonies at the University of California, San Diego, on June 14, 1997, the president made a broad appeal for racial reconciliation and called upon the nation to engage in a one-year dialogue to work through the controversial issues associated with race. To inspire a national dialogue on these vexing problems and help him articulate his vision of racial reconciliation, Clinton appointed a seven-member advisory panel.[16] The appointees included the eminent African-American historian John Hope Franklin, the former governor of New Jersey Thomas Kean, labor leader Linda Chavez-Thompson, and the Reverend Susan D. Johnson, senior pastor of the Bronx Christian Fellowship Church in New York City. The advisory panel for the president's initiative on race, headed by an executive director appointed for a twenty-month period, will have a $30 million budget and a staff of twenty people.[17]

The advisory board will host town hall meetings, conduct race relations educational forums, do research on the history of race relations over the past fifty years, and make proposals designed to reduce racial conflict and provide improvements for minorities in education, employment, housing, health care, and the administration of criminal justice. Based on what is learned from the meetings and research, Mr. Clinton, working closely with the board, will write a report summarizing his vision for a racially diverse society. The president's report will also outline steps that churches, businesses, individuals, and government (at all levels) can take to improve race relations.

Bill Clinton is mindful of the fact that a candid racial dialogue among Americans will not be easy at first. He understands that we will have to get past defensiveness, fears, "political correctness," and other barriers that prevent us from honestly confronting our thoughts and emotions in the perplexing arena of race. But ultimately, the push for an interracial dialogue must come from the people. In December 1955, Rosa Parks did not wait for church leaders, social activists, politicians, or the president of the United States to do the right thing. She stood up, stepped forward, took the risk, and ignited a series of changes that touched the core of American society. It's time for the undiscovered Rosa Parkses—Black and White, male and female—to step up and start the next phase of racial progress. The nation is waiting; it's time to get moving.

NOTES

Chapter 1

1. Richard Lacayo, A critical mass: Report on the Million Man March. *Time,* October 30, 1995, pp. 34–36.

2. Follow-up to Million Man March. *Los Angeles Times,* July 28, 1996, p. A13.

3. Kenneth Turan, The bus stopped here. *Los Angeles Times,* October 16, 1996, pp. F1, F6.

4. Ellis Cose, Watch what they do. *Newsweek,* October 7, 1996, pp. 62–63.

5. Clarence Page, A whole deck of race cards. *Los Angeles Times,* October 9, 1995, p. B9.

6. The Gallup Organization, The Gallup poll social audit on Black/White relations in the United States, Executive Summary, June 10, 1997, pp. 1–27.

7. Paul Richter, Beneath the bitterness over race. *Los Angeles Times,* August 13, 1991, pp. A1, A10.

8. Sylvester Monroe, The mirage of Farrakhan. *Newsweek,* October 30, 1996, p. 52.

9. Ruth Rosen, Which of us is taking welfare. *Los Angeles Times,* December 29, 1994, p. B7.

10. David Rosenbaum, Liberals move to fight corporate welfare. *New York Times,* March 13, 1997, p. A3.

11. Jesse Jackson, Democrats must hold fast to dreams of justice. *Los Angeles Times,* April 8, 1990, p. M7.

12. Jeffery Birnbaum, Turning back the clock. *Time,* March 3, 1994, pp. 36–37.

13. David Lesher, Willie Brown fervently defends affirmative action. *Los Angeles Times,* February 15, 1995, pp. A1, A29.

14. James Washington, ed., *Testament of Hope* (New York: Harper, 1996).

15. Stephen B. Oates, *Let the Trumpet Sound: The Life of Martin Luther King, Jr.* (New York: Harper & Row, 1982).

Chapter 2

1. Martin Bernal, *Black Athena: The Afroasiatic Roots of Classical Civilization,* Vol. 1: *The Fabrication of Ancient Greece 1785–1985* (New Brunswick, NJ: Rutgers University Press, 1987), p. 8. See also Andrew Billingsley, *Climbing Jacob's Ladder: The Enduring Legacy of African-American Families* (New York: Simon & Schuster, 1992); Cheikh Anta Diop, *The African Origin of Civilization: Myth or Reality* (Chicago: Lawrence Hill, 1974); Carter G. Woodson, *African Background Outlined* (Washington, DC: Association for the Study of Afro-American Life and History, 1936); Carter G. Woodson, *The Mis-Education of the Negro* (Washington, DC: Associated, 1933); Ivan Van Sertima, *They Came Before Columbus: The African Presence in Ancient America* (New York: Random House, 1976); Yosef A. A. ben-Jochannan, *African Origins of the Major "Western Religions"* (Baltimore: Black Classic Press, 1988); John Henrik Clarke, *Africans Away from Home* (Washington, DC: Institute of Independent Education, 1992); and Asa G. Hilliard III (with Larry Williams and Damali Nia), *The Teachings of Ptah Hotep: The Oldest Book in the World* (Atlanta: Blackwood Press, 1987).

2. For a discussion of some of the relevant issues in the controversy over race by anthropologists and psychologists, see *Anthropology Newsletter,* April 1997, vol. 38, no. 4, and October 1997, vol. 38, no. 7 through May 1998, vol. 39, no. 5. See also Halford H. Fairchild, A. H. Yee, Gail E. Wyatt, and F. M. Weizmann, Readdressing psychology's problems with race. *American Psychologist, 50,* no. 1 (1995): 46–47; and A. H. Yee, H. H. Fairchild, F. Weizmann, and G. E. Wyatt, Addressing psychology's problems with race. *American Psychologist, 48,* no. 11 (1993): 1132–1140.

3. Luigi Luca Cavalli-Sforza, Genes, people and languages. *Scientific American,* November 1991, pp. 104–110; L. L. Cavalli-Sforza, Genes, people and languages. *Proceedings of the National Academy of Sciences of the United States of America,* July 22, 1997, pp. 7719–7724.

4. Useni E. Perkins, *Harvesting New Generations: The Positive Development of Black Youth* (Chicago: Third World Press, 1985).

5. Robert Staples and Leanor B. Johnson, *Black Families at the Crossroads: Challenges and Prospects* (San Francisco: Jossey-Bass, 1993).

6. Herbert Ekwe-Ekwe and Femi Nzegwu, *Operationalising Afrocentrism* (London: International Institute for Black Research, 1994).

7. Wade Nobles, African philosophy: Foundations for Black psychology. In *Black Psychology,* ed. Reginald L. Jones (New York: Harper & Row, 1972), pp. 18–22.

8. Jerome Schiele, Afrocentricity: Implications for higher education. *Journal of Black Studies, 25,* no. 2 (1994): 150, 169.

9. Nilgun Okur, Afrocentricity as a generative idea in the study of African-American drama. *Journal of Black Studies, 24,* no. 1 (1993): 88, 108.

10. Molefi K. Asante, *The Afrocentric Idea* (Philadelphia: Temple University Press, 1987).

11. Alfred B. Pasteur and Ivory L. Toldson, *Roots of Soul: The Psychology of Black Expressiveness* (New York: Doubleday, 1982).

12. Geneva Smitherman, *Talkin' and Testifyin': The Language of Black America* (Boston: Houghton Mifflin, 1977).

13. Alex Haley, *Roots* (New York: Doubleday, 1976).

14. Sharon Harley, *The Timetables of African-American History* (New York: Simon & Schuster, 1995).

15. Staples and Johnson, *Black Families at the Crossroads.*

16. Stanley Elkins, *Slavery: A Problem in American Institutions and Intellectual Life* (Chicago: University of Chicago Press, 1968).

17. Orlando Patterson, *The Sociology of Slavery* (London: Granada, 1967).

18. Uirich Phillips, *American Negro Slavery* (Baton Rouge: Louisiana State University Press, 1918).

19. Nathan Glazer and Daniel Moynihan, *Beyond the Melting Pot* (Cambridge, MA: MIT Press, 1963).

20. Melville Herskovits, *The Myth of the Negro Past* (Boston: Beacon Press, 1941).

21. John Blassingame, *The Slave Community* (New York: Oxford University Press, 1972).

22. George Rawick, *From Sundown to Sunup: The Making of the Black Community* (Westport, CT: Greenwood, 1972).

23. Joseph White, *The Psychology of Blacks: An Afro-American Perspective* (Englewood Cliffs, NJ: Prentice Hall, 1984).

24. Staples and Johnson, *Black Families at the Crossroads.*

25. Rawick, *From Sundown to Sunup.*

26. John Hope Franklin, A historical note on Black families. In *Black Families,* 2nd ed., ed. Harriett Pipes McAdoo (Newbury Park, CA: Sage, 1988).

27. Frederick Law Olmsted, *A Journey in the Seaboard Slave States with Remarks on Their Economy* (New York: Putnam, 1955).

28. Carter G. Woodson, *The Negro in Our History* (Washington, DC: Associated Press, 1927).

29. Joseph Carroll, *Slave Insurrections in the United States, 1800–1865* (New York: New American Library, 1938).

30. Dorothy Sterling, *Captain of* The Planter (Garden City, NY: Doubleday, 1958).

31. Vincent Thompson, Leadership in the African diaspora in the Americas prior to 1860. *Journal of Black Studies, 24,* no. 1 (1993): 42–76.

32. Frederick Law Olmsted, *The Cotton Kingdom* (New York: Knopf, 1953).

33. Janice Hamlet, Religious discourses as cultural narrative: A critical analysis of African-American sermons. *Western Journal of Black Studies, 18,* no. 1 (1994): 11–17.

34. Ibid.

35. Rawick, *From Sundown to Sunup.*

36. Eric Lincoln, *The Negro Pilgrimage in America: The Coming of Age of Black Americans* (New York: Bantam, 1967).

37. Audrey Smedley, *Race in North America: Origin and Evolution of a World View* (Boulder, CO: Westview, 1993).

38. Charles Carroll, *The Negro as a Beast: or, In the Image of God* (St. Louis, MO: American Book and Bible House, 1900).

39. William Lee Howard, The Negro as a distinct factor in civilization. *Medicine, 60* (May 1903): 434.

40. George Frederickson, *The Black Image in the White Mind: The Debate on Afro-American Character and Destiny 1817–1914* (Hanover, NH: Wesleyan University Press, 1971).

41. Hugh Pearson, *The Shadow of the Panther: Huey Newton and the Price of Black Power in America* (Reading, MA: Addison Wesley, 1994).

42. James Davis, *Who Is Black? One Nation's Definition* (University Park: Pennsylvania State University Press, 1991).

43. Frederickson, *The Black Image in the White Mind.*

44. Upton Sinclair, *The Jungle* (New York: New American Library, 1906; reprint 1964).

45. Thomas Dixon, Jr., *The Clansman: An Historical Romance of the Ku Klux Klan* (New York: A. Wessels, 1905).

46. Donald Bogle, *Toms, Coons, Mulattoes, Mammies, and Bucks: An Interpretive History of Blacks in American Films,* 3rd ed. (New York: Continuum, 1994).

47. Rayford Logan, The Negro as portrayed in representative northern magazines and newspapers. In *White Racism,* ed. Barry N. Schwartz and Robert Disch (New York: Holt, 1970), pp. 393, 398.

48. Theodore Cross, *The Black Power Imperative: Racial Inequality and the Politics of Non-Violence* (New York: Faulkner Books, 1987).

49. Earl Ofari Hutchinson, *Assassination of the Black Male Image* (Los Angeles: Middle Passage Press, 1994).

50. Tom P. Brady, *Black Monday* (Winona, MS: Association of Citizens' Councils, 1955), p. 11.

51. Cross, *The Black Power Imperative.*

52. Ibid.

53. Pearson, *The Shadow of the Panther.*

54. Michael Friedly and David Gallen, *Martin Luther King, Jr.: The FBI File* (New York: Carroll & Graf, 1993).

Chapter 3

1. Ralph Ellison, *Invisible Man* (New York: Random House, 1947), p. 3.

2. Molefi K. Asante, *The Afrocentric Idea* (Philadelphia: Temple University Press, 1987).

3. Joseph White and Thomas Parham, *The Psychology of Blacks: An African-American Perspective,* 2nd ed. (Englewood Cliffs, NJ: Prentice Hall, 1990).

4. Faith Berry, *Langston Hughes: Before and Beyond Harlem* (Westport, CT: Lawrence Hill, 1983).

5. James Baldwin, *The Fire Next Time* (New York: Dell, 1963).

6. Geneva Smitherman, *Talkin' and Testifyin': The Language of Black America* (New York: Houghton Mifflin, 1977).

7. White and Parham, *The Psychology of Blacks.*

8. Otto Kerner, *Report of the National Advisory Commission on Civil Disorders. U.S. Riot Commission Report* (New York: Bantam, 1968).

9. Henry H. Mitchell and Nicholas Cooper-Lewter, *Soul Theology: The Heart of Black American Culture* (New York: Harper & Row, 1986).

10. Wayne Blake and Carol Darling, The dilemmas of the African-American male. *Journal of Black Studies, 23,* no. 4 (1994): 460, 471.

11. Andrew Billingsley, *Climbing Jacob'sLadder: An Enduring Legacy of African-American Families* (New York: Simon & Schuster, 1992).

12. Linda Callahan, A critical scene within Jesse Jackson's rhetorical vision. *Journal of Black Studies, 24,* no. 1 (1993): 3–15.

13. James Cones, *The Spirituals and the Blues* (New York: Orbis, 1992).

14. Rose Finkenstaedt, *Face to Face, Blacks in America: White Perceptions and Black Realities* (New York: William Morrow, 1994).

15. Daniel Wolff, *You Send Me: The Life and Times of Sam Cooke* (New York: William Morrow, 1995).

16. Kenneth Estell, *African-America: Portrait of a People* (Detroit: Visible Ink Press, 1994).

17. Alfred B. Pasteur and Ivory L. Toldson, *The Roots of Soul: The Psychology of Black Expressiveness* (New York: Doubleday, 1982).

18. Finkenstaedt, *Face to Face.*

19. Lawrence W. Levine, *Black Culture and Black Consciousness: Afro-American Culture from Slavery to Freedom* (New York: Oxford University Press, 1971).

20. Nelson George, *Elevating the Game: Black Men and Basketball* (New York: HarperCollins, 1992).

21. Ira Berkow, *The Du Sable Panthers* (New York: Atheneum, 1978).

22. E. Franklin Frazier, *The Black Bourgeoisie* (New York: Free Press, 1957).

23. David Halberstam, *The Fifties* (New York: Villard Books, 1993).

24. Pasteur and Toldson, *The Roots of Soul.*

25. Shelley F. Fishkin, *Was Huck Black? Mark Twain and African-American Voices* (New York: Oxford University Press, 1993).

26. Anthony DePalma, Huck Finn's voice is heard as Twain meets Black youth. *New York Times,* July 7, 1992, pp. A1, A9.

27. Finkenstaedt, *Face to Face.*

28. W. E. B. Du Bois, *The Souls of Black Folks* (Chicago: McClurg, 1903).

29. William H. Grier and Price M. Cobbs, *Black Rage* (New York: Basic Books, 1968).

30. Stephen B. Oates, *Let the Trumpet Sound: The Life of Martin Luther King, Jr.* (New York: Harper & Row, 1982).

31. Hugh Pearson, *The Shadow of the Panther: Huey Newton and the Price of Black Power in America* (Reading, MA: Addison-Wesley, 1994).

32. Du Bois, *The Souls of Black Folks.*

Chapter 4

1. Howard Rosenberg, Check on Blacks' progress in T.V. land. *Los Angeles Times,* February 19, 1997, pp. F1, F12.

2. Mel Watkins, *On the Real Side* (New York: Simon & Schuster, 1994).

3. Gregg Braxton, Roots plus 20 years. *Los Angeles Times Calendar,* January 26, 1996, pp. 8, 9, 79.

4. Donald Bogle, *Toms, Coons, Mulattoes, Mammies, and Bucks: An Interpretive History of Blacks in American Films,* 3rd ed. (New York: Continuum, 1994).

5. Braxton, Roots plus 20 years.

6. Mitchell Duneier, *Slim's Table: Race, Respectability, and Masculinity* (Chicago: University of Chicago Press, 1992).

7. Nicholas Lemann, *The Promised Land* (New York: Knopf, 1991).

8. Elijah Anderson, The code of the streets. *Atlantic Monthly,* July 1994, pp. 80–94.

9. Ibid.

10. Margot Slade, At the bar, the urban survival syndrome. *New York Times,* May 29, 1994, p. A14.

11. Sharon Elise and Umoja Adewole, Spike Lee constructs the new Black man: Mo' better. *Western Journal of Black Studies, 16,* no. 2 (1992): 82–89.

12. Ibid.

13. Bogle, *Toms, Coons, Mulattoes, Mammies, and Bucks.*

14. Nelson George, *Blackface: Reflections on African-Americans and the Movies* (New York: HarperCollins, 1994).

15. Elise and Adewole, Spike Lee constructs the new Black man.

16. Cathleen Decker, Race often plays a real, but unspoken role in politics. *Los Angeles Times,* October 16, 1994, pp. A10, A40.

17. Ken Englade, *Murder in Boston* (New York: St. Martin's Press, 1990).

18. Don Terry, Woman's false charge revives hurt for Blacks. *New York Times,* November 6, 1994, p. A12.

19. Elijah Anderson, *Streetwise: Race, Class, and Change in an Urban Community* (Chicago: University of Chicago Press, 1990).

20. Duneier, *Slim's Table.*

21. Studs Terkel, *Race: How Blacks and Whites Think and Feel About the American Obsession* (New York: New Press, 1992).

22. James M. Jones, Psychological models of race: What have they been and what should they be? In *Psychological Perspectives on Human Diversity in America. Masters Lectures in Psychology,* ed. Jacqueline P. Goodchilds (Washington, DC: American Psychological Association, 1991), pp. 3–46.

23. Raymond Hernandez, Rutgers' chief seemingly aloof, now hurts. *New York Times,* February 13, 1995, p. E4.

24. Julie Cart and Dean Murphy, Two L.A.P.D. stops harassment, says Olympian. *Los Angeles Times,* May 9, 1992, p. A37.

25. Stephen Holmes, Behind a park mirror: Traditional victims give vent to racism. *New York Times,* February 13, 1994, p. E4.

26. Douglas Rose and Gary Esolen, DuKKKe for governor. In *The Emergence of David Duke and the Politics of Race,* ed. Douglas Rose (Chapel Hill: University of North Carolina Press, 1992), pp. 197, 241.

27. Ellis Cose, To the victor, few spoils. *Newsweek,* March 29, 1993, p. 54.

28. David Gates, White male paranoia. *Newsweek,* March 29, 1993, pp. 48–53.

29. Terkel, *Race.*

30. Joe R. Feagin and Melvin P. Sikes, *Living with Racism: The Black Middle-Class Experience* (Boston: Beacon Press, 1994).

31. Stephen Braun and Ron Russell, For veterans of Watts: Riots are a violent re-run. *Los Angeles Times,* May 4, 1972, pp. A1, A11.

32. Ellis Cose, *Rage of a Privileged Class: Why Are Middle-Class Blacks Angry? Why Should Americans Care?* (New York: HarperCollins, 1993).

33. Brent Staples, The cruelest game: High school players in Coney Island buy a ticket out of the ghetto on train that doesn't run. *New York Times Book Review,* November 13, 1994, p. 1.

34. Darcy Frey, *The Last Shot: City Streets, Basketball Dreams* (Boston: Houghton Mifflin, 1994).

Chapter 5

1. Richard Majors and Janet M. Billson, *Cool Pose: The Dilemma of Black Manhood in America* (New York: Lexington, 1992).

2. Gwendolyn Brooks, *The World of Gwendolyn Brooks* (New York: Harper & Row, 1971), p. 315.

3. Albert Camus, *The Stranger,* trans. S. Gilbert (New York: Knopf, 1946).

4. Cornel West, *Race Matters* (Boston: Beacon Press, 1993).

5. Joseph White, *The Troubled Adolescent* (New York: Pergamon Press, 1989).

6. Maulana Karenga, *Kwanzaa, Origin, Concepts, Practice* (Los Angeles, Kawaida Publications, 1976).

7. Kenneth Estell, *African-America: Portrait of a People* (Detroit: Visible Ink Press, 1994).

8. Jack Cheevers, Songs of violence top the charts. *Los Angeles Times,* April 3, 1995, pp. A1, A20.

9. Jessie Katz, Rock furor: New evil or new story. *Los Angeles Times,* August 5, 1995, pp. A1, A22.

10. Bakari Kitwana, *The Rap on Gangsta Rap* (Chicago: Third World Press, 1994).

11. Michel Marriott, Shot silences angry voice. *New York Times,* September 16, 1996, pp. A1, A13.

12. John Leland, Requiem for a gangsta. *Newsweek,* March 24, 1997, pp. 74–78.

13. Robert Hilburn, No easy answers for violence in gangsta rap. *Los Angeles Times,* March 10, 1997, p. A18.

14. Michel Marriott, Before he was B.I.G., rap star shadowed by trouble. *Los Angeles Times,* March 17, 1997, p. A13.

15. Matt Lait and Chuck Philips, Motives sought in rap slaying. *Los Angeles Times,* March 11, 1997, p. A15.

16. Leland, Requiem for a gangsta.

17. Michael Dyson, When gangstas grapple with evil. *New York Times,* March 30, 1997, Sec. II, p. 34.

18. John Leland, Rap and race. *Newsweek,* June 29, 1992, pp. 47–51.

19. James Romero, Hip-hop resonates worldwide. *Los Angeles Times,* March 14, 1997, pp. A1, A30, A31.

20. Lynn Hirschberg, The godfather of gangsta rap and his family values. *New York Times Magazine,* January 14, 1996, pp. 24–31.

21. Christopher Farley, From the driver's side. *Time,* September 20, 1996, p. 70.

22. Cheevers, Songs of violence top the charts.

23. Romero, Hip-hop resonates worldwide.

24. Paula Nechak, Rhyme documents ghetto life. *Seattle Post-Intelligencer,* March 5, 1995, p. C5.

25. Allen Abrahamson and Chuck Philips, Rap records mogul gets nine year sentence. *Los Angeles Times,* March 1, 1997, p. A12.

26. Robert Hilburn and Cheo Coker, Future cloudy at Death Row Records. *Los Angeles Times,* September 14, 1996, pp. F1, F6.

27. Chuck Philips, Tupac's mom sues. *Los Angeles Times,* April 19, 1997, p. A20.

28. Allison Samuels, Live from death row. *Newsweek,* May 18, 1998, pp. 78–79.

29. Hirschberg, The godfather of gangsta rap and his family values.

30. Hilburn and Coker, Future cloudy at Death Row Records.

31. Alex Raskin, A rapper's message for the eyes, not ears. *Los Angeles Times,* April 1, 1993, p. E5.

32. Jim Newton, Witnesses tell jury of Fuhrman epithets. *Los Angeles Times,* September 6, 1995, pp. A1, A8.

33. Katz, Rock furor.

34. Brent Staples, The politics of gangster rap. *New York Times,* August 27, 1993, p. A14.

35. Leland, Rap and race.

36. Kitwana, *The Rap on Gangsta Rap.*

37. Romero, Hip-hop resonates worldwide.

38. Ibid.

39. Ibid.

40. Leland, Rap and race.

41. West, *Race Matters.*

42. Jawanza Kunjufu, *Hip-Hop Visits MAAT: A Psychological Analysis of Values* (Chicago: African-American Images, 1993).

43. Kitwana, *The Rap on Gangsta Rap.*

44. Perry Hall, Beyond Afro-centrism: Alternatives for African-American studies. *Western Journal of Black Studies, 16,* no. 2 (1991): 207, 212.

45. Robert Fullilove and Mindy Fullilove, Black men, Black sexuality, and AIDS. In *Black Male Adolescents: Parenting and Education in a Community Context,* ed. Benjamin P. Bowser (Lanham, MD: University Press of America, 1991), pp. 214–227.

46. Estell, *African-America.*

47. Cheo Coker, Gangsta rap performer notorious B.I.G. slain. *Los Angeles Times,* March 10, 1997, p. A1.

48. Allison Samuels and David Gates, Last tango in Compton. *Newsweek,* January 25, 1997, pp. 74–75.

49. Jerry Crowe, Rappers call for truce in hip-hop. *Los Angeles Times,* February 13, 1997, p. A36.

50. Set to tour. *Los Angeles Times,* April 5, 1997, p. F1.

51. Steve Houchman and Cheo Coker, Rap summit is called. *Los Angeles Times,* April 18, 1997, pp. F1, F16.

52. Cheo Coker, Prophets answer to the rap question. *Los Angeles Times,* March 22, 1997, pp. F1, F16.

Chapter 6

1. Na'im Akbar, *Visions for Black Men* (Nashville, TN: Winston-Werek, 1991).

2. James Doyle and Michele Paludi, *Sex and Gender* (Dubuque, IA: William C. Brown, 1991).

3. Akbar, *Visions for Black Men.*

4. Molefi K. Asante, *The Afrocentric Idea* (Philadelphia: Temple University Press, 1987).

5. James Jones, Psychological models of race: What have they been and what should they be? In *Psychological Perspectives on Human Diversity in America. Masters Lectures in Psychology,* ed. Jacqueline D.

Goodchilds (Washington, DC: American Psychological Association, 1991), pp. 3–46.

6. William Cross, *Shades of Black: Diversity in African-American Identity* (Philadelphia: Temple University Press, 1991).

7. Ibid.

8. Ibid.

9. Bailey Jackson, Black identity development. *Journal of Educational Diversity and Innovation, 2* (1979): 19, 25.

10. Thomas Parham, Cycles of Nigrescence. *Counseling Psychologists, 17,* no. 2 (1989): 1187–1226.

11. Jonathan Agronsky, *Marion Barry, The Politics of Race* (Latham, NY: British American Publishing Co., 1991).

12. NOMAS—National Organization for Men Against Sexism, Statement of principles. In *Men's Lives,* ed. Michael S. Kimmel and Michael A. Messner (New York: Macmillan, 1992), p. 553.

13. Jerry Adler, Drums, sweat, and tears. *Newsweek,* June 24, 1991, pp. 46–51.

14. Ibid.

Chapter 7

1. John Leland and Allison Samuels, The generation gap. *Newsweek,* March 17, 1997, pp. 53, 55.

2. William Julius Wilson, When work disappears. *New York Times,* August 18, 1996, Sec. 6, pp. 26–31, 48–55.

3. Kurt Eichenwald, The two faces of Texaco. *New York Times,* November 10, 1996, Sec. 3, pp. 10–11.

4. Thomas Mulligan and Chris Kraul, Texaco settles race bias suit for $176 million. *Los Angeles Times,* November 16, 1996, pp. A1, A21.

5. Eichenwald, The two faces of Texaco.

6. Ibid.

7. Jolie Solomon, Texaco's troubles. *Newsweek,* November 25, 1996, pp. 48–49.

8. Jim Fitzgerald, Texaco settles race lawsuit. *Orange County Register,* November 16, 1996, p. A1.

9. Glenn Loury, The racism we condemn. *New York Times,* November 26, 1996, p. E15.

10. Mulligan and Kraul, Texaco settles race bias suit for $176 million.

11. Edward Barnes, Can't get there from here. *Time,* February 19, 1996, p. 33.

12. Bob Herbert, Bias intensified by inertia. *New York Times,* January 24, 1997, p. A15.

13. Don Terry, Chicago neighborhood reveals an ugly side. *New York Times,* March 27, 1997, p. A10.

14. Jewelle T. Gibbs, Young Black males in America: Endangered, embittered, embattled. In *Young, Black, and Male in America: An Endangered Species,* ed. Jewelle T. Gibbs (Westport, CT: Auburn House, 1988), pp. 1–36.

15. Ex-G.I. gets life term in racial killings. *New York Times,* February 7, 1997, p. A8.

16. Joe R. Feagin and Melvin P. Sikes, *Living with Racism: The Black Middle-Class Experience* (Boston: Beacon Press, 1994).

17. Gibbs, Young Black males in America.

18. Warren Leary, Discrimination may impair Blacks' health. *New York Times,* October 24, 1996, p. A12.

19. Nancy Krieger and Stephen Sidney, Racial discrimination and blood pressure. *American Journal of Public Health, 86,* no. 10 (October 1996): 1370–1378.

20. James Moss, Hurtling oppression: Overcoming anomie and self-hatred. In *Black Male Adolescents: Parenting and Education in a Community Context,* ed. Benjamin P. Bowser (Lanham, MD: University Press of America, 1991), pp. 282–297.

21. Richard Wright, *Native Son* (New York: Harper & Row, 1940).

22. James Baldwin, *The Fire Next Time* (New York: Dial Press, 1963).

23. Joseph White, *The Troubled Adolescent* (New York: Pergamon Press, 1989).

24. William Oliver, Black males and social problems: Prevention through Afro-centric socialization. *Journal of Black Studies, 20,* no. 1 (1989): 15–39.

25. Samuel R. Delaney and Joseph Beam, The possibilities of possibilities. In *In the Life: A Black Gay Anthology,* ed. Joseph Beam (Boston: Alyson Publications, 1986); and Kenneth Monteiro and Vincent Fuqua, African American gay youth: One form of manhood, *The High School Journal* (Chapel Hill: University of North Carolina Press, 1993/1994).

26. Ibid.

27. Frederick Ernst, Rupert Francis, Harold Nevels, and Carol Lemeh, Condemnation of homosexuality in the Black community: A gender-specific phenomenon? *Archives of Sexual Behavior, 20,* no. 6 (1991): 579–585.

28. Brenda Crawley and Edith Freeman, Themes in the views of older and younger African-American males. *Journal of African-American Male Studies, 1,* no. 1 (1993): 15–29.

29. Daniel J. Levinson et al., *The Seasons of a Man's Life* (New York: Knopf, 1978).

30. Sylvester Monroe and Peter Goldman, *Brothers: Black and Poor—A True Story of Courage and Survival* (New York: William Morrow, 1988).

Chapter 8

1. Sanyika Shakur (Kody Scott), *Monster: The Autobiography of an L.A. Gang Member* (New York: Atlantic Mercury Press, 1993).

2. Nathan McCall, *Makes Me Wanna Holler: A Young Black Man in America* (New York: Random House, 1994).

Chapter 9

1. Brent Staples, *Parallel Time: Growing Up in Black and White* (New York: Random House, 1994).

2. Henry Louis Gates, *Colored People* (New York: Knopf, 1994).

3. Sylvester Monroe and Peter Goldman, *Brothers: Black and Poor—A True Story of Courage and Survival* (New York: William Morrow, 1988).

4. Ellis Cose, *Rage of a Privileged Class: Why Are Middle-Class Blacks Angry? Why Should Americans Care?* (New York: HarperCollins, 1993).

5. Sam Fulwood, The rage of the middle class. *Los Angeles Times Magazine,* November 3, 1991, pp. 22, 52–57.

6. Ken Hardy, War of the worlds. *Networker,* July–August 1993, pp. 50–57.

7. Joe Klein, Can Powell reach them? *Newsweek,* October 30, 1995, p. 48.

8. William Henry, Pride and prejudice. *Time,* February 28, 1994, pp. 21, 25.

9. Arthur Magida, *Prophet of Rage: A Life of Louis Farrakhan and His Nation* (New York: Basic Books, 1996).

10. Howard Fineman and Vernon Smith, An angry charmer. *Newsweek,* October 30, 1996, pp. 32, 38.

11. Henry, Pride and prejudice.

12. Howard Ramseur, Psychologically healthy adults: A review of theory and research. In *Black Adult Development in Aging,* ed. Reginald L. Jones (Berkeley, CA: Cobb and Henry, 1989).

13. Audrey Edwards and Craig Polite, *Children of the Dream: The Psychology of Black Success* (New York: Doubleday, 1992).

14. Ramseur, Psychologically healthy adults.

Chapter 10

1. Daniel Patrick Moynihan, *The Negro Family: The Case for National Action* (Washington, DC: U.S. Government Printing Office, 1965).

2. Charles Willie, Social policy and social theory derived from the Black experience. *Journal of Black Studies, 23,* no. 4 (1993), 451–459.

3. Marco Williams, In search of our fathers. *Frontline Series,* Public Broadcasting System, November 24, 1992.

4. Nancy Boyd-Franklin, *Black Families in Therapy: A Multi-Systems Approach* (New York: Guilford Press, 1989).

5. Ibid.

6. Andrew Billingsley, *Climbing Jacob's Ladder: The Enduring Legacy of African-American Families* (New York: Simon & Schuster, 1992).

7. Nicholas Cooper-Lewter and Henry Mitchell, *Soul Theology: The Heart of American Black Culture* (San Francisco: Harper & Row, 1986).

8. Billingsley, *Climbing Jacob's Ladder.*

9. Keith Parker and Earl Smith, Religious participation among Black men. *Journal of African-American Male Studies, 1,* no. 1 (1993): 38, 46.

10. Billingsley, *Climbing Jacob's Ladder.*

11. Maxine Baca Zinn and D. Stanley Eitzen, *Diversity in Families,* 3rd ed. (New York: HarperCollins, 1993).

12. Lynn Smith, Single mothers go it alone. *Los Angeles Times,* July 22, 1993, pp. E1, E4.

13. Linda Dixon, The future of marriage and family in Black America. *Journal of Black Studies, 23,* no. 4 (1993): 472, 491.

14. David Blankenhorn, *Fatherless America* (New York: Basic Books, 1995).

15. Tamar Lewin, Rise in single parenthood is reshaping U.S. *New York Times,* October 5, 1992, pp. A1, A16.

16. Brent Staples, *Parallel Time: Growing Up in Black and White* (New York: Random House, 1994).

17. Elijah Anderson, The code of the streets. *Atlantic Monthly,* May 1994, pp. 80–94.

18. Ron Harris, Youth isn't kids' stuff these days. *Los Angeles Times,* May 12, 1991, pp. A1, A22–A23.

19. Noel A. Cazenave, Middle income Black fathers: An analysis of the provider role. *The Family Coordinator,* 28 (October 1979): 583, 593.

20. Sylvester Monroe and Peter Goldman, *Brothers: Black and Poor—A True Story of Courage and Survival* (New York: William Morrow, 1988).

21. Nathan McCall, *Makes Me Wanna Holler: A Young Black Man in America* (New York: Random House, 1994).

Chapter 11

1. Moshe Smilansky, *Friendship in Adolescence and Young Adulthood* (Gaithersburg, MD: Psychosocial and Educational Publications, 1991).

2. Harry Stack Sullivan, *The Interpersonal Theory of Psychiatry* (New York: Norton, 1953).

3. John Mitchell, Gangs rise in affluent Black turf. *Los Angeles Times,* November 13, 1992, pp. A1, A28.

4. Henry Louis Gates, *Colored People* (New York: Knopf, 1994).

5. Nathan McCall, *Makes Me Wanna Holler: A Young Black Man in America* (New York: Random House, 1994).

6. Clyde W. Franklin II, *The Changing Definition of Masculinity* (New York: Plenum, 1984).

7. Joseph White, *The Psychology of Blacks: An Afro-American Perspective* (Englewood Cliffs, NJ: Prentice Hall, 1984).

8. Alexander Jesseson, Connecting. *New York Times Magazine,* October 30, 1994, pp. 20–22, 36–37.

9. Sanyika Shakur (Kody Scott), *Monster: The Autobiography of an L.A. Gang Member* (New York: Atlantic Mercury Press, 1993).

10. Jesseson, Connecting.

11. Leon Bing, *Do or Die: For the First Time, Members of L.A.'s Most*

Notorious Teenage Gangs—the Crips and the Bloods—Speak for Themselves (New York: HarperCollins, 1991).

12. Jessie Katz, A gang ethic dies with gang sheet. *Los Angeles Times*, April 14, 1996, p. A1.

13. Ibid.

14. Tracy Wilkinson and Stephanie Chavez, Elaborate death rites of gangs. *Los Angeles Times*, March 2, 1992, p. A1.

15. Ibid.

16. Don Terry, Boy sought in teenager's death is latest victim of guns. *New York Times*, September 2, 1994, pp. A1, A9.

17. Don Terry, Two brothers held in slaying of murder suspect. *New York Times*, September 3, 1994, p. A5.

Chapter 12

1. Annie E. Casey Foundation, *Kids Count—Data on Asian, Native American, and Hispanic Children* (Baltimore, 1996).

2. Elijah Anderson, The code of the streets. *Atlantic Monthly*, May 1994, pp. 81–94.

3. Joe Sexton, Dispute in Brooklyn subway ends in killing of student, 16. *New York Times*, April 5, 1994, p. A15.

4. Isabel Wilkerson, Two boys, a debt, a gun, a victim: The face of violence. *New York Times*, May 16, 1994, pp. A1, C16.

5. Fox Butterfield, Seeds of murder epidemic: Teenage boys with guns. *New York Times*, October 19, 1992, p. A8.

6. National Urban League, Inc., *The State of Black America* (New York, 1996).

7. Susan Chira, Teenagers, in a poll, report worry and distrust of adults. *New York Times*, July 10, 1994, pp. A1, A9.

8. National Urban League, *The State of Black America*.

9. Ron Harris, For youths, fear for lives is part of living. *Los Angeles Times*, May 13, 1991, pp. A1, A16.

10. Ibid.

11. Mary Taylor Previte, What will they say at my funeral? *New York Times*, August 7, 1994, p. 17.

12. Harris, For youths, fear for lives is part of living.

13. Chira, Teenagers, in a poll, report.

14. Harris, For youths, fear for lives is part of living.

15. Michel Marriott, Grief tinged with anger over two deaths. *New York Times,* August 26, 1996, p. A11.

16. David Elkind, Understanding the young adolescent. *Adolescence, 13* (Spring 1978): 127–134.

17. Richard Wright, *Black Boy* (New York: Harper, 1945).

18. Jolia Wright, Out of blind anger, insight. *Los Angeles Times,* May 9, 1994, p. B8.

19. Celia W. Dugger, A boy in search of respect discovers how to kill. *New York Times,* May 15, 1994, pp. A1, A17.

20. Don Terry, Gangs: Machiavelli's descendants. *New York Times,* September 18, 1994, p. A14.

21. Dale Davis, Let me tell you. *New York Times,* November 5, 1994, p. A5.

22. Ron Suskind, Against all odds: In rough city schools, top students struggle to learn—and escape. *Wall Street Journal,* May 26, 1994, pp. A1, A8.

23. Felicia R. Lee, A drug dealer's rapid rise and ugly fall. *New York Times,* September 10, 1994, pp. A1, A10.

24. John Mitchell, Gangs rise on affluent Black turf. *Los Angeles Times,* November 11, 1992, pp. A1, A28–A29.

25. Michael Quintanilla, Looking bad. *Los Angeles Times,* March 6, 1992, pp. E1, E9.

26. Mitchell, Gangs rise on affluent Black turf.

27. Ibid.

28. David Ferrell, Lure of the streets puts promising L.A. youth on road to prison. *Los Angeles Times,* June 27, 1992, p. A30.

29. Ibid.

Chapter 13
1. Richard G. Majors, Conclusions and recommendations: A reason for hope—An overview of the new Black male movement in the United States. In *The Black American Male: His Present Status and Future,* ed. Richard G. Majors and Jacob U. Gordon (Chicago: Nelson Hall, 1994), pp. 299–316.

2. Al Stantoli, They turn young men into fathers. *Parade* magazine, May 29, 1994, pp. 16–17.

3. Noel A. Cazenave, Middle income Black fathers: An analysis of the provider role. *Family Coordinator, 28* (October 1979): 583, 593.

4. Jonathan Rabinovitz, A Hartford program to put fathers back in the family. *New York Times,* June 16, 1996, pp. A1, A12.

5. Ibid.

6. David Blankenhorn, *Fatherless America: Confronting Our Most Urgent Social Problem* (New York: Basic Books, 1995).

7. Sheryl Stolberg, No longer missing in action. *Los Angeles Times,* June 16, 1996, pp. A1, A18.

8. Ibid.

9. Alex Haley, *Roots* (New York: Doubleday, 1976).

10. Nathan Hare and Julia Hare, *Bringing the Black Boy to Manhood: The Passage* (San Francisco: The Black Family Think Tank, 1985).

11. Nsenga Warfield-Coppock, *Afrocentric Theory and Applications,* Vol. 1: *Adolescent Rites of Passage* (Washington, DC: Baobab Associates, 1990).

12. Hare and Hare, *Bringing the Black Boy to Manhood.*

13. Erik Erikson, *Childhood and Society* (New York: Norton, 1963).

14. Andrew Trotter, Rites of passage: In an urban school, students build on their roots. *Executive Educator* (September 1991): 48–49.

15. Courtland Lee, *Empowering Young Black Males* (Ann Arbor, MI: ERIC Clearinghouse, 1992).

16. Lynn Smith, Roland Gilbert's mentors for men in the making. *Los Angeles Times,* July 13, 1993, pp. E1, E8.

17. Lee, *Empowering Young Black Males.*

18. Richard Majors and Susan Wiener, *Programs That Serve African-American Male Youth* (Washington, DC: The Urban Institute, 1995).

19. Michel Marriott, Manhood training at the mosque: Hope, discipline, and defiance. *New York Times,* March 5, 1994, pp. A1, A8.

20. Lee, *Empowering Young Black Males.*

21. Majors, Conclusions and recommendations.

22. William Celis III, Cities innovate search for minority men to teach. *New York Times,* November 3, 1993, pp. A1, B9.

23. Detroit's African-centered academies disarm skeptics, empower boys. *Black Issues in Higher Education,* February 24, 1994, pp. 18–21.

24. Ronnie Hopkins, *Educating Black Males: Critical Lessons in Schooling, Community, and Power* (Albany: State University of New York Press, 1997).

25. Ibid.

26. Clifford Watson, *Educating African-American Males: Detroit's Malcolm X Academy Solution* (Chicago: Third World Press, 1996).

27. Joy G. Dryfoos, *Full-Service Schools: A Revolution in Health and Social Services for Children, Youth, and Families* (San Francisco: Jossey-Bass, 1994).

28. Margot Hornblower, It takes a school. *Time,* July 3, 1994, pp. 36, 38.

29. Sylvester Monroe and Peter Goldman, *Brothers: Black and Poor—A True Story of Courage and Survival* (New York: William Morrow, 1988).

30. Susan Chira, Smaller schools better? Educators now say yes. *New York Times,* July 3, 1993, pp. A1, A10.

31. Ibid.

32. Bob Herbert, Jewels in Harlem. *New York Times,* February 16, 1994, p. A14.

33. Anita Merina, From dispute to dialogue. *NEA Today,* February 19, 1995, pp. 10–11.

34. Michael Quintanilla, The age of rage. *Los Angeles Times,* March 10, 1994, pp. E1, E6.

35. Fox Butterfield, Program seeks to stop trouble before it starts. *New York Times,* December 30, 1994, p. A11.

36. Rodney Hammond, *Dealing with Anger: A Violence Prevention Program for African-American Youth* (Waterloo, Ontario: Research Press, 1992).

37. Merina, From dispute to dialogue.

38. Jennifer Steinhauer, Support groups are rapidly increasing for teens in high school. *New York Times,* February 2, 1995, p. A8.

Chapter 14

1. Joe Klein, Shepherds of the inner city. *Newsweek,* April 18, 1994, p. 28.

2. Isabel Wilkerson, Doing whatever it takes to save a child. *New York Times,* December 30, 1994, pp. A1, A24.

3. To stem the tide of violence [editorial]. *Boston Globe,* April 29, 1991, p. A13.

4. Peter Applebome, Crime is seen as forcing changes in youth behavior. *New York Times,* January 12, 1996, p. A12.

5. Ibid.

6. Fox Butterfield, Federal program will track gun sales to youth. *New York Times,* July 7, 1996, p. A1.

7. Applebome, Crime is seen as forcing changes.

8. Carla Power and Allison Samuels, Battling for souls. *Newsweek,* October 30, 1995, pp. 46–47.

9. Francis Clines, Ex-inmate returns to area of crime to help. *New York Times,* December 30, 1991, pp. A1, A16.

10. Fox Butterfield, More Blacks in their '20s have trouble with the law. *New York Times,* October 5, 1995, p. A18.

11. Ibid.

12. Rehabilitation: Way to conquer crack. *Los Angeles Times,* May 20, 1990, p. M6.

13. Jessie Katz, Summit of gangs to end violence. *Los Angeles Times,* May 12, 1993, pp. A3, A25.

14. Don Terry, Chicago gangs, extending turf, turn to politics. *New York Times,* October 25, 1993, p. A12.

15. Mitchell Duneier, *Slim's Table: Race, Respectability, and Masculinity* (Chicago: University of Chicago Press, 1992).

16. *MAD DADS National Information Sheet.* (Omaha, NE: MAD DADS, 1997).

17. Denise Wagner and Daniel Anderson, Faith in the future: The Black church tries to redefine its mission. *Orange County Register,* March 7, 1994, p. A12.

18. Arthur J. Magida, *Prophet of Rage: A Life of Louis Farrakhan and His Nation* (New York: Basic Books, 1996).

19. Power and Samuels, Battling for souls.

20. Ibid.

Chapter 15

1. W. E. B. Du Bois, *The Souls of Black Folks* (Chicago: McClurg, 1903).

2. Clarence Page, A whole deck of race cards. *Los Angeles Times,* October 9, 1995, p. B9.

3. Paul Richter, Beneath the bitterness over race. *Los Angeles Times,* August 13, 1991, pp. A1, A10.

4. J. Anthony Lukas, Race matters [review of *Racial Healing,* by Harlon L. Dalton]. *New York Times Book Review,* October 1, 1995, p. 10.

5. David Lamb, Workshop on Whiteness explores unearned rights. *Los Angeles Times,* November 19, 1996, p. A5.

6. Donald Bogle, *Toms, Coons, Mulattoes, Mammies, and Bucks: An Interpretive History of Blacks in American Films,* 3rd ed. (New York: Continuum, 1994).

7. Ellis Cose, Beneath the "code of silence." *Newsweek,* January 10, 1994, pp. 22–23.

8. Lisbeth Schorr and Daniel Schorr, *Within Our Reach: Breaking the Cycle of Disadvantage* (New York: Anchor/Doubleday, 1988).

9. Eric Harrison, A Christian coalition offers Black repentance funds. *Los Angeles Times,* June 16, 1994, pp. A1, A12.

10. Jason DeParle, The Christian right confesses its sins of racism. *New York Times,* August 14, 1996, p. E5.

11. Laurie Goodstein, Putting politics aside. *Washington Post,* October 6, 1997, pp. A1, A10.

12. Ellis Cose, *Color Blind: Seeing Beyond Race in a Race-Obsessed World* (New York: HarperCollins, 1996).

13. Ellis Cose, *Rage of a Privileged Class: Why Are Middle-Class Blacks Angry? Why Should Americans Care?* (New York: HarperCollins, 1993).

14. Cose, *Color Blind.*

15. Sam Fulwood, Panel on race wants Clinton to do more. *Los Angeles Times,* February 10, 1997, p. A5.

16. Alison Mitchell, Defending affirmative action, Clinton urges debate on race. *New York Times,* June 14, 1997, pp. A1, A14.

17. Eric Pooley, Fairness or folly? *Time,* June 23, 1997, pp. 32–36.

Index